The Complete Idiot's Quick Paint Shop Pro Cheat Sheet

Standard Toolbar

D0245803

Button	Tool	Shortcut	Button	Tool	Shortcut
	Arrow	J		Color Repla...	
	Zoom	G		Retouch	Z
	Deform	D		Eraser	E
	Crop	R		Scratch Remover	K
	Mover	V		Picture Tube	.
	Selection	S		Airbrush	U
	Freehand Selection	A		Flood	F
	Magic Wand	M		Text	X
	Eye Dropper	Ctrl		Draw	I
	Paint Brush	B		Preset Shape	/
	Clone Brush	N		Object Selector	Q

Showing/Hiding Screen Features

Feature	Shortcut	Feature	Shortcut
Toolbars	T	Histogram window	H
Tool palette	P	All current	Tab
Color palette	C	Open all	Shift+Ctrl+T
Tool Options palette	O	Title, status, and	Shift+A
Overview window	W	menu bars	
Layer palette	L	Image information	Shift+I

File Commands

Command	Shortcut	Command	Shortcut
New Image	Ctrl+N	Print Image	Ctrl+P
Open Image	Ctrl+O	Browse Images	Ctrl+B
Save Image	Ctrl+S	Load Workspace	Shift+L
Save As	F12	Save Workspace	Shift+S
Save Copy As	Ctrl+F12	Delete Workspace	Shift+D

cut here

alpha
books

Node Editing Mode Commands

Command	Shortcut	Command	Shortcut
Drawing/Edit Mode	Ctrl+E	Cusp Node	Ctrl+X
Join	Ctrl+J	Smooth/Tangent Node	Ctrl+T
Merge	Ctrl+M	Convert to Line	Ctrl+L
Break	Ctrl+K	Line Before	Ctrl+B
Close	Shift+Ctrl+C	Line After	Ctrl+F
Reverse Contour	Ctrl+R	Curve Before	Ctrl+1
Reverse Path	Shift+Ctrl+R	Curve After	Ctrl+2
Asymmetric Node	Shift+Ctrl+S	Quit Editing	Ctrl+Q
Symmetric Node	Ctrl+S		

Selection and Editing Commands

Command	Shortcut	Command	Shortcut
Select All	Ctrl+A	Paste as Transparent Selection	Shift+Ctrl+E
Select None	Ctrl+D		
Show/Hide Marquee	Shift+Ctrl+M	Paste into Selection	Shift+Ctrl+L
Cut	Ctrl+X	Paste as New Vector	Ctrl+G
Copy	Ctrl+C	Clear Selection	Del
Copy Merged	Shift+Ctrl+C	Flip	Ctrl+I
Paste as New Image	Ctrl+V	Mirror	Ctrl+M
Paste as New Layer	Ctrl+L	Rotate	Ctrl+R
Paste as New Selection	Ctrl+E	Crop to Selection	Shift+R

Window and View Commands

Command	Shortcut	Command	Shortcut
New Window	Shift+W	Full Screen Preview	Shift+Ctrl+A
Duplicate Window	Shift+D	Rulers	Ctrl+Alt+R
Fit to Window	Ctrl+W	Grid	Ctrl+Alt+G
Full Screen Edit	Shift+A		

Image Adjustment

Command	Shortcut	Command	Shortcut
Resize	Shift+S	Down to 16 Colors	Ctrl+Shift+2
Brightness/Contrast	Shift+B	Down to 256 Colors	Ctrl+Shift+3
Gamma Correction	Shift+G	Down to 32K Colors	Ctrl+Shift+4
Highlight/Midtone/Shadow	Shift+M	Down to 64K Colors	Ctrl+Shift+5
Hue/Saturation Lightness	Shift+H	Down to X Colors	Ctrl+Shift+6
Red/Green/Blue	Shift+U	Up to 16 Colors	Ctrl+Shift+8
Load Palette	Shift+O	Up to 256 Colors	Ctrl+Shift+9
Set Transparency	Shift+Ctrl+V	Up to 16M Colors	Ctrl+Shift+0
Down to 2 Colors	Ctrl+Shift+1		

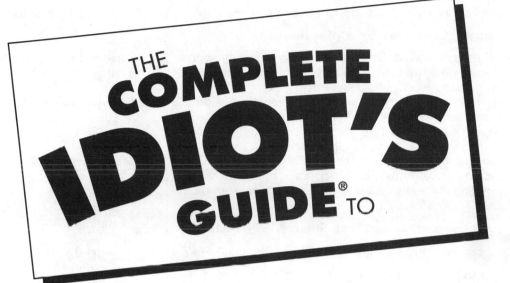

THE COMPLETE IDIOT'S GUIDE® TO

Paint Shop Pro™ 7

Nat Gertler

alpha books

201 West 103rd Street, Indianapolis, Indiana 46290

Complete Idiot's Guide to Paint Shop Pro™ 7

Copyright © 2001 by Alpha Books

All rights reserved. No part of this book shall be reproduced, stored in a retrieval system, or transmitted by any means, electronic, mechanical, photocopying, recording, or otherwise, without written permission from the publisher. No patent liability is assumed with respect to the use of the information contained herein. Although every precaution has been taken in the preparation of this book, the publisher and author assume no responsibility for errors or omissions. Nor is any liability assumed for damages resulting from the use of the information contained herein.

International Standard Book Number: 0-7897-2460-X

Library of Congress Catalog Card Number: 00-105439

Printed in the United States of America

First Printing: October 2000

03   02   01   4   3   2

Trademarks

All terms mentioned in this book that are known to be trademarks or service marks have been appropriately capitalized. Alpha Books cannot attest to the accuracy of this information. Use of a term in this book should not be regarded as affecting the validity of any trademark or service mark.

Warning and Disclaimer

Every effort has been made to make this book as complete and as accurate as possible, but no warranty or fitness is implied. The information provided is on an "as is" basis. The author and the publisher shall have neither liability nor responsibility to any person or entity with respect to any loss or damages arising from the information contained in this book.

Associate Publisher
Greg Wiegand

Acquisitions Editor
Angelina Ward

Development Editors
Laura Norman
Sarah Robbins

Managing Editor
Thomas F. Hayes

Senior Editor
Susan Ross Moore

Copy Editors
Cynthia Fields
Kate O. Givens
Kay Hoskin
Molly Schaller

Indexer
Chris Barrick

Proofreader
Lisa Wilson

Technical Editor
Jim Grey

Illustrator
Judd Winnick

Team Coordinator
Sharry Gregory

Interior Designer
Nathan Clement

Cover Designer
Michael Freeland

Production
Stacey DeRome
Ayanna Lacey
Julie Swenson

Contents at a Glance

Table of Contents

Appendixes

Foreword

Art Made Easy

Whoever said "art isn't easy" obviously never met Jasc Paint Shop Pro.

With Jasc Paint Shop Pro 7, digital art is easier than ever before. You can edit and enhance photos. Draw. Paint. Even animate. It's an all-in-one, easy-to-use, affordable software solution. So whether you're a digital photographer, home or business user, or Web designer, a newcomer to digital imaging or a graphics guru, Paint Shop Pro gives you the power to unleash your inner artist.

To help you get started, we're pleased to point you to this great new book, *The Complete Idiot's Guide to Paint Shop Pro 7*. It's got all you need to know about Paint Shop Pro, right at your fingertips. It couldn't be easier than this.

Armed with this book and a copy of Paint Shop Pro 7, you'll soon be taking the art world by storm. Just remember to tell the Museum of Modern Art we said hello.

From the whole Jasc Software team, I also want to say thank you for choosing Paint Shop Pro. We appreciate your interest and your support. Now get ready to start creating!

Kris Tufto
Chief Executive Officer
Jasc Software, Inc.

About the Author

If you thought of **Nat Gertler** simply as a former computer programmer and trainer who has written such computer books as *Multimedia Illustrated*, *The Complete Idiot's Guide to PowerPoint*, and *Easy PCs*, then you'd be missing a large part of his creative side. As a comic book creator, he has crafted comics for dozens of publishers, including spinning tales about Speed Racer, the Flintstones, and Richard Petty. His own original comics creation, *The Factor*, brought him a nomination for the prestigious Eisner award, and has also been optioned for television. Nat's fiction appears in books, in magazines, and on television, while he contributes a column and crossword puzzles to *Hogan's Alley*, a magazine of the cartoon arts. In his dubious spare time, he runs the online Peanuts book and video catalog AAUGH.com. If for some crazed reason you want to know more about Nat, stop by www.Gertler.com.

Tell Us What You Think!

As the reader of this book, *you* are our most important critic and commentator. We value your opinion and want to know what we're doing right, what we could do better, what areas you'd like to see us publish in, and any other words of wisdom you're willing to pass our way.

As an Executive Editor for Que, I welcome your comments. You can fax, email, or write me directly to let me know what you did or didn't like about this book—as well as what we can do to make our books stronger.

Please note that I cannot help you with technical problems related to the topic of this book, and that due to the high volume of mail I receive, I might not be able to reply to every message.

When you write, please be sure to include this book's title and author as well as your name and phone or fax number. I will carefully review your comments and share them with the author and editors who worked on the book.

Fax: 317-581-4666

Email: desktop_pub@macmillanusa.com

Mail: Beth Millett
          Executive Editor
          Que Corporation
          201 West 103rd Street
          Indianapolis, IN 46290 USA

Introduction

Welcome to *The Complete Idiot's Guide to Paint Shop Pro*, your user-friendly, low-calorie guide to using Paint Shop Pro. Paint Shop Pro (which is sometimes lazily referred to as PSP, to save my tired little typing fingers) is a first-class graphics program at a bargain-basement price. With PSP (see?) you can touch up photographs, create drawings, invent logos, and craft some fascinating graphics for your Web site. It can be a great productive tool—or it can be a great way to waste time, drawing moustaches on photographs of your new niece.

This Book Is Full of Good Stuff

The basics of using Paint Shop Pro are found early in the book, helping you to quickly start designing images. Later in the book you get to see more of PSP's special features so that you can make fancier images, and ones that look exactly like you want them to. You get advice on making creative decisions to give your image impact. There's so much good stuff in here that you won't believe it's fat-free!

Browsing Through the Book

If you're as lazy as I am (and that's saying something!), you probably don't want to spend a lot of time reading about things you're never going to use—and odds are that with all of PSP's features, you'll never use them all. This book is broken into chapters. There are a few core chapters you have to read to get the hang of the program, but most chapters you can skip until you decide to learn about that specific topic. Each chapter starts with a list of the things you learn when reading that chapter, so you can decide whether to skip it. Think of it as a buffet of knowledge, and you can always come back for seconds!

Part 1: The Basics

The chapters are grouped into parts. The first part is designed to make you comfortable with Paint Shop Pro. Chapter 1, "Test Driving Paint Shop Pro," walks you through making a very simple drawing, so that you can understand the basics of how PSP works. Chapter 2, "Helllllllp!," teaches you how to use the program's help system to get quick answers to basic questions, as well as points out some other sources of PSP assistance. These are short chapters, and they help you to learn the terminology for the rest of the book, so be sure to read them.

Part 2: A Beginner's Paint Shopping Spree

This string of chapters covers the basics of using Paint Shop Pro: how to select colors, what the basic drawing tools are, how to use an existing photograph or image, how to save your work, and how to print it. By the time you reach the end of Part 2, you're able to do some good strong basic graphics work. Read all of these chapters.

Part 3: Painting Outside the Lines

As you see in Part 2, Paint Shop Pro's tools fall into two categories. *Raster* tools deal with your picture as a series of little dots; *vector* tools create shapes made up of lines and curves. You'll almost certainly end up using both types of tools. Part 3 focuses on the raster tools, teaching you to use some of the fancier features of *brushes* to draw different styles of lines, and *fills* to fill in areas. If you find it hard to draw with a mouse, you can use a device called a *pressure-sensitive tablet* to improve your precision. You see how to use deformation commands to warp your image, and you learn how *effects* and *filters* can give your image a special appearance. Skip any of these chapters that you don't want to read, but at least flip through the pictures. There are some pretty nifty tricks in these chapters that can bring a professional polish to your work.

Part 4: Vector Victories and Layer Lay-Ups

The first couple chapters of Part 4 cover actions that are best done with vector tools: adding shapes and adding text. Then we move on to different tools to handle *layers*, (building an image by building and arranging different objects that make up that image). You learn how to use special layers that can have special effects on parts of your image. Again, you can pick and choose your chapters to learn the topics in which you're most interested, and save the others for later.

Part 5: Painting the World Wide Web

Paint Shop Pro is a great tool for designing graphics for Web sites. If that's your goal, read these chapters. You learn how to optimize your graphics so that they look good and load quickly on the Web. Chapter 25, "Watermarking: The Stain that Protects," covers marking your graphics with a *digital watermark*, so you can prove that someone has reused your art on their Web site. Chapter 26, "Animation Shop 101: Picture Motions," and Chapter 27, "Animation Shop 201: Transformations and Tricks," cover using Animation Shop, a program that comes free with Paint Shop Pro. This program helps you to create animated graphics.

Part 6: Advanced Concerns

The chapters in Part 6 are aimed at people who are looking to get the most out of Paint Shop Pro. These chapters are specifically devoted to touching up photos and creating logos. Chapter 30, "Your Own Custom Paintshop," concentrates on customizing Paint Shop Pro to make it better fit your needs. Chapter 31, "Digital Laundry Day: Separating and Correcting Colors," you see how to use PSP as a color separation and proofing tool for advanced printing needs. You can skip over any chapter in which you're not interested. Never mind that I spent weeks slaving over a hot keyboard to get those chapters just right (sniff). You just go have fun with your friends instead.

The Rest of the Book

The table of contents in the front and index in the back of the book are both handy, but I doubt you'll sit down and read them. Appendix A tells you how to install Paint Shop Pro, if you're not lucky enough to have someone install it for you. If you're fairly new to Windows, or aren't fully comfortable with the terminology, the Appendix B tells you about how to use Windows and what the various parts of it are called.

The Speak like a Geek section is a glossary full of techno-terms you might run into and what those terms mean to folks who aren't computer art geeks. This section is a handy reference.

Before Part 1 there's an introduction, but it's too late to decide if you want to read that, because you're already most of the way through it!

The Language of the Book

A few standard tricks are used in this book to make things clear. For example, if I tell you to hit a key, click on a button, or select a command, the command name, button name, or key is printed **like this**. If I want you to hold down the Shift, Alt, or Ctrl keys and press another key, it will look like: press **Shift+G** to get a capital G.

If I tell you to type something, the phrase that you type will look `like this`. When I give you a definition to a word, the new word appears in *italics* (slanted letters).

Throughout the book are a number of *sidebars*, gray separate sections that are not part of the normal reading. The following text shows the sidebars you'll run into later in the book.

Tricks'N'Tips Sidebars

Sidebars with this picture are used to tell you about special features and other little bits of information that might be handy to know. This is where you'll find shortcuts for doing hard tasks, and other ways of saving time.

The Science of Art Sidebars

This picture means that the sidebar is letting you know some technical details about how something works. You don't need to know this stuff to use Paint Shop Pro. If you understand the technical side of computing, it might be interesting, and if you don't understand technical, this is a good place to learn. Don't let this symbol scare you away!

New in Paint Shop Pro 7

This picture is used to let you know when there's a new useful feature that was not in older versions of Paint Shop Pro. Don't worry if you're using an earlier version, though; most of the important things haven't changed (and probably won't change in the next version, either, so you won't be caught off-guard).

Ack! Nowledgements!

I'd like to thank the gang at Que for dragging me into yet another one of these books. Particular thanks go to Angelina Ward for calling on me at just the right time. Small mounds of karmic chocolate to Laura Norman, Sarah Robbins, and Susan Moore for their editorial work on this book. I'd also like to thank the people involved in my various Web site, TV, and comics projects for their patience during the writing of this tome. And, for the last time, let me thank my girlfriend Lara Hughes for her support; by the time I write my next book (barring the unforeseen), she'll have undergone a metamorphosis into Dr. Lara Gertler.

I'll Trade These Marks for Other Marks!

Paint Shop Pro is a trademark of Jasc Software, Inc., so don't go trying to name your kid that. The name is taken.

Dedication

This book is dedicated to the memory of Charles M. Schulz, creator of *Peanuts*. I have been immersed in his cartoons since I was very young, and his influence on me is so vast and ever-present that it is almost undetectable, much in the way that we seldom notice air. Have you shared *Peanuts* with anyone lately?

—Nat Gertler

Part I

The Basics

It's time to dangle your feet in Paint Shop Pro—the program, I mean. If you dangled your feet in a real paint shop, you'd probably just end up with various colors of latex enamel on your toes. (That could be very handy if you're trying to hide in a bag of M&Ms.)

In Part 1 you take a quick run through the program, do some simple exercises, and learn how to get help if you have questions or problems (and if you get trapped in a bag of M&Ms, that sounds like a problem!).

Chapter 1

Test Driving Paint Shop Pro

In This Chapter

➤ Starting the program

➤ Drawing a happy face

➤ Saving your drawing

➤ Exiting the program

Paint Shop Pro sounds like the name of a good blue-collar job for someone with a good color sense and a high tolerance for latex fumes. Actually, it's the name of a great graphics program, one that makes it easy to draw, to work with photographs, to design logos, and to make really sharp-looking "kick me" signs to stick to your boss's back.

Paint Shop Pro might look intimidating. There are so many buttons and menus and toolbars that it looks like it's impossible to figure out. It's not. Consider how your great grandmother, who used to drive a Model A, would feel if she were plunked down behind the wheel of your new VW Beetle. Suddenly, she sees a dashboard with dozens of buttons and controls, and she thinks the car is hard to drive. But those controls are for the radio and the air conditioner and the remote door locks, and she doesn't need those to drive. You show her the key, the steering wheel, the gas pedal, and the brake—all things that she's familiar with from her Model A. Within a minute, she's driving (if a bit timidly) down the driveway.

This chapter aims to show you Paint Shop Pro's steering wheel, as well as the gas and brake pedals, and get you moving slowly but confidently down the graphics driveway. Then you can go through the rest of the book, learning how to use the other buttons and switches. By the time you reach the end of the book, you'll be running the Beetle at high speeds down twisty roads, up on two wheels with your windows rolled down and your favorite They Might Be Giants song blaring from the speakers.

Turning On the Ignition

I'm assuming that you actually have Paint Shop Pro installed on your PC. If you don't, flip to Appendix A in the back of the book, for instructions on installing the software. Don't worry, we'll wait right here while you take care of that.

Ready? Good. To start the program, click the **Start** button on your Windows taskbar. From the menu, click **Programs**. On the submenu, click **Paint Shop Pro 7**. The program starts up.

Go Away, You Little Windows

If you're using the *evaluation version* of PSP, a window appears showing you how many days you have left in your free trial. Click **Start** to continue.

Tricks 'n' Tips

Evaluation Over?

If you're running out of time on your 30-day free trial evaluation version of Paint Shop Pro, click **Order** on the opening screen. You're taken to a page with an order form for ordering the you–can–use–it–forever version. If you want to get the final version as quick as possible, point your Web browser to www.jasc.com where you can pay some money and download a file that takes away the time limit immediately. If you want the program on CD-ROM rather than going through the trouble of downloading, head over to www.MillionsOnTheInternet.com, where you'll find an offer to get the program at a discount.

A **Tip of the Day** window appears (unless someone else has been using your computer and turned off the Tip Of The Day function). Click **Close** to get rid of this window.

A dialog box may open with a list of types of files that PSP can understand, with checks next to some of them, as seen in Figure 1.1. Click **OK**, and PSP will set itself up to be the main program to handle the checked files.

Which File Formats?

You may want to clear the checkbox for every format but the PSP format, if you're just evaluating Paint Shop Pro. That way, you're not interfering with any other programs that may be set up to handle other file formats. To tell Paint Shop Pro to take control of more formats later, choose **File, Preferences, File Format Associations** and the File Format Associations dialog box reappears.

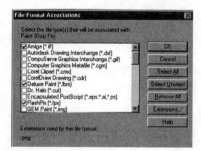

Figure 1.1

Pick PSP as your program for perusing a plethora of picture types.

Look at All Them Fancy Controls

At this point, you should have a window that looks something like Figure 1.2. The toolbars shown in Figure 1.2 might not be exactly like toolbars on your screen (particularly if someone else has been using your computer), but they should look roughly the same.

Each part of the window has its own function:

➤ **Title bar** Displays the name of the program you're running. (Hint: it's an anagram for short hippo nap!)

➤ **Menu bar** Lists the words used to select commands. It works like the menu bars in most Windows programs.

➤ **Tool bar** Houses buttons used for loading and saving, undoing commands, and opening other windows and sets of buttons. If you don't see the toolbar, press **T**.

➤ **Tool palette** Includes buttons for each of the different tools that you use to draw and rearrange the parts of your picture. If you don't see this, press **P** or click the **Toggle Tool palette** button.

➤ **Color palette** Displays the color your tools are using and shows which colors you can choose from. If you don't see it, press **C** or click the **Toggle Color Palette** button.

Figure 1.2

Paint Shop Pro is ready to go!

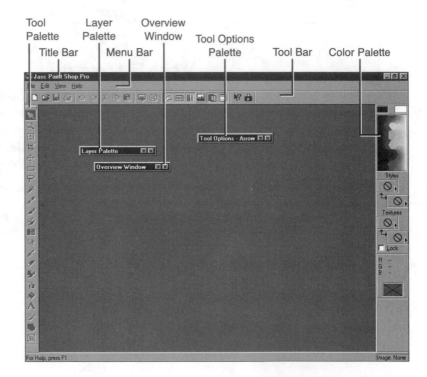

Get a Blank Sheet

Now that we see that we have all of our drawing tools in place, we need something to draw on. If we were drawing away from the computer, we'd be looking for a new sheet of paper. On the computer, we want a nice new image document instead. Click the **New** button (shortcut: **Ctrl+N**), and a New Image dialog box (as shown in Figure 1.3) shows up, wanting to know what size and color an image you want to start with.

Let's make a drawing 4 inches high and 4 inches wide. Select **Inches** from the drop list, next to the height and width fields. Type 4 into the **Width** field, and another 4 into the **Height** field. (After you enter each number, PSP turns them into 4.000, to show that they are precisely four.)

12

Figure 1.3

Pick the proper portion of pixels for your picture.

Below the Height field is the Resolution field. When a computer displays or prints out a picture, the image is made up of a grid of little dots, called *pixels*. The smaller the pixels, the sharper the image looks. Your printer probably prints dots small enough that it takes anywhere from 300 to 2400 dots to make up a one-inch line. But we won't be printing out the picture we're about to draw. We'll just view it on the screen, which uses much bigger dots. Type 72 into the Resolution field, and select **Pixels/inch** from the drop-down list.

Seventy-Two?

Seventy-two seems like a strange number, and it is. It's the standard estimate for how many dots make up a one-inch line on your monitor, but it's a very rough estimate. Everyone has different size monitors and different settings. Because of this, your picture might actually look larger or smaller than 4 inches across while you're working on it.

What color paper do you want to draw on? Let's keep it simple and use white. From the **Background Color** drop-down list, choose **White**.

Using the Image type drop list, you can choose how many different colors you're allowed to work with. Let's be greedy; choose **16.7 Million Colors (24 bit)** from this list.

Finally, click **OK**, and your new blank sheet appears!

Time for a Face-Off

Okay, now you have a sheet of paper. It's time to start the fun stuff!

 On the Tool palette, click the **Paint Brush** button (shortcut: **B**). Move your cursor over to the rectangle of colors at the top of the color palette, and click an area of nice dark blue. That is the color that your paint brush will paint with.

On your sheet, click where you want the left eye. A dot of blue appears. Move your brush a bit to the right, and click the right eye into place. The eyes that appear might be circular, or they might be square, or even some other shape if you or someone else has left a different shape selected in the Paint Brush's options (I'll show your how to change that shape just a little later).

Move your pointer to one end of where you want the mouth to be. Hold down the left mouse button, and drag the pointer along in the shape of a mouth. As you drag the pointer, you leave a trail of color on the screen. When you're done with the mouth, release the button.

Getting a Head

 We have a face, but now we need a head—a perfectly round head. To draw a perfect shape, click the **Preset Shapes** button on the Tool palette (shortcut: **/**).

This button is designed to make all sorts of different shapes, but we want a very specific shape. We want a circle, and we have to tell the system what we want. To do this, we have to set the options for this tool.

 There's probably already a bar on your screen marked *Tool Options*. If not, click the **Toggle Tool Option Window** button (shortcut: **O**) and the bar appears (see Figure 1.4). Point to the bar, and it will expand into a dialog box.

Figure 1.4

The Tool Options dialog box changes based on which tool is chosen.

From the **Shape Type** drop-down list on the first tab of the Tool Options dialog box, choose **Ellipse**. (We really want to draw a circle, but a circle is just a very specific type of an ellipse, much like how a square is a specific type of rectangle.) If the **Create as Vector** option or the **Retain Style** option is checked, click the check box to clear the check. (Those options would add some features to the circle that we don't need now.)

14

Over on the Color palette, directly under the word Style, are two rectangles. The top one shows what color our circle will be *stroked* (outlined) with, and the bottom shows what color the center should be *filled* with. However, we don't want our circle filled with any color; we want to leave it clear so that the beautiful eyes and mouth you've drawn show through. Point to the lower box and hold your left mouse button down. A row of buttons appears, as seen in figure 1.5. Click to the last button on the right, which shows a circle with a slash through it (the international No symbol). Release the mouse button. The No symbol will now be in the style rectangle, showing that we want no color filling this circle.

Figure 1.5
The pop-up style toolbar.

Move your pointer to where your face's nose would be (we must be rhinophobes; we skipped the nose altogether). This is where the center of the circle will be. Hold down the right mouse button, and drag the pointer away from the center. An outline of the circle appears. After the outline is big enough that the eyes and face are inside, release your mouse button.

Why Is Right Right?

You used the right mouse button in this case because that tells PSP you're starting where you want the center of the item. If you'd used the left button, you would've been indicating the outside edge of the area you wanted the circle in.

The circle appears. Violà! The face is done.

Saving Face

If you followed my directions exactly, you now have the finest work of art in history. Such art must be preserved for the ages!

 Click the **Save** button (shortcut: **Ctrl+S**) and the Save As dialog box appears. Type a name for your file (smiley) into the **File name** field. In the **Save as type** field, make sure **Paint Shop Pro Image** is selected. Click **Save**, and your file is saved to disk.

We're Outta Here!

Click the **Close** (**X**) button on the upper corner of smiley's window to close smiley. Click the **Close** (**X**) button on the upper-right corner of the Paint Shop Pro window, and it's gone. Your computer is once again freed up for more important things, such as Tetris and passing on email chain letters!

The Least You Need to Know

➤ To start Paint Shop Pro, click the **Start** button and select **Programs**, **Paint Shop Pro 7**.

➤ To start a new image document, click the **New** button.

➤ To pick the color with which to paint, click the color display at the top of the Color palette.

➤ To pick a drawing tool, click the Tool palette.

➤ Use the Tool Options dialog box to set the details of how your selected tool works.

➤ Click the **Save** button to save the image document to your hard disk.

Chapter 2

Helllllp!

In This Chapter

➤ Using Paint Shop Pro's online help system

➤ Find out what different buttons are and what they do

➤ Get your Tip of the Day

➤ Get help from friends and strangers on the Internet

As you work with Paint Shop Pro, you are apt to have some questions such as "How do I print several images on the same page?" or "What does this button do?" or "When are the Chicago Cubs going to win the World Series?" Although questions like that last one have kept philosophers boggled for millennia, answers to the others are available if you know where to look.

This Book Is Helpful

This book is designed to be a good first place to turn with your Paint Shop Pro questions. The table of contents in the front and the index in the back make it easy to track down the topic at hand. The Speak Like a Geek glossary, just before the index, is filled with definitions for confusing terms. This book is also very effective tool for whomping spiders, should any come at you while you're reading it.

But this book can't answer everything, and you might not always have this book with you (if you find yourself sneaking back into the bookstore and reading this book off the shelf whenever you have a question, it's time to buy your own copy). Luckily, the program has a number of built-in help features that are able to answer most of your vital PSP questions (although they are no good against attacking spiders).

The Online Help System

Choose **Help**, **Help Topics** from the menu, and a window like the one in Figure 2.1 appears. This is your gateway to the online help system.

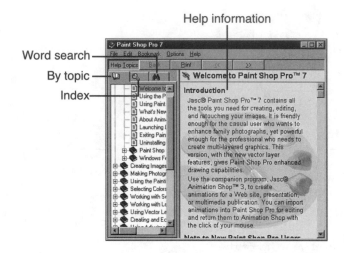

Figure 2.1

Help is on its way!

To Pick a Topic

In the left portion of the Help window, a bunch of pictures of little books are lined up, each with a topic listed next to it. Double-click on the topic that interests you, and the list expands to show a list of subtopics within that topic. Some of these topics have pictures of pieces of paper next to them; others will have pictures of books. Try to find a piece of paper with the specific topic you want to learn about; you might have to double-click through several levels of books to find it.

When you find that piece of paper, click on it. The information about that topic appears on the right side of the window. This help information might include text, screenshots, or even a *hyperlink* (different-colored text that you click to get further information on a given subtopic).

The Index Is Indexpensive and Indexpensible

The books-and-pages way of finding a topic is a good method for browsing through all the contents of the help system. If you really know what it is you want, though, you'll find it faster using the index. Click the **Index** tab (the one with a picture of a key), and the index appears, organized in alphabetical order. Start typing the name of the feature with which you want help. The page automatically scrolls to the part of the index that covers the topic you've typed. Click the topic or subtopic you want, and help appears on the right *or* a list of subtopics appears. If the subtopics appear, click on one and the relevant information appears on the right.

Find Every Little Word

If you couldn't find what you were looking for in the index, it doesn't mean that your topic isn't covered. It may be that what you're looking for is mentioned on one of the help pages, but whoever made the index didn't consider it a separate topic.

To search through every topic for a given word, click the **Find** tab (the one with binoculars on it). If this is the first time you've used the Find function, a dialog box tells you that it has to build a database of the words in the help files. Click **Next**, then click **Finish**. This database only takes a few seconds to build.

Synonyms

If the index or search doesn't have the term you typed, try typing another word or term that means the same thing.

The Find tab has three fields, as seen in Figure 2.2. After you type the word you're searching for into field 1, a list of words appears in field 2. These are all the words that begin with what you type and that show up anywhere in the help pages.

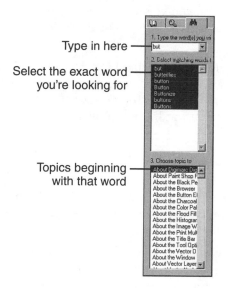

Type in here ——

Select the exact word
you're looking for ——

Topics beginning
with that word ——

Figure 2.2

The Find tab is useful for those of us who couldn't find our butterflies with both hands.

When you click the exact word you want to find, a list of help pages with that word in it shows up in field 3. Click on the help page you want, and the page is displayed.

If you type more than one word into field 1, field 3 shows a list of any topic that has all of those words in it. For example, if you typed abandoned, bleeding, you'll find a page with both words. (That sounds like it would be a rather horrible page, doesn't it? Actually, it's a page about *dithering*, a technique in which PSP mixes dots of two different colors to trick you into thinking you see a third color.) Typing in multiple words is often handy if your first word brings up too many entries.

Other Help Page Tricks

The help display has a row of useful buttons. Clicking **Help Topics** turns on or off the display of the index. Clicking **Back** returns you to the previous help topic you were viewing. Clicking **Print** prints the content of the current help topic so that you can carry it with you or make a paper airplane out of it.

If you press the **F1** key at any time, the help display opens, and it tries to open to a topic relevant to whatever you're doing. When the display opens this way, it doesn't have the index section on the left. Click the **Help Topics** button to make it appear.

Every Button Tells a Story

The little pictures on the buttons of computer programs are designed by people who spent a lot of time in design school. Apparently, most of that time was spent playing tic-tac-toe or figuring out where to buy black clothing in bulk. Not enough time was spent figuring out how to design meaningful little button pictures. Sure, some of the pictures make sense, or are at least familiar, because you've seen them before. But if you're like me, there is always a batch of buttons that you just stare at and wonder what they do.

If you point your pointer at a button, a description of what that button does will show up at the bottom of the PSP window. Leave the pointer hovering over the button for a second, and a little *tooltip* with the name of the button appears. (Be patient while doing this; if you keep moving your pointer around, the tooltip won't appear!)

Button Help with the Help Button

 Click the **Help** button and your pointer changes. When you click this pointer on any other button, a page pops up with information about how that button is used. This trick also works with menu commands: Click the **Help** button, then select the menu command, and you see a help page relevant to that command.

Now here's the thing that boggles my mind: If you click the **Help** button, then use the help pointer to click the **Help** button, you get a page of help about help. But obviously, you don't need help with the help button! If you didn't know how to use the help button, you wouldn't have been able to get the help screen that tells you about the button. I feel so confused...

A Web of Help

Jasc Software, the makers of Paint Shop Pro, maintains a support Web site at www.jasc.com/techsup.asp? (seen in Figure 2.3) that includes tips, hints, and answers. It also is the place to find updates to your software.

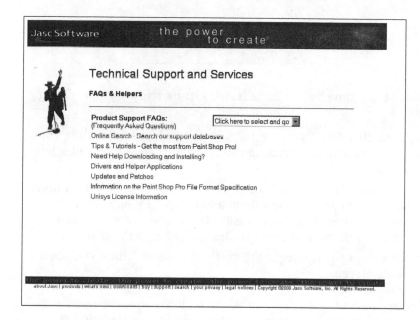

Figure 2.3

The World Wide Web's wonderful website for whats and whys!

Those of you who use *Usenet* (the Internet's bulletin board system) should know that there is a newsgroup devoted to Paint Shop Pro. Set your newsgroup readers to comp.graphics.apps.paint-shop-pro to find an active group of folks sharing tips and hints and answering questions about the program.

If you can't find the information you're looking for, you can email Jasc's technical support department. To do this, choose **Help**, **Jasc Software Online**, **Email Technical Support.** PSP starts up your email program and opens an email address to the support department.

A Tip of the Hat to the Tip of the Day

Paint Shop Pro has a nice little feature called Tip of the Day (see Figure 2.4). When I first saw this feature, I was disappointed because it wasn't what I thought it would be: a gratuity guide. ("Today's going tip for waitresses is 16.13% of the check. There has been little change today in tips for cabbies, it's almost all bills.") Instead it's a feature that gives you a nice little tip to using PSP each time you start the program.

Figure 2.4

Tip of the Day has a new tip everyday for months!

You can view these tips at any time by choosing **Help**, **Tip of the Day**. The dialog box has three features:

➤ A checkbox you put a check in if you want a new tip displayed every time you start the program. (If you're tired of getting those tips, just clear that check box by clicking in the box.)

➤ The **Next Tip** button advances through the tips. That's right; you're not limited to one tip a day! You can breeze through them all at once, if you want, but I wouldn't recommend it. After all, you can easily absorb one or two tips at a time; if you read a dozen or more at once, you're apt to forget them all.

➤ The **Close** (**X**) button tells the tip display to go away. The next time you open it, a different tip is displayed.

There are dozens of tips to be had. After you run through all the tips, the tips repeat. That way, if you failed to remember something the first time you saw it, you get another shot at it!

The Least You Need to Know

➤ To pull up the help system, choose **Help**, **Help Topics**.

➤ The help system has an index tab (with a picture of a key). This index feature is generally the fastest way to find what you need.

 ➤ To find out more about a button or command, click the **Help** button, then click the button or select the menu command you want to know more about.

➤ You can find further help at www.jasc.com/techsup.html on the Web.

➤ Choose **Help**, **Tip of the Day** to look at one tip from a list of dozens.

Part II

A Beginner's Paint Shopping Spree

It's time to start getting to know your tools. By the end of this part, a paintbrush, an airbrush, an eraser, a magnifying glass, a lasso, a magic wand, an eyedropper, and 16.7 million crayons will all be at your beck and call. I hope you have a lot of pockets.

Chapter 3

All 16.7 Million Colors of the Rainbow

HOLY MACKEREL.

In This Chapter

➤ How computers handle color

➤ Working with a limited color palette

➤ Selecting colors

➤ Re-using colors

Whenever you create an image, you deal with color. This is the case even if the image is in black and white—well, black and white *are* colors, aren't they? Granted, they aren't very *colorful* colors (the white crayon was never the most useful crayon in the box), but they are colors nonetheless.

The Big Box of Crayons

Your computer can handle a lot more than black and white. It can handle more colors than you can name (which isn't that surprising; after naming about a dozen colors you're apt to find yourself stretching for terms like *ecru* and *aquamarine* and *Pepto-Bismol pink*). How many different colors can your computer handle? A bunch. Sixteen million, seven hundred and seventy-seven thousand, two hundred and sixteen—to be precise. That's a lot of crayons. It's also a very strange number, but there's a reason for it, as you'll see shortly.

Is Your Screen Holding You Back?

Even though the hardware of almost every PC sold for years can show 16.7 million colors, some displays have been configured to show only 256 (or even fewer!) colors. To check your system, right-click your Windows desktop and choose **Properties** from the pop-up menu. On the Display Properties dialog box that appears, click the **Settings** tab. In the Colors field, select **True Colors (24 bit)**. While you're checking this out, make sure that the Screen Area is set to **800 × 600 pixels** or higher. If Windows doesn't let you have that large a screen area and True Colors at the same time, you might have to settle for **High Color (16 bit)** in the Colors field. Click **OK**. (Your system might tell you that you have to reboot your machine before these settings take effect.)

Primary Colors

You might remember *primary colors* from your grammar school days, filed somewhere in your brain along with the chief export of Albania (chrome) and the capital of Liechtenstein (a capital L.) By mixing together the three primary colors of light you can make any color. Your computer monitor works on a similar concept. Every point on the monitor has a dot of red, a dot of green, and a dot of blue. By adjusting the brightness of these dots, different colors can be made. To make purple, for example, your computer makes the blue and red dots bright, but leaves the green dot dark.

Why 256?

Computers count using *binary*, a system using only 0 and 1 rather than using the numbers 0 through 9. Using eight binary digits, the computer can count from 0 to 255.

Each colored dot can be set to any one of 256 levels of brightness, anywhere from 0 (the dot is off) to 255 (the dot is as bright as can be). To make black, for example, all three dots are set to zero. To make bright white, all three dots are turned to full, 255. When you set the red to 200, and set the blue and green to 100, you get a dull red. Every combination makes a different color, and with 256 settings for each color, the number of combinations is 256 times 256 times 256, which multiplies out to that 16 million number.

This is about at the limit that the human eye can discern. Using a thousand different levels for each color wouldn't make the images look any better.

Picking Colors

Move your pointer over the Available Colors display of colors at the top of the color palette (as seen in Figure 3.1). In the Current Color display below it, you see a rectangle of the color you are pointing to, as well as the amounts of red, green, and blue in that color—marked R, G, and B, respectively. (If you see H, S, and L instead, choose **File**, **Preferences**, **General Program Preferences**. Click the **Dialogs and Palettes** tab, and click the **Display colors in RGB format** option.)

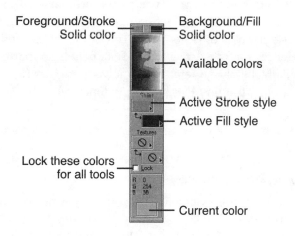

Foreground/Stroke Solid color
Background/Fill Solid color
Available colors
Active Stroke style
Active Fill style
Lock these colors for all tools
Current color

Figure 3.1

The color palette probably looks a lot more colorful on your screen than it does in this black and white picture.

Click a color in the Available Colors display, and it is displayed in the Foreground/Stroke Solid Color panel. It should also be displayed in the Active Stroke Style panel. If not, point to the Active Stroke Style box and hold the left mouse button down. Four buttons will appear. Release the mouse button, and then click the left-most of the four buttons (it looks like a paint brush). The color you selected is now your main color. If you were to start painting, it would be in that color.

Right-click on the Available Colors area, and that color is displayed in the Background/Fill Solid Color panel. It should also be displayed in the Active Fill Style panel. If not, point to the Fill Style box and hold the left mouse button down. Four buttons will appear. Release the mouse button, and then click the left-most of the four buttons (the one that looks like a paint brush). This is a secondary color. When, for example, you use the shape-drawing tool to draw a circle with an outline, the outline will be in the Stroke color (*stroke* means *outline*, in art-speak) but it will be filled inside with the Fill color.

Put a check in the **Lock** check box. Without this check, the colors would change whenever you picked a different art tool from the Tool palette (which can actually be handy, since that also means that when you switch back to that tool, it still has the color you last used with it).

Stylish Pseudonyms

The fine folks who created PSP gave each of the Style panels *two* names. The upper one is called the *Active Stroke Style* panel when using it with some tools, and the *Active Foreground Style* panel with other tools. This is just too confusing, so in this book I'll always refer to it as the *Active Stroke Style* panel, no matter what tool is being used. Similarly, I'll always refer to the lower panels at the *Active Fill Style* panel, even though the fine PSP folks sometimes call it the *Active Background Style* panel.

Precise Picking for Pickier Pickers

Picking the exact color you want from the Available Colors display is not only difficult, it can be impossible. This is because the area only has space for less than five thousand of the sixteen million possible colors. If you don't have any images open, or if you're working on an image that was set to let you use all 16.7 million colors (as we set up that smiley picture to be), you can use a much richer color selection tool.

Color Fast

Right-click the Stroke or Fill style box instead of clicking it, and you'll be shown 10 standard colors and several of your most recently used colors. Click one of these, and you're on your way.

Click on the **Active Stroke Style** panel, and the Color dialog box shown in Figure 3.2 appears. (This same trick works with the Active Fill Color box.)

Click any spot on the hue wheel to choose the basic color you want. The box inside the wheel shows a range of versions of that color, with different amounts of light and color saturation. Click the spot on the box that shows the color you want.

Click to select one
of 48 standard colors

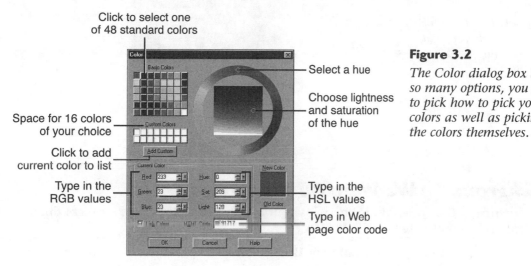

Space for 16 colors
of your choice

Click to add
current color to list

Type in the
RGB values

Select a hue

Choose lightness
and saturation
of the hue

Type in the
HSL values

Type in Web
page color code

Figure 3.2
*The Color dialog box has
so many options, you get
to pick how to pick your
colors as well as picking
the colors themselves.*

You can also quickly get one of 48 preset colors by clicking the Basic Colors grid. If you frequently find yourself using colors that aren't on the Basic Colors grid, select that color using the color wheel, and then click **Add Custom**.

You can also select a color by entering the red, green, and blue values into the fields marked **Red**, **Green**, and **Cheese Sandwich**. (Oh, okay, I made that last one up.) You can return to the existing stroke color by clicking **Old Color**.

After you select your color, click **OK**! That color is now your new foreground/stroke solid color (unless you clicked your Active Fill Style to begin with, in which case this is your new background/fill solid color). And here's a neat little trick: To quickly switch your Active Fill Style and Active Stroke Style, just click the little arrow that's on the lower left of the Styles display!

First Blush: Your Initial Color Choices

When you click the **New** button, the New Image dialog box presents you with two different color-related decisions that you have to make (see Figure 3.3). You have to choose your background color, and you have to choose how many colors you're allowed to play with. Both of these options are in the Image Characteristics area of the dialog box.

Figure 3.3

Ah, if only I had as much control over my personal image as I do over a new PSP image....

Backgrounds: We Were All Born Young

The first option you have to choose is your background color. There are eight different possibilities here:

➤ Choose **Foreground Color** or **Background Color** if you want to use one of the colors you've selected as your Stroke/Foreground Solid Color or Fill/Background Solid Color. (And if you think you're the only one who finds it weird that there are options besides Background Color to select for a background color, you're right!)

➤ Choose **White**, **Black**, **Red**, **Green**, or **Blue** to get a background of one of those colors. If you're looking for a red, green, or blue background, however, you might do better to select it using the Foreground Color or Background Color options. Otherwise, you might not get the right *shade* of those colors.

➤ **Transparent** is an option that's there so that you can create images that aren't rectangular. If you choose this, there is no background in the image itself; if you put it on a Web page or a document, the page color shows through anywhere you have not painted. (While you're working on the image, Paint Shop Pro displays a checkerboard pattern in the background. Don't worry; that pattern doesn't show up on your finished image.)

Image Type: How Many Crayons Will We Use?

The next selection deals with how many different colors you will actually be able to use in your image. The first instinct is to say "I want to be able to use them all!" But that's like seeing the dessert cart and saying you want everything. It might not end up being the best choice.

The more colors you tell Paint Shop Pro that you want to use, the more disk space the file you end up making fills. This is true even if you only actually have two colors in your picture. Using more colors also means that Paint Shop Pro runs a bit slower, particularly if you're making a large image on a computer without much RAM memory.

Is Hue For You?

In addition to the red, green, blue method of color selection, the color selector also offers you the chance to use the *hue, saturation, light* method. The three values you set are:

➤ **Hue** The base color. There's no easy way to remember which color goes with which number, but you don't have to. Just click the color wheel, and on the center of the box inside the color wheel to set the Hue value for that color.

➤ **Saturation** The richness of the color. A low value gives you a dull color, and a high value gives you a rich color. When you set it to zero, you end up with gray.

➤ **Light** The brightness of the color. The higher the value, the brighter the color. When you set it zero, it is so dark that it will be black, no matter what hue you picked. Set it to 255, and it will be pure white. In between, you get the hue you chose in various levels of brightness.

Most people working with computer graphics prefer to work with the red, green, blue (*RGB*) method rather than the hue, saturation, light (*HSL*) method (sometimes called *hue, saturation, value* or *HSV*). This is because the RGB method is a little more precise, and exactly matches the way the computer handles color internally. HSL values have to be converted to RGB values before the color is displayed. However, it's often easier to fine-tune a color in HSL; get your hue right, and then make small adjustments to your saturation and light settings.

With this color selector, you don't have to choose one way or the other. You can make adjustments in any way you choose.

By using the **Image Type** drop-down list, you can select from the following amounts of colors:

➤ **2 Colors** sets up a black-and-white drawing (no shades of gray).
➤ **16 Colors** gives you 16 basic colors to draw with.
➤ **Greyscale** offers you the use 256 different shades of grey, like a black-and-white photo.

➤ **256 Colors** gives you a pretty good set of colors. (This is the largest number of colors that you can use if you're trying to create non-rectangular graphics for the Web.)

➤ **16.7 Million Colors** is definitely what you want if you're working with color photographs.

When you're a beginner—playing around and seeing what all the Paint Shop Pro tools can do—you're best off working with 16.7 million colors. The mode is more flexible, and some of the tools don't work in the fewer color modes. And it's more fun!

Easier Choices: Picking from Fewer Colors

If you're working in a less-than-16.7-million color mode, picking your Stroke and Fill colors work a little differently. After all, you have to be able to click from a very limited set of colors, called the *palette*. Things are going to get a little confusing here, because the fine folks behind Paint Shop Pro use the word *palette* to mean two very different things:

➤ *Palette* is sometimes used to refer to the limited set of colors you get to choose from.

➤ *Palette* is also used to describe portions of the Paint Shop Pro display. For example, the group of buttons with painting tools on them is called the *Tool palette*. To make it worse, the color selecting area is called the *Color palette*.

I'm working hard to make sure that it's clear which word *palette* I'm using whenever I use the word. As long as you know that the word has two meanings, you shouldn't get confused.

To pick a color in these fewer-color modes, you can still click the Available Colors display. You can also click the Active Stroke or Fill Style panel. When you do this, you don't get the same fancy dialog box shown in Figure 3.3. Instead, you'll get the straightforward color selector you see in Figure 3.4.

Simply click on the color you want to use, then click **OK**. You'll be using the color you chose.

You can rearrange the colors being displayed, making it easier to find the one that you want. To do that, use the **Sort order** drop-down list. You can sort by **Palette Order** (a set of internal numbers that the computer uses to keep track of your limited palette), **By Luminance** (brightness), or **By Hue**.

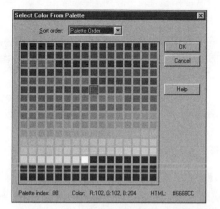

Figure 3.4

In fewer-color modes, you can see every color available to you.

The Science of Art

Any Color You Like—as Long as It's Black

When you are working in 256-color mode, and you choose a color, you find that a lot of the colors look the same. There are dozens of slots that display the exact same shade of black. This is because the palette was designed for people creating Web graphics. Although many Web viewers can support 16.7 million colors, others can only handle 216 different colors. The 256-color palette is made up of those 216 colors, plus 40 extra copies of the color black.

Getting the Right Sixteen Colors

Just because you're working with a small palette doesn't mean that you're stuck with the palette that PSP offers you. You can pick and choose your own colors to fill that palette. If you want to draw with 16 different colors of blue, you can. If you're working in two-color mode, those colors don't have to be black and white; they can be ecru and aquamarine.

To change the colors you're using, choose **Colors**, **Edit Palette** (shortcut: **Shift+P**). The Edit Palette dialog box appears. It looks a lot like the Select Color From Palette dialog box, displaying all the colors in your current palette. Double-click on a color that you don't want, and the color selector from Figure 3.3 appears. You can use this to select any of the 16.7 million colors to use in place of the color you didn't like. (Beware! If you've already used that color in your drawing, and you change the palette, the new color takes the old color's place in your image.)

Recycling Colors

If you have a palette you like and you might want to reuse it on another image some other time, save it! Choose **Colors, Save Palette**, and a file selector appears. Type in a name for your palette, and click **Save**. Your palette is saved in a file.

To reuse the palette on a new image, use the **New** button to create a new image window, then choose **Colors, Load Palette** (shortcut: **Shift+O**), and select the palette you want from the list of palette files.

Color Count Correction

If you've ever tried throwing a party, you know that estimating is impossible. If you only order enough pizza for the 10 people you expect, then the entire senior class will show up (free pizza is a powerful lure). If you order enough olives for 150 people, only three will show up and you'll find yourself eating nothing but olives for the next month.

I'm Using Eleventeen Colors

To find out how many different colors are actually in your image, choose **Colors, Count Colors Used**.

Similarly, when you start an image, you might mis-guess how many colors you need. If you think you need 13 colors, you might need 130. You might start out in 16.7-million-color mode, and discover that you've only used ecru and aquamarine.

Luckily, you can change the number of colors available at any time. To increase the number of colors, choose **Colors, Increase Color Depth**, and select from the three options of numbers of colors.

Decreasing the number of colors is a little trickier. Choose **Colors, Decrease Color Depth**, and then select the size of palette that you want from the menu that appears. When you do this, the Decrease Color Depth dialog box shown in Figure 3.5 appears.

Figure 3.5

Reducing the color depth requires certain decisions to be made.

What colors should be in the palette?

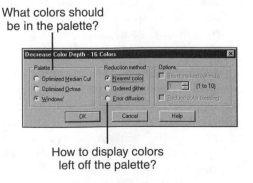

How to display colors left off the palette?

First, you have to choose how Paint Shop Pro selects which colors to keep and which to throw away. With the **Optimized Median Cut**, Paint Shop Pro makes a good guess at which colors are most important, and then matches those colors fairly well. This is usually your best choice. **Optimized Octree** doesn't do as good a job of picking the important colors, but it does a better job of matching the colors you do pick. **Standard/Web-Safe** (available only if you're reducing to 256-color mode) uses a palette made up of the 216 colors that all color Web displays can show. **Windows** (available only when reducing to 16 colors) uses the 16 standard colors that your operating system uses.

Hey, I Couldn't Pick Those Numbers

The color depth reduction menu includes options for **32K** (geek-speak for 32,000) and **64K** (64,000). These are used mainly for creating images for certain types of computers that can only display that many colors. If you do this conversion, Paint Shop Pro eliminates the extra colors, but it leaves the image in 16.7-million-color mode. So if you work more on the image, you might increase your total number of colors. If you want to end up with an unusual exact number of colors—for example, 57 or 173—choose **X Colors** from the Decrease Color Depth menu. It can handle any number between 2 and 256, and creates the number of colors you want using 16- or 256-color mode.

Next, choose what you want PSP to do with the colors that are in your image but won't be in your new palette. The **Nearest Color** option simply replaces the missing color with the nearest color that is in the palette (this makes sure that solid areas of color remain solid.) The **Ordered Dither** method (available only with the Standard/Web-Safe and Windows options) and the **Error Diffusion** method try to fake the missing colors by creating a dot pattern of different colors. For example, if you had pink in the drawing and it doesn't show up in the palette, PSP might replace the pink area with a mixture of red and white pixels. Experiment with this, and see how you like the effects.

Click **OK**, and Paint Shop Pro reduces the colors in your image.

The Least You Need to Know

➤ Computers treat all colors as a numerical mixture of red, green, and blue.

➤ When starting a new image, you have to select the background color and the number of colors in the image.

➤ Choosing to have more colors available to you makes for larger files and slower program times.

➤ To set the Foreground/Stroke Solid Color, click on the **Available Color** display. Right-click that area to set the Background/Fill Solid Color.

➤ Clicking the **Active Stroke Style** or **Active Fill Style** panel opens a dialog box that you use to select the exact color you want from the available colors.

➤ When working in a fewer-color mode, you can change the colors in your palette by choosing **Colors**, **Edit Palette** then double-clicking the color you want to change.

Chapter 4

The First Coat of Paint

In This Chapter

➤ Paint with the paintbrush and airbrush, and unpaint with the eraser

➤ Replace one color with another

➤ Draw shapes

➤ Fill in areas

That's enough talk about picking palettes and color ranges. It's time we get down to actually slapping some digital paint down on the digital canvas! Make sure you're wearing your digital smock, because we're going to be tossing around pixels with abandon.

In this chapter, you cover the basics of all the *raster* drawing tools, the tools that directly set the color of each pixel. Some of these tools have so many features that they need their own chapters to really cover them in detail, so I've given them their own chapters later in the book. But after reading this chapter, you'll have basic knowledge of a good set of tools, and you'll be able to do some nice computer paintings. Press **Ctrl+N** to open up a new window (go for 16.7-million-color mode), and let's get painting!

Without the Paint Brush, the Program Would Just Be "Pro"

 The paint brush is your numero uno basic painting tool. Click the **Paint Brush** button (shortcut: **B**) then move your pointer to an open image window, and your pointer turns into a little picture of a paint brush. Press your mouse button and drag the mouse, and your Paint Brush leaves a line of the foreground color. That, plain and simple, is the very basic of the Paint Brush.

But of course that's not all there is to it. Try holding down the right mouse button and dragging the mouse. Now you're painting with the fill color.

Straight Talk About Straight Lines

As a part-time comic book writer, I spend a fair amount of time at comic book conventions, autographing my work. There's usually an artist sitting next to me, autographing his or her work and doing sketches. Some fan usually looks on in awe, saying, "That's amazing. I couldn't draw a straight line!" The artists always grin.

You see, they can't draw straight lines either. They cheat. They use rulers or straight edges.

Drawing a straight line with a mouse is actually harder than drawing one with a pencil, but Paint Shop Pro lets you cheat. With your Paint Brush tool, click where you want one end of the line to be. A dot shows up. Now hold down **Shift** and click where you want the line to end. A straight line appears between the point at which you first clicked and where you just clicked. If you keep holding down **Shift** and clicking in different spots, you end up with a series of straight lines going from spot to spot.

One nifty trick you can pull with this straight-line system is to alternate between left-clicking and right-clicking while you hold down **Shift**. This results in you drawing a series of lines alternating between the stroke and fill colors.

Size Matters

You can draw with brushes of different thickness; you can use a small brush for drawing details, a large brush for filling in large areas quickly, or a teeny tiny brush if you have a large area to fill in and are getting paid by the hour.

To change the size of the brush, point to the Tool Options title bar (if the title bar isn't displayed, press the letter **O** on the keyboard). It expands to display the dialog box seen in Figure 4.1.

Click to keep option
window open

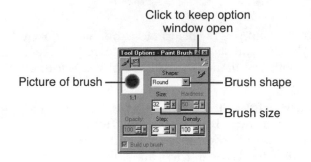

Picture of brush ⟶   ⟵ Brush shape

⟵ Brush size

Figure 4.1

Changing the width and point of your brush is easier on the computer—you don't have to lick it!

Fruitful Roll-Ups

Most users leave their PSP tool options in *roll up* mode, which means than only the title bar is displayed. When you point to the title bar, the rest of the dialog box appears. When you're done setting options, it rolls back up. If you want to lock the dialog box into its rolled down mode, click the down arrow button next to the close (**x**) button; it turns into an up arrow button, and the dialog box locks open. If you never want such things to roll up, choose **File, Preferences, General Program Preferences**, then on the **Dialogs and Palettes** tab, clear the **Enable automatic palette roll-ups** checkbox.

The Size field on the first tab of the dialog box lists the brush width in pixels. You can change this size in a number of ways:

➤ Type a number into the Size field.

➤ Click the up and down arrows right next to the Size field to increase or decrease the size.

➤ Click anywhere on the two-colored line beneath the size field to set a width ranging from 1 to 255 pixels.

➤ Click on the drop-down arrow at the far right of the Size field. While you hold the mouse button down, a measuring stick appears. Drag your pointer along the measuring stick; your brush will be as wide as the distance from the left end of the measuring stick to where you drag the pointer to.

If it's possible to have *too* many ways to set the same number, I think this is a clear example! (Many of the number-selecting fields in PSP work in this same way.)

Shape Shifting

Click on the **Shape** drop-down list, and you're able to pick from half a dozen different shapes for your brush tip. Usually, you should use **Round** (which makes it easier to keep curved lines looking smooth and natural) or **Square** (if you want pointy corners).

The other four shapes (**Left Slash**, **Right Slash**, **Horizontal**, and **Vertical**) are good for drawing lines of variable thickness. For example, the Horizontal brush is wide but not very tall. This makes up-and-down lines come out thick, but side-to-side lines come out thin. Take some time to play with these and see what I mean.

And All the Rest

The other settings on the first tab of the Paint Brush Tool Options palette are advanced features you use to create brushes with special textures. You learn about these in Chapter 12, "Fuller Brush Knowledge." For now, just leave Hardness, Opacity, and Density set to 100, and leave Step set to 1.

An Eraser That Looks Like a Brush

 The **Eraser** tool (shortcut: **E**) works exactly like the Paint Brush tool, with one exception: When you hold down the left mouse button, it paints with the fill color, and the right mouse button paints the stroke color, instead of vice versa.

Whoopee. There hardly seems to be a point to having an eraser at all, if it works just like a brush, right? But actually, there is a point to this. You set the Paint Brush and Eraser tool options separately. That way, you can have a big round paintbrush and a little square eraser without having to keep switching options.

The Eraser tool has one other important trick: if your image has a transparent background, erasing with the left mouse button simply removes the paint, leaving transparency in its wake.

'ow to 'andle an 'airbrush

 The **Airbrush** tool (shortcut: **U**) works a lot like the paint brush, with one main exception: The paint it puts down looks like it came out of a spray can, so it's heaviest in the center and is thinner at the edges. If you keep running the Airbrush over a single spot in your picture, the paint becomes heavier and heavier.

The real difference between the Airbrush and the Paint Brush is the tool option settings for Hardness, Opacity, and Density. Don't mess with those, or you'll ruin the effect.

Tricks 'n' Tips

Undo: The Right Way to Correct Missteaks

People who aren't artists usually think that erasers are there to correct a pencil error you just made. If you just made an error with a brush, however, the Eraser tool doesn't actually erase what you did. Instead, you end up painting over it. It's hard to paint exactly over it. Even if you can paint exactly over it, you're just painting a solid color; you aren't restoring any detail that you actually painted over.

 If you make a mistake, click **Undo** (shortcut: **Ctrl+Z**). PSP undoes the last change you made to your drawing. You can click **Undo** multiple times to step back a few steps. Note: Undo does not undo changes in tool options and does not unsave files. It really only undoes changes that alter the appearance of your current image.

 If you click Undo too many times, click **Redo** (shortcut: **Ctrl+Alt+Z**). This re-does the step you just undid. (You have to do this before you do anything else to the drawing, however. After you change the drawing, you lose the ability to redo.)

If you need to undo more than a few steps, or if you want to see exactly what commands you're undoing, choose **Edit, Command History** (shortcut: **Shift+Ctrl+Z**). A display appears, showing a long list of the individual steps used to make up this picture. Click on the earliest step you want to undo, then click **Undo**; that step and every step since are undone.

Color Recycling: Reuse Those Hues

After you've worked on your image for a while, you've probably changed your stroke color several times. What if you want to resume working with a color you used earlier? Sure, you could look through all 16.7 million colors hoping to happen upon the right one, which is a fine way to spend time if there's nothing good on TV.

 Oh, who am I kidding? There's *always* something good on TV. Luckily, there's also an easy way to reuse any color you're already using. Click **Dropper** (so named because you use it to pick up colors; what do you expect from folks who created a tool that paints over things and then called it *Eraser*?) and a little eyedropper icon appears. On your image, click any spot that has the color you want to reuse. Violà, it becomes your stroke color! To select fill color, right-click with the Dropper.

The Science of Art

A Little Paint with Big Requirements

Airbrush is designed to work in 16.7-million-color mode, where it can paint lightly over existing colors by tinting them with the spray color. Airbrush is much less subtle in lower-color modes, where those small variations in color aren't available.

A Quicker Picker-Upper

You can get the Dropper while using any painting tool without clicking on any screen buttons. Just hold down the **Ctrl** key, and you have the Dropper. That way, you can quickly pick up a color and then go back to using the tool you were already using just by releasing the Ctrl key.

Being able to select an existing color is very important if you're going to try (time for some big letters now) …

Color Replacing: Turning Your Blues into Roses

You've just finished painting a beautiful picture of your girlfriend and her beautiful blue eyes. Then your best friend looks over your shoulder and points out that your girlfriend's eyes are really green. What do you do? Do you start all over? Do you tear out your hair in frustration? Do you start to get very worried that your best friend has been paying close attention to your girlfriend's eyes? No! You just use the Color Replacer tool.

 When you click **Color Replacer** (shortcut: **,**—the comma key) you find yourself working with a brush that works like the other brushes, with one major exception: it won't paint over most colors. It only paints over the currently selected fill solid color, and colors that are very similar to that.

Tricks 'n' Tips

How Close Is Close?

The Color Replacer doesn't require an exact color match to replace a color. That way, you can use it to work on a photo of Mom and repaint her hair purple without worrying about the fact that her real hair is not all the exact same shade. You can actually adjust how precisely the color has to match; on the second tab of the **Tool Options** palette for the Color Replacer, there is a **Tolerance** field. Reduce the number in this field, and the match has to be more precise. Increase the number, and a looser match is fine. Don't increase it *too* much, or you'll start painting over colors you didn't mean to replace.

Use the Dropper to pick the color from your picture's eyes (right-clicking so that it gets picked up as the fill color), then select the correct color for her eyes from the Available Color display. Now you can run the Color Replacer brush quickly over her eyes, without worrying about accidentally painting her eyelashes green.

Retouch Me, Baby!

 The **Retouch** tool (shortcut: **Z**) is another brush, but it doesn't paint with the Stroke or Fill color. Instead, it messes with the colors you already have.

How does it mess with them? That depends on the *Retouch mode* you select from the second tab of the Retouch Tool Option palette, as shown in Figure 4.2.

Figure 4.2

With the second tab of the Retouch tool options, you can burn your image.

Retouch has 19 different modes, each with a different effect. You can see the affect of these effects in the first two pages of this book's color inset section.

➤ *Lighten RGB* and *Lightness Up* both lighten the color wherever you paint with this brush. (The difference between them is slight, having to do with how the lighter color is calculated.) Similarly, *Darken RGB* and *Lightness Down* causes darker colors wherever you paint.

➤ *Soften* blurs the edges of adjacent colors together; *Sharpen* makes the edges more distinct.

➤ *Emboss* turns everything gray, and creates shadows and light at the edges of your figure, making it look like it's pressed into a metal plate.

➤ *Smudge* and *Push* smear paint around. Smudge smears all the paint you move across; Push keeps smearing the color from where you start dragging.

➤ *Burn* causes already dark areas to become darker, while leaving lighter areas alone. *Dodge* does just the opposite, lightening darker areas while leaving light areas alone.

➤ *Saturation Up* makes the color more vibrant; *Saturation Down* makes it duller, bringing it down to gray.

➤ *Hue Up* and *Hue Down* replace your colors with other colors. This can be a very psychedelic effect.

➤ *Saturation to Target*, *Hue to Target*, *Lightness to Target*, and *Color to Target* make whatever you paint over more like your currently selected stroke color. If you want to see what your brother would look like if he held his breath until he turned blue, you could use a photo of him, select a blue color from your palette, and use **Hue to Target**.

Retouch only works in 16-million-color mode and in greyscale mode. Some of the retouch styles (the ones based on hue, saturation, and lightness) don't even work in greyscale mode.

No-Frills Fills

 The **Flood Fill** tool (shortcut: **F**) is designed to quickly have an effect on an area of a single color. Usually, it's used to fill that area with another color, or a pattern. You can change that blue sky to a green one with a single click.

To use the Fill tool to fill with a solid color, you need to check your settings on your Flood Fill Tool Option palette, as seen in Figure 4.3.

Figure 4.3

Flood Fill can do a lot of neat tricks. To keep things simple, use these settings.

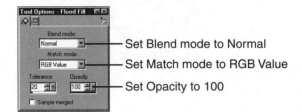

— Set Blend mode to Normal
— Set Match mode to RGB Value
— Set Opacity to 100

With these settings in place, simply click on the area of the picture that you want to fill. A click fills with the stroke color, and a right-click fills with the fill color. The fill spreads out to every connected pixel of the same color (or similar color—this tool uses the tolerance setting just like the retouch tool did, so you can require things to be the exact same color or you can have the fill spread to anything of similar color).

Fancier Fills

The Flood Fill tool can also fill the selected area with patterns, or with another image, or perform a tint or other nifty effect on the area. In fact, there are so many tricks that you can do with fills that I couldn't even begin to squeeze them all into this chapter. They deserve a chapter of their own, and they've got one: Chapter 11, "Fun with Fills."

Circles and Arrows and Squares, Oh My!

 When you click **Preset Shapes** (shortcut: **/**) you're ready to spend the day drawing all the circles, arrows, rectangles, and stars you want. (Me, I'd settle for three squares a day.)

The settings for this tool (seen in Figure 4.4) are easy. Use the **Shape Type** field to select what sort of shape you're drawing. This offers 15 different shapes, ranging from your basic triangle to ellipses, hexagons, octagons, to happy faces and helicopters.

Figure 4.4

Here's where you preset your preset shape.

Use the **Line width** selector to choose the width of the line you stroke with. If you're working with this tool now, make sure that the **Create as vector** checkbox is cleared. If you leave a checkmark in there and then draw a shape, you'll find that most of your tools are no longer available. There's a good reason for this, which you learn about in upcoming chapters. For now, trust me and leave it clear.

If you have a check in the **Retain style** option, the shape will be drawn in the colors it appears in on the Tool Options palette. With this option turned off, the shape will be outlined with your current stroke color, and filled with your current fill color. If you don't want the shape filled in, point to the Active Stroke Style panel and hold your mouse button down. Four buttons appear; release your mouse button and then click the right-most of the four. The Stroke Style display now shows a circle with a slash through it, meaning that there will be no stroke. Similarly, if you want to draw an unfilled outline, do the same action with the Active Fill Style panel.

Shaping the Shape

The way that you put down the shape varies a little depending on the sort of shape you're putting down.

To draw any other object, mentally picture a rectangle that fits tightly around the fill area of this object. Drag from the upper-left corner of that rectangle to the lower-right corner. When you release your mouse button, your shape appears.

If you drag down toward the left, rather than toward the right, the object you draw will be the mirror reflection of how it's pictured on the Preset Shape Tool Option palette. If you drag upwards instead of downwards, the shape will appear upside-down. Of course, with some

Pick Your Center

If you need a shape centered on a certain spot, point to that spot then hold down the right mouse button instead of the left when dragging.

objects this won't make much difference; an upside-down and backwards ellipse is still an ellipse.

What Is "Alias," and Why Are We Against It?

The option marked *antialias* might have caught your eye. Computer images are made up of pixels, those nicely lined-up little rectangular dots. That's really great if you want to make a smooth horizontal line (a row of pixels in one color) or a vertical line (a column of pixels). But what if you want to make a diagonal line, or a curve?

Building a curve out of rectangular pixels is a lot like trying to build a curve out of Lego blocks. The best you can hope for is a rough curve shape made up of little angled steps. This curve might look fine from a distance, but if you get a good close look at it, you see the angled edge of every Lego. The lower the resolution your computer image is, the more likely that the little steps (called *jaggies*, after Lego block inventor Antoine Jaggie) will be visible. (I admit it: that bit about Antoine Jaggie is made up. Everyone knows Lego blocks were invented by Nancy Legoblock, herself.)

Recognizing this problem, alert computer graphics geeks (fueled, as always, by intense curiosity and excessive amounts of cola) came up with a technique called *antialiasing*. This technique blurs the edges of the curve, blending the color of the curve with the color behind the curve. As you can see in Figure 4.5, this creates a smoother-looking image.

Figure 4.5

This is a close-up of two copies of the same line. The right curve uses the antialiasing option, the left one does not. Don't run your finger on those jaggies; they're sharp!

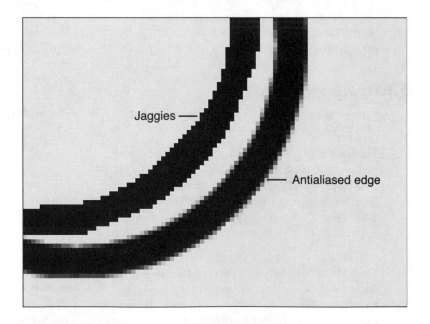

Jaggies ——

—— Antialiased edge

Why not always use antialiasing? There are two main times when you want to avoid it. The first is if you're going to try to be using a flood fill or some other tool that needs to identify the edges of the curve. Because it's using variable colors, it's hard to identify the edge of an antialiased curve.

The other reason not to use it would be file size. If you're designing screen buttons for your Web site, for example, antialiasing could double the size of your image file, slowing down your page.

Clone Brush: Nice Tool, Scary Name

 Reach for the **Clone Brush** (shortcut: **N**) when you want to copy a little detail or texture from one part of your image to another. It's a nifty tool, and (like real cloning) can be used to create mutants, as Figure 4.6 shows.

Copy to pointer

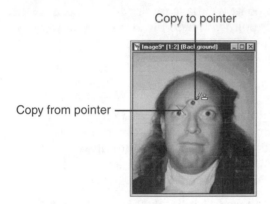

Copy from pointer

Figure 4.6

Ben Franklin didn't need bifocals any more after growing a third eye.

To use the Clone Brush tool, right-click on the spot that you want to copy from. Then go to where you want the copy to end up, press down the left mouse button, and start brushing. As you brush, you see two pointers: a brush pointer where you're painting, and an X where you're copying from. As you move the brush, the X moves in conjunction with it. That way, you can copy from all around the original spot.

The Clone Brush isn't the best way to copy full objects or large areas. (You'll see better tools to do that in Chapter 5, "Selecting and Cropping: Tools for a Picky Farmer.") What it's great for is copying subtle textures. Let's say you want to create an image of a leatherbound book entitled *Why I Love Canned Zucchini*. You have a picture of a nice leatherbound book, but unfortunately it has the title *The Lonely Man's Guide to Piranha Care* on the cover. With the Clone Brush, you can copy some of the leather

Tricks 'n' Tips

Clone From Another World

The Clone Brush can be used to copy from one picture to another that's using the same color mode. Open both pictures, right-click the one you're copying from, then paint on the one you're copying to.

texture over those words. Because it's a brush, there won't be a hard edge showing where you copied.

Clone Alignment: Political Problem of the Future?

On the first tab of the tool options for the Clone Brush are the same options that you saw for the other sorts of brushes. The second tab has an interesting option that's just for cloning: *Clone mode*.

Select **Aligned**, and the distance between the copy-from and the copy-to point stays the same until you right-click a new copy-from point. This helps you if you're not copying all in one smooth stroke. For example, after you're done painting Ben Franklin's eye, you can release the mouse button, roll the mouse down and to the left, and start painting again. Your copy-to point will have moved to Ben's eye on the right side of the picture, and the copy-from point will be on his nose. If you were to start dragging here, you'd be painting the nose on top of the eye.

Selecting **Non-Aligned**, however, resets the copy-from point to the original copy-from point every time you stop dragging the mouse. This is handy if you want to copy one object to many different spots on the screen. If you just copied Ben Franklin's eye to his forehead, then released the mouse button and pointed to Ben's cheek, the copy-to point will have moved to his cheek but the copy-from point will still be on his eye. Start painting again, and you'll copy his eye onto his cheek. This way, you can paint eyes all over his face without having to right-click on the eye each time.

And that would be quite appropriate. After all, wasn't it Ben Franklin who said, "My only regret is that I have but two eyes to give for my country?"

No, I guess it wasn't.

The Least You Need to Know

 ➤ Use the Paint Brush to paint with the current foreground color.

 ➤ The Airbrush paints with softer edges.

 ➤ Click the Dropper on the picture to reuse an existing color for your new foreground color.

 ➤ The Flood Fill tool can be used to fill a single-color area with a different color or a pattern.

➤ The Preset Shape tool can draw circles, rectangles, arrows, and other shapes.

➤ The Clone Brush copies one area of the image to another.

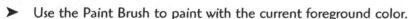

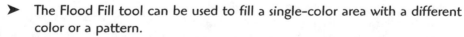

Chapter 5

Selecting and Cropping: Tools for a Picky Farmer

In This Chapter

➤ Selecting and indicating a portion of your image

➤ Copying your selection

➤ Moving your selection

➤ Trimming off the edges of your image

Sometimes you might want to do something to just part of your picture. For example, you might have a bunch of lovely photos of your trip to Italy last year. The only problem is, that pain-in-the-neck that you were dating (for reasons that you can no longer recall) is in every shot. You want to cut that particular mistake out of those shots, to paint over, erase, or otherwise eliminate this person from your shots. (Except maybe the shot of the Leaning Tower of Pisa, where it looks like it's about to collapse on your ex-lover—that one brings a smile to your face.)

To do something to part of your picture, you have to show Paint Shop Pro the part of the picture you're concerned about. That's what *selecting* is.

Selecting is easy—it usually takes just a couple mouse clicks. The reason selecting takes up a whole chapter is not because it's complicated, but because PSP provides so many different sorts of selecting tools, each designed to make a different sort of selecting easy.

Selecting Rectangular Areas and Square People

 The **Selection** (shortcut: **S**) tool is used to select an area that's a simple shape. Usually, it's used to select a rectangular area of the image, but if you explore the Tool Option palette for this tool, you see it can also be used to select shapes such as circles, arrows, stars, and some of the other marshmallow shapes from Lucky Charms.

To select a rectangular shape, point to one corner of the area that you want to select. Drag to the rectangle's opposite corner. A moving dotted line appears, showing you the area that you've selected. This line is called the *marquee*, named after the Marquee De Queensbury, who invented the rules for boxing. (Or maybe it is named after Marquee Mark And The Funky Bunch, I'm not sure.)

If you set the shape to Circle or Ellipse on the Tool Options palette, then the first point you click is the center of the selection, and the point you drag to is the outside edge of the selected area. If your shape is Arrow 3, the arrow aims from where you start dragging and goes to where you stop dragging. Choose any other shape, and the selected area is the biggest version of that shape that fits into the area you dragged.

Selections at Work

To see the effect selecting has, use the Paint Brush and try to paint across the edge of the selected area. As you can see in Figure 5.1, the Paint Brush works fine inside the selected area, but it doesn't paint at all outside the selection.

Figure 5.1

The scribbling stops automatically at the marquee that marks the selection edge.

Smoothing Sharp Edges

The Tool Options palette for the Selection tool (seen in Figure 5.2) has two different ways of removing the sharp edges from what you select. When you put a check in the **Antialias** checkbox (only available in 16 million color and greyscale modes) and move or copy the selected area to somewhere else, the edges are antialiased against what you put it against. This helps hide the edges where you pasted the new object, so there isn't a telltale sharp band of color showing that it is pasted into place.

The Mystery of the Missing Marquee

If the marquee annoys you or blocks your view of something you need to see, press **Shift+Ctrl+M** to make it disappear. To make it reappear, press **Shift+Ctrl+M** again

Figure 5.2

You have the option of selecting options for the Selection tool in the Selection Tool Option palette.

Selecting a number for the **Feather** field has a somewhat similar effect. *Feathering* is an artists' term for fading in or out at the edges. When you feather the edge of the selection, PSP takes a little of the color from a band around the edge of the selection and leaves a little of the color there (the number you set in the field is the width of the band, in pixels). This way, when you paste the selection into something, the selection is surrounded by a mixture of the colors from the old location and from the new. It's kind of like how the Empire State Building would stick out like a sore thumb if you put it in the middle of sleepy Riverton, New Jersey (my home town). But if you took a handful of

Precision Selection

Double-click the **Selection** button on the tool palette and the Select Area dialog box appears. You can use this to create a selection area with a specific width and height.

smaller New York buildings along with it, it would look a little less out of place—but just a little. Feathering really works properly only in 16 million color and greyscale modes. In modes with fewer colors, it expands the selection area but selects all of the expanded area, rather than fading out to the edges.

Freehand Cowhand: Lasso Irregular Shapes and People

Not everything in life is a rectangle, a circle, or even a hexagon. Crullers, for example, aren't rectangles. Nor are banana splits, chicken drumsticks, or those little snack crackers shaped like goldfish. Oh, there are probably some non-food items that are also non-rectangular, but I don't think about those so much.

 When you click the **Freehand** button, you activate one great tool for selecting irregular shapes. Actually, you get *three* great tools, all wrapped up in one little button. The three different tools can be selected from the Selection Type drop-down menu in the Tool Options palette.

Freehand Freehand: A Tool so Great They Had to Name It Twice

Select the **Freehand** option from the Selection Type field, and you have the tool that's the simplest to understand (but probably the hardest to use accurately). With the mouse button held down, draw a line around whatever you want to select. (That's the tricky part, trying to draw a smooth and exact shape around an object using the mouse.)

Why Did the Selection Get Bigger?

If the selection seems to expand when you release the mouse button, you probably have left a number in the Feather field. Set it to zero, and this problem stops.

When you've followed the full path, release the mouse button. The area within the path you traced is now selected. If you release the mouse button without bringing the path back to where you started, PSP completes the path by drawing a straight line between where you started and where you ended.

If you're as bad a mouse-drawer as I am (as shown in Figure 5.3), you've probably ended up with a very irregularly shaped blob. You have to have a truly steady hand to capture exactly what you want and no more.

The Point of Point To Point

The **Point to Point** setting in the Selection Type field is a great tool for precisely selecting an area. With this option in place, click at points around the edge of the area you want to select, as though you're putting up fence posts to build a fence right on the border of the area. As you lay down each post, the path is drawn from the previous post to this one.

Figure 5.3

I tried to select the circle using the freehand option, but as you can see by the marquee, I didn't do a very good job.

After you place the last point, right-click once. Paint Shop Pro connects the last point to the first. The area within your "fence" is now selected.

The Smart Edge for Fuzzy People

But what if you have an item to select that doesn't have a nice, clean edge? What if you have a picture of a fuzzy lady in a fuzzy sweater eating a fuzzy sandwich? How do you select anything within that fuzz?

Tricks 'n' Tips

Fix It in Post-Production

If you place a point badly, press **Delete** to get rid of it, then continue placing points.

When it's hard to place fence posts right around the image, choose **Smart Edge** in the Selection Type field. You still click from point to point around the image, but (as you can see in Figure 5.4) when you put down each point, Paint Shop Pro displays a rectangle leading from the previous point. You don't have to place the points precisely; just make sure the edge of the object stays inside that rectangle.

When you click the point into place, Paint Shop Pro finds an edge within the rectangle. (It detects the edge by seeing where one color ends and the next one begins.) On a fuzzy object or a photograph, this isn't a straight line; it is a wiggly edge, but it should contain what you're trying to capture. The more careful you are in setting your points, the better PSP will be at finding what you want.

As with the point to point tool, after you click the last point into place, right-click. The first point and the last point are automatically connected. Pressing **Delete** undoes the most recently set point.

Figure 5.4

Sometimes, the Smart Edge freehand tool can really get my goat!

The existing path   Keep the edge within this rectangle

The Magic Wand: It's Wanderful!

 Click the **Magic Wand** button when you want to quickly select a large area of a similar color or brightness. The Tool options for the Magic Wand include the Match Mode field, where you can choose pixels based on the following criteria:

➤ **RGB Value**   Find the group of connected pixels that closely match the color of the one you clicked.

➤ **Hue**   Include those pixels of the same hue, even if they are different levels of brightness or saturations. For example, dark red areas and light red areas are both included.

➤ **Brightness**   Match pixels with similar degrees of white. This is good for picking out the silhouette of a man standing in front of a bright sunset, or a glowing man standing in front of a dark moonset. (The Hue and Brightness settings for the magic wand only work with 16.7 million color images.)

➤ **All Pixels**   Use this on pictures with transparent areas. It selects everything connected to the click point that's not transparent.

The Tolerance field is used to set how close the match between pixels has to be. The lower the number, the closer the match has to be.

By using the Magic Wand tool, you can pick up some very irregular areas. Because each pixel in the area is tested, the wand frequently drops a lot of individual pixels from the area. (This makes the marquee look very complex and busy, because it has to show an outline around every pixel it drops out.)

The Magic Wand only selects pixels that are connected in a group. If you want to include every area in the picture that matches a given pixel, first use the Magic Wand to select that pixel, then choose **Selections**, **Modify**, **Select Similar** (which only works in 16 million color and greyscale modes).

To clear the selection altogether, just right-click with the Magic Wand. It disappears like magic!

Simplifying the Selection

To recapture all the dropped-out pixels, choose **Selections**, **Modify**, **Expand**, then enter 3 to expand the selection by three pixels. Choose **Selections**, **Modify**, **Contract**, and enter 3 to trim the added pixels from the outside rim.

Everything: The Unselective Selection

To select the entire picture, choose **Selections**, **Select All** (shortcut: **Ctrl+A**). Now you can copy the whole thing, or paint on the whole image—both of which you could do if you had nothing selected at all!

Muscling Up and Trimming Down Your Selection

Normally, starting a new selection deselects the selection you already have. And that's usually what you want it to do. But let's say you're trying to select an ice cream cone (I select pistachio cones, myself) from a picture of a girl holding two ice cream cones. If you click the Magic Wand on the ice cream, you just select the ice cream, and ice cream without a cone is a mess. If you then click the cone with the Magic Wand, the cone becomes selected, but the ice cream is deselected—and a cone without ice cream is a tragedy!

If you select the cone then hold down the **Shift** while clicking the ice cream, both items are selected, as you can see in Figure 5.5. Any selecting you do with the **Shift** key held down, no matter which tool you use, is added to the previous selection.

Figure 5.5

Hold down the Shift key, and you can select both the cone and the ice cream. (I select sugar cones and pistachio ice cream, myself.)

Making a More Selective Selection

You can remove parts of your selection. Just hold down the **Ctrl** key while using any selection tool, and the tool becomes a deselection tool, trimming away from the already selected area. (Remember, feathering also works on deselection, so your edges might not come out just as you expect them to.)

Growing Concerns

If you just want to expand the selection area, choose **Selections**, **Modify**, **Expand**. A dialog box appears asking for a number of pixels. Type in how many pixels you want to expand the edge by, and press **Enter**.

Similarly, to trim a few pixels around the edge of the selection, choose **Selections**, **Modify**, **Contract**, and then enter the number of pixels. Enter a number high enough, you end up with nothing selected!

Everything but the Girl

Sometimes, you want to select everything *but* a certain object. To do that, select the item you want to exclude. Choose **Selections**, **Invert** (shortcut: **Shift+Ctrl+I**) and you'll still see the marquee around your original selection, but you'll see a marquee around the edge of the image as well. What's selected now is everything between the two marquees, which is everything *but* your original selection. (If your original selection touched the edge of the image, then you'll just see one marquee, which scoots around your original selection to exclude it.)

Not Even the Girl

To deselect everything, just right-click on the picture with any selection tool. Alternatively, you could deselect by hitting **Ctrl+D** (the shortcut for **Selections**, **Select None**), saving you from having to switch tools.

It's Selected; Now What?

There's more to selecting than getting that nifty marquee effect around the picture of your dog. As mentioned earlier, after you select an area, most of the paint tools work only on the selected area. (This isn't true of the Preset Shape tool, by the way.) The selected item can also be copied, moved, resized, flipped, and toasted in various forms.

Faith Can Move Mountain Goats

If you point your selection tool to the inside of the selection, the pointer turns into a four-headed arrow (which is very hard to string into a bow without hurting yourself). You can use this pointer to drag the selection to another part of the image. As you can see in Figure 5.6, the area that the selected item took up is now filled with the current Background/Fill Solid Color.

Feather–Plucking

To get rid of the edge created by the antialiasing or feathering features, choose **Selections**, **Matting**. Then choose **Remove White Matte** if it has a white background, **Remove Black Matte** if it has a black background, or **Defringe** if it has a color background.

If you hold down the **Alt** key while dragging the selection, you don't leave a hole where the selection had been. Instead, you get a second copy of your selection to drag around.

You can also make very exact moves by holding down the **Shift** key and pressing the keyboard arrow keys. Each press moves the selection one pixel in the direction of the arrow. Hold down **Ctrl+Shift**, and the arrow keys move the selection 10 pixels at a time.

Figure 5.6

If you move a mountain goat, you leave a mountain goat-shaped hole.

Sliding Stylish Selection Shapes

 Here's a keen little trick: If you use the **Mover** tool to *right-drag* (drag holding down the right mouse button, rather than the left) the selection, you move the marquee without moving its contents. Suddenly (as you'll see in Figure 5.7), you have a selected area that's the shape of a mountain goat even though it doesn't have a mountain goat inside it! (This trick only works if you haven't already moved the selection.)

Figure 5.7

Admittedly, you'll rarely have to select an area the same shape as a mountain goat that doesn't contain the mountain goat.

Cuttin' Up and Pastin' Down

You can make copies of your mountain goat to sprinkle around your picture or add to other pictures. (You can even copy images that aren't mountain goats, if there aren't any mountain goats in your image. But golly, why would you want to make an image without mountain goats?)

 Click **Copy** (shortcut: **Ctrl+C**), and a copy of your selected area is stored in an area of computer memory called the *clipboard*. (It's a cheap clipboard; it can only hold one thing at a time. When you copy something onto the clipboard, whatever was previously on the clipboard is replaced with the new item.)

One Clipboard Fits All

All the programs you use work with the same clipboard. The good news is that you can use the clipboard to move images from one program to another. The bad news is that if you copy some text in your email program (for example), you wipe out the picture you had stored on the clipboard.

 Cut (shortcut: **Ctrl+X**) works a lot like copy, except that when it puts your selection on the clipboard, it removes it from your image.

While you have the image on your clipboard, you can paste it down on this image or on other images. Several different paste commands, each with its own special magic, exist for your pasting and placement pleasure. When you choose **Edit**, **Paste** a submenu that includes the following selections appears:

➤ **As New Image** (shortcut: **Ctrl+V**) creates a brand new image with the clipboard contents. If your copied selection is a rectangle, the image is now the size of that rectangle. If your selection is anything else, the image size is the smallest rectangle possible that holds the image. All the space outside of the selected item is transparent.

➤ **As New Selection** (shortcut: **Ctrl+E**) copies the material from the clipboard onto the currently selected image. This is true even if the current image is a different image than the one you copied the selection from, as shown in Figure 5.8.

➤ **As Transparent Selection** (shortcut: **Shift+Ctrl+E**) works the same as As New Selection, except that any part of the clipboard image that matches the currently selected background color becomes transparent, showing through to the image on which it was pasted.

➤ **Into Selection** (shortcut: **Shift+Ctrl+L**) can be used to stretch or shrink the item from the clipboard. Before you use this command, use the rectangular select tool to select where you want the image to appear.

Figure 5.8

"Mommy, how did the mountain goat get in the house?"
"It was pasted as a new selection, dear."

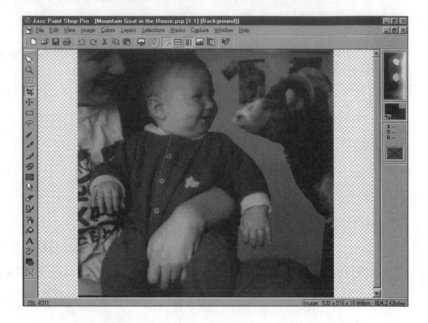

Once an image is on the clipboard, you can paste it repeatedly, until you cut or copy something else onto the clipboard.

There are several other selections on the Paste sub-menu. Those work with other PSP features, and are described in the appropriate sections of the book.

Floating Your Goats and Other Selections

When you move your selection or paste an item as a new selection, the selection *floats*. That means that it's not actually part of your image yet. It's hovering above the image. It becomes stuck into your image when you deselect it.

If you want to stick the selection into your image without deselecting it, choose **Selections**, **Defloat** (shortcut: **Shift+Ctrl+F**). To get rid of your selection altogether, press **Delete**.

Tricks 'n' Tips

Floating Motionless

To make your selection float without moving it, press **Ctrl+F**.

Flipping and Tipping

You can spin your selected object, reversing it, rotating it, or turning it upside-down. (Just be careful if you do all this to a mountain goat; there's nothing worse than a mountain goat with motion sickness.) The commands to do this are:

➤ **Image, Flip** (shortcut: **Ctrl+I**) flips your selection upside down. (This is different from rotating it upside down. When you flip your mountain goat upside down, the feet will be at the top, but the nose will still be at the left. If you were to rotate your mountain goat 180 degrees, the feet would be in the air but the nose would now be at the right.)

➤ **Image, Mirror** (shortcut: **Ctrl+M**) creates a mirror image of your selection. In other words, your goat's nose is now be where his other end was, and vice versa.

➤ **Image, Rotate** (shortcut: **Ctrl+R**) brings up the dialog box seen in Figure 5.9. You can rotate the image at nice right angles (90°, 180°, or 270°—in other words, a quarter turn, a half turn, or a three-quarters turn), which keeps the image perfectly sharp. You can also rotate at any other angle, which fuzzes the picture a bit. The higher the resolution of your image, the less the fuzzing is visible.

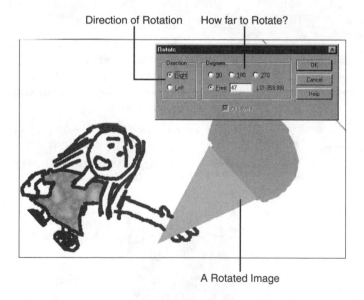

Direction of Rotation   How far to Rotate?

A Rotated Image

Figure 5.9

Rotate: *The command so cruel, it knocks over little girls with ice cream.*

Crop: Turn Paint Shop Pro into a Chop Shop

You've got this really great picture of your son, running down the road carrying the Little League Most Valuable Player trophy triumphantly over his head. At least, that's what the left side of the picture is. The right side shows the kid next door chasing after your son, trying to get back the trophy that that your son stole from him. It would be nice if you could just keep one side of the picture and get rid of the rest, and that's where the Crop tool comes in.

Selected Cropping

If the part you want to crop to is already selected and the selection isn't floating, choose **Image, Crop to Selection** (shortcut: **Shift+R**). This will crop to the closest possible rectangle containing the selection.

Crop by Number

Double-click the **Crop** button, and a Crop Area dialog box appears. You can use this to create a cropping area with precise dimensions.

Click **Crop** (shortcut: **R**), then point to one corner of what you want your image to include. Drag to the opposite corner, and a rectangle appears, surrounding everything included in your final image.

You can adjust the edges of this rectangle. Point to a top or bottom edge, and your pointer becomes a two-headed arrow. You can now drag that edge up or down. Similarly, point to a side edge, and you can drag that edge side-to-side.

When you have the edges where you want them, double-click inside the rectangle. Everything outside the rectangle is eliminated, as you can see in Figure 5.10!

Figure 5.10

By cropping, you can reduce an image to its most interesting part. Or you can reduce it to a goat head.

The Least You Need to Know

➤ Use the **Selection** tool to select rectangular areas.

➤ The **Freehand** tool helps you select irregular shapes.

➤ Click the **Magic Wand** on a pixel to select all the similarly colored pixels surrounding it.

➤ Dragging the selected area moves it to another part of the image, leaving an empty shape behind.

➤ Dragging the selected area while holding down the **Alt** key makes a copy of the selection and moves that.

➤ Click **Copy** to copy the selection onto the clipboard, from which you can paste it using the **Edit, Paste** commands.

➤ To trim a picture, use the **Crop** tool to select the area of the picture you want to keep, then double-click inside that area.

Zooming In and Moving Things About

This chapter covers nothing about changing your image. Read through the entire thing, and you won't find a single mention of anything that will change the color, fix the shape, or rearrange the pieces of your image.

So what exactly is in this chapter? Thrilling tales of the Space Bunny Patrol!

No, wait. My editor (the incredibly talented Sarah Robbins) says I have to talk about Paint Shop Pro. So I'll talk about the various ways that you can change your view of your image to make it easier to work on. And I'll also complain about how editors can add words like "the incredibly talented" when you aren't looking.

Zoom In for a Close-Up

When you look at your image on the screen, it looks nice and smooth. That's very nice for enjoying your picture, but when working with it you often have to be able to see individual pixels of your image clearly.

To zoom in on your picture, choose **Zoom**, then click your picture. Click once, and every pixel in your image file shows up on your screen as two pixels wide and two pixels high. Click again, and each one is three pixels wide and three pixels high. You can keep enlarging your image this way until each pixel is shown at thirty-two times its normal height and width. Remember, when you do this, you aren't actually changing your image at all—you're just holding a magnifying glass up to it.

The Tool Options palette for the Zoom tool has a single drop-down list from which you can directly pick the degree of zoom.

You can also zoom in using the menus. Choose **View, Zoom In By 1** to increase the pixel width by 1. If you want a larger zoom, choose **View, Zoom In By 5**. You can always tell what ratio you're viewing at by looking at the title bar of your image window. If it says 10:1, for example, that means that each pixel is being shown at 10 times its normal size.

If there's a specific area that you want to close in on, point the Zoom tool to the upper right-hand corner of the area; then drag down to the lower left.

Songs in the Key of Zoom

To zoom in using the keyboard, press **+** on the number pad on the right side of your keyboard. This works no matter what tool you have selected.

The New Zoom

The ability to drag an area with the Zoom tool and zoom right into it is brand new in PSP version 7.

The Zoom-Out Key

Pressing the minus sign (–) on the number pad zooms the current window out by one—no matter which tool is currently selected.

Zoom Out for a Far–Up

Click **Normal Viewing** (shortcut **Ctrl+Alt+N**) to return to viewing at a 1:1 ratio. But what if you want to zoom out further than that? If you're designing something like a magazine cover or working with large photographs, you need a way to shrink your image.

Choose **Zoom**, then right-click your picture. Suddenly, your ratio is 1:2—you only see every other pixel from every other row. Click it again, and at 1:3, you see every third pixel from every third row. Obviously, you aren't able to see every detail of your image, but you should be able to see enough to work with it (and yes, you can use all the normal image tools on a zoomed-in or zoomed-out image).

Zoom out also supports menu commands (**View, Zoom Out By 1** and **View, Zoom Out By 5**). The maximum zoom-out ratio is 24:1.

Overlooking the Overview Window Would Be an Oversight

Pressing the **W** button opens the Overview Window, a small display of your entire image. This can be handy when you're zoomed in, so you don't lose track of where you are and what you're doing. If your image is larger than the window you're editing in, the Overview Window shows a black frame around the area that's in the window. You can drag this frame to another part of the image, and that portion will show up in your editing window.

If your Overview Window has just a title bar, click the little triangle button next to the Close (X) button. This opens the window and keeps it stuck open until you click the button again.

Zooming on Wheels

If you have a mouse with a wheel on it, rolling that wheel forward zooms in, while backwards zooms out.

Overnew

The Overview Window is new in version 7 of PSP.

Two Views: I've Looked at Space Bunnies from Both Sides, Now

You can open two windows on the same image. That way, you can look at the details of one part of the image while you see the whole picture (as seen in Figure 6.1), or you can look at details in two different spots.

To do this, choose **Window, New Window** (shortcut: **Shift+W**). You can open as many windows as you want with the same image. When you make a change to the image on any one window, you see the change copied onto other windows. You can close any one of the windows by clicking the **Close** (**X**) button on the right end of the window's title bar; as long as at least one window of the image remains open, Paint Shop Pro doesn't think you're closing the image altogether.

Normal view   Zoom ratio   Close-up view

Figure 6.1

The New Window com-
mand gives you a close-up
view of a Space Bunny in
one window, while keep-
ing him at a distance in
the other.

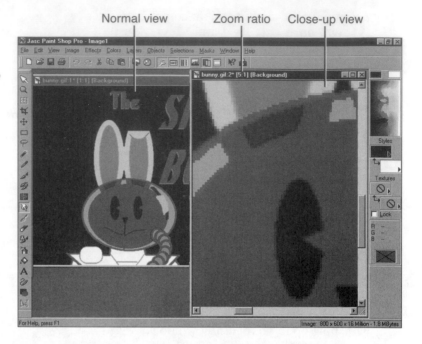

Getting the Most Space for Your Image

Your monitor is only so big (unless you've paid for one of those large monitors, in which case it's *soooooo* big, but even so it's only so big), and at times you want to use as much of that space as possible to view your image, so you can see a lot of it. There are many things you can do to get rid of other onscreen items to make more space for your image:

➤ If your Paint Shop Pro window isn't already taking up your full screen, double-click on the window's title-bar. It expands to fill the screen.

➤ Double-click on your image window's title bar, and it expands to take up as much of the Paint Shop Pro window as possible.

➤ Press **Tab** to hide your Tool Options dialog box and other small palettes. (Pressing it again makes them reappear.)

➤ Press **T** to hide your toolbar, **C** to hide your color palette, and **P** to hide your tool palette. (You can also open or close any of these items by right-clicking on any one of them, and selecting the item from the list that appears.)

➤ Choose **View, Full Screen Edit** (shortcut: **Shift+A**) to get rid of the title bar and menu bar.

To really make the best use of these features, try to get used to using keyboard shortcuts as much as possible.

Pinpointing Particular Pixels Precisely

Drawing with your mouse doesn't tend to be very precise, which is fine if your goal is to be the next Pablo Picasso. If your goal is to be more precise (like, say, Bob Picasso or Julia Picasso), you should take advantage of some fine PSP tools. Read on, and I'll write on about them!

Minimal Palettes

If you have your Tool Options palette open, then you really don't need your Tool Palette. Click the magnifying glass icon on the upper right of your Tool Options palette, and a menu appears from which you can choose any tool.

The Rulers: Kings of the Screen

When you choose **View**, **Rulers** (shortcut **Ctl+Alt+R**), measuring guides appear at the left and top edges of your image window, as seen in Figure 6.2. As you move your pointer, indicators along the rulers show how far from the upper right-hand corner of the image your pointer is.

Vertical Indicator   Horizontal Indicator

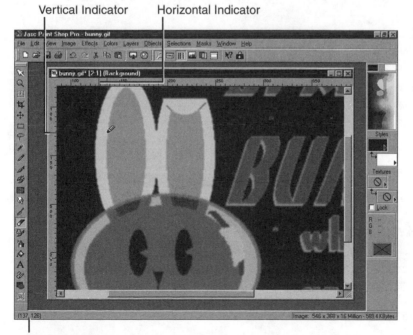

Pixel Location

Figure 6.2

The rulers show us locations on our space bunny. In the future, space bunnies might be our rulers!

Pixel Placement

Except in full screen mode, the current placement of your pointer is always listed in the lower left of the PSP window. The first number is the cursor's distance (in pixels) from the left, and the second is its distance (in pixels) from the top. While dragging a rectangle, this area lists where you started, where you ended, and the size of the rectangle.

You can set the rulers to show distance in pixels, inches, or centimeters (alas, the space bunnies that use the program can't get their measurements in light years). Choose **File, Preferences, General Program Preferences** and the Paint Shop Pro Preferences dialog box appears. On the **Rulers and Units** tab (shown in figure 6.3), use the **Display units** drop-down list to select the units you want, then click **OK**. Generally, if you're designing images to be shown on computer monitors, you want to stick with pixels. If you're designing something to be printed, you may want to use inches or centimeters (although many graphic artists work in pixels even then.)

Figure 6.3

The Rulers and Units tab of the Paint Shop Pro Preferences dialog box simply defies any good humorous caption.

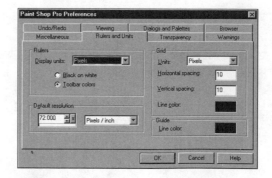

Grid: A Street Map for Your Picture

The *grid* feature helps you line up items in your image and keeps track of the number of pixels between items. It displays a series of horizontal and vertical lines in front of your image that you can use as guidelines, as seen in Figure 6.4. Don't worry, these lines don't actually become *part* of your image. It's just like looking at your image through a screen door!

To turn on the grid, choose **View, Grid** (shortcut: **Ctrl+Alt+G**), which happens to be the same command you use to turn off the grid when you're done with it.

Figure 6.4

The grid: Just the thing we need to catch a space bunny!

Tricks 'n' Tips

Precise Pointing

Normal pointers can make it hard to tell what you're pointing at. On any Tool Option dialog box, click the last tab and put a check the **Precise Cursor** option. Now your pointer is an exactly-aimable crosshair, rather than a picture of your tool.

You can set the grid spacing by choosing **File**, **Preferences**, **General Program Preferences**. On the **Rulers Units** tab, you can select whether the spacing between the grid lines should be measured in pixels, inches, or centimeters using the **Units** field. You can also set the distance between lines using the **Horizontal Spacing** and **Vertical Spacing** fields. You can even pick what color the lines should be by clicking the **Line Color** field to get a color selector. After you've chosen your settings, click **OK**.

What Colors Do I Lean On?

Pressing the **H** key brings up the Histogram window (see Figure 6.5). The word *histogram* is obviously an anagram for *am so right*, which makes sense because the Histogram Window is so right about how much of the basic colors make up your image.

To make the Histogram window, PSP checks every pixel of your image for how much red, green, blue, brightness, hue, saturation, and lightness it contains. From this information, it builds a graph with seven lines. The vertical measurement is *how many pixels* and the horizontal is *how much of this attribute*. If the red line is high at the left end of the chart, that means that you have a lot of pixels (high) without much red (the left end). If it's low at the right end, there aren't many pixels with a lot of red in them.

Imagine Information

For more information on your image, choose **View, Image Information** (shortcut: **Shift+I**). This shows the file size, image size, and other useful info.

Similarly, a blue line shows the amount of blue, a green line shows the amount of green, and a black line shows the amount of greyscale (brightness—although why black represents brightness is a question I cannot answer). Cyan represents the amount of hue, magenta shows the amount of saturation, and yellow shows the amount of lightness (which is very similar to brightness, but calculated a different way, so the lines won't quite line up).

There are checkboxes that you can use to separately turn on or off each line. If you want to, turn them all off and have a graph that shows you absolutely nothing! Otherwise, you can use this to make sure the line you want to see isn't blocked or lost amidst a bunch of other lines.

Figure 6.5

The Histogram window shows the mix of primary colors and brightness in your image.

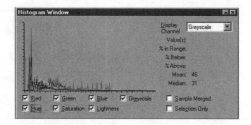

The Least You Need to Know

➤ Use the **+** on your keyboard's number pad to zoom in on the image, and the **–** key above it to zoom out.

➤ Choose **View, Full Screen Edit** (shortcut: **Shift+A**) to hide the title bar and menu bar, making more room for your picture.

➤ Choose **View, Rulers** to display rulers along the top and left of your image.

➤ Choose **View, Grid** to display a grid over your image.

➤ Choose **File, Preferences, General File Preferences** and select the **Rulers and Units** tab (or just double-click your ruler) to find and adjust the settings for the ruler and the grid.

➤ Press **H** to view the Histogram Window, which shows the distribution of the intensities of the primary colors in your image.

I'M THE MAN WITH THE PLAN.

THE PLAYER WITH LAYERS.

Becoming a Player with Layers

Many good things come in layers. Snow, bed sheets, and chocolate cakes all come in layers. So do Paint Shop Pro images.

Layers: We Don't Mean Hens

You can build an image by taking different pieces of the image and putting them in separate overlapping sections, called *layers*. I can't think about layers without thinking about animated cartoons. When I was a kid, I knew that cartoons were drawn frame by frame. I thought those must be the most amazing artists in the world—I'd see the Tasmanian Devil spinning around Bugs Bunny on a desert island, and notice that the artists had managed to draw the desert island exactly the same every frame. There wasn't a little wiggle in the lines from them messing up.

Then I learned the truth. Animators are lazy. Some of them are among the hardest-working lazy people I know, but none of them would ever redraw the same desert island shot over and over. They drew the desert island *once* as a nice wide painting called a *background*. Bugs Bunny never got painted onto the background. Instead, Bugs got painted onto a clear sheet called a *cel*. Put that cel on top of the background, and suddenly it looks like Bugs is standing on the island. The Tasmanian Devil was painted onto his own cel. If you put the Tasmanian Devil's cel on top of Bugs', it looks like he is whirring in front of Bugs. If you put the Tasmanian Devil's cel between the Bugs Bunny cel and the background, it looks like the Tasmanian Devil is whirring behind Bugs.

Layers are just like animation drawings. You have a layer with the background image at the bottom, which you can overlap with layers that have other images in them. You can add layers, rearrange them, and remove them at will.

Why Use Layers?

Why make a bunch of images when you're only going to end up with a single image? Isn't making one layer hard enough? Isn't it hard enough to get out of bed in the morning? Doesn't that all make life so hard that you find yourself turning to donuts and other intoxicating substances?

Actually, layers make life easier in a number of ways. Oh, they won't help you out of bed or do the morning donut run, but there are many reasons why layers come in handy.

Reason Number One: It's Easier to Make Adjustments

Your friend Claudine calls you and asks you to touch up a family photo. She wants you to draw balloons into each of her kids' hands, put a silly hat on her, and replace Harold's head with a giant tomato. You do this and email her the file. She emails you back telling you that there's been a mistake; it's not her *husband* Harold that should have the tomato-head, it's her pet kangaroo Harold who is standing beside them. If you didn't use layers, you drew the tomato right into the photo, wiping out the husband's face. To fix this photo, you'd either have to carefully redraw his face by hand, or start over again from scratch and redraw everything else.

Ah, but if you added the original touch-ups on a layer, then you haven't wiped out any of the original picture. In fact, if you drew the tomato on a separate layer from the other items you added, all you have to do is slide the layer with the tomato on it. When you do so, the tomato uncovers Harold-the-husband's face on the lower layer, and now covers Harold-the-kangaroo's face.

Reason Number Two: Layers Are Recyclable

Let's say you're a magazine designer. You design covers for the magazine, which means that you have to put the title, the price, the UPC code, and all the other little bits of fun on the cover of every issue. You could spend time every month getting things just right, or you could set it up in a layer with all these elements and put that layer in front of a different picture each issue (as seen in Figure 7.1).

Figure 7.1

Seeing that you can reuse the layer with the basic cover design is a good sign indeed!

Reason C: Virginia Is for Lovers, but Layers Are for Tracers

Let's say you want to make a drawing of your favorite band, Angry Black T-Shirts, and you have a photograph to work from. If you scan the photo into Paint Shop Pro, and then put a new clear layer over it, that layer can be used as tracing paper. With your painting tools, copy the picture to the best of your ability, and then delete the original photo layer. All you're left with is your drawing!

Reason Seventy-Two: Layers Can Do Different Things

There are three different types of layers for different uses:

➤ **Raster layers** are image layers in which the image is designed as a grid of pixels. Everything in the book up to this point has been about raster layers.

➤ **Vector layers** are image layers in which all the shapes are defined as a set of easily-reshapable lines and curves. You'll see more about vector layers in the next chapter, "Vector Frankenstein: The Science of Making Vector Objects."

➤ **Adjustment layers** don't contain actual images. Instead, they change the appearance of the layers below them. For example, you might use an adjustment layer to brighten parts of your image and darken others. Adjustment layers are covered in Chapter 22: "Layers of Adjustment."

Be a Layer Creator

Whenever you start a new image, all it has is a single raster layer (the background). You can add a new layer by clicking **Layers** and selecting **New Raster Layer** or **New Vector Layer**. When you do this, a big dialog box with a whole mess of settings appears, as seen in Figure 7.2.

Figure 7.2

The Layer Properties dialog box has a whole mess of settings, which is better than having an incomplete mess of settings.

For now, the only setting we need to worry about is the one marked **Name**. Enter a name for the layer into that field, then click **OK**. Your new layer is set into place. You don't actually see any difference in your image, because the new layer starts out totally transparent; but don't worry, it's there.

The Science of Art

Layer Limits

Paint Shop Pro can handle up to 100 layers per image. However, each layer takes up memory; so if you're dealing with a large image, go easy on the layers. Images that aren't in 16 million color or greyscale mode can only have one raster layer and no adjustment layers, but you can still have plenty of vector layers.

Layered Pastry: Pasting in a Layer

When you're pasting something, it's often a good time to start a new layer. That way, the new item merely hides—rather than obliterates—whatever is under it. To paste something down as a new layer, choose **Edit, Paste, As New Layer** (shorcut: **Ctrl+L**).

If the object currently on your clipboard is a vector object, the new layer is a vector layer. If it's an object copied from a raster layer, the new layer is also a raster layer.

If a Meta Picture Import dialog box (seen in Figure 7.3) appears, this means you're copying something from another program that isn't a simple raster object. (This usually happens to me when I'm using my word processor and Paint Shop Pro at the same time, and have forgotten that the last thing I copied was word processor text.) Paint Shop Pro lets you set the width and height that you want this new item to be. After you do that, click **OK**, and the clipboard will be pasted as a raster layer.

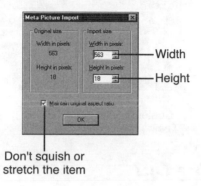

Width

Height

Don't squish or
stretch the item

Figure 7.3

If you leave the Maintain Original Aspect Ratio option checked, you can change the height and Paint Shop Pro changes the width to match, or vice versa.

Accidentallayerly

New users (and even more practiced folks) often create new layers by accident. It's easy to do. Several of the tools on your Tool palette can be used to create raster items or vector items. If you're working on a raster layer, and you tell the tool to make a vector item, it automatically creates a vector layer. Similarly, if you're working in vector mode and create a raster item, it creates a new raster layer for it. (You see, the computer thinks you know what you're doing. It's eager to do whatever you tell it—whether or not it's what you *mean* it to do! Sometimes, it's nice to be thought infallible.)

 The Shape tool is a good example of this. If you click **Preset Shapes**, your Tool Options palette includes a Create As Vector option. With a check mark in that option check box, Paint Shop Pro thinks you're trying to make a vector object. With no check box, it thinks you're making a raster object. If you're not working on the appropriate type of layer, it creates one.

The Layer Palette: Layer Player Central

 Click **Toggle Layer Palette**, or press **L**, to see the *layer palette* (like that one in Figure 7.4). This is your main control for selecting layers, rearranging layers, hiding layers, adding layers, deleting layers, renaming layers, merging layers, and a million other uses! And that's not all! Order now, and you'll also get this handy dandy video tape, *The Complete Idiot's Guide To Turning On Your VCR!*

The layers are shown in the order of the layer pile. The layer at the top of the list is the one on the top of the pile and isn't blocked by anything, and the one on the bottom of the list is on the bottom of the pile and is hidden behind the rest.

Figure 7.4

The layer palette makes working with layers palatable!

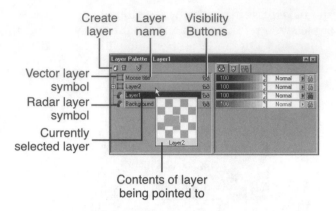

Create layer Layer name Visibility Buttons

Vector layer symbol

Radar layer symbol

Currently selected layer

Contents of layer being pointed to

Which Layer Am I Working On?

Your tools only work on one layer at a time. (The exception to this is the Crop tool, which cuts through all the layers at once. Now that's a powerful blade!)

Tricks 'n' Tips

Quicker Creator

Click the **Create Layer** button on the Layer palette to make a new raster layer. If you hold down **Shift** while clicking it, you can skip the Layer Properties dialog box. Right-clicking the button lets you choose the type of layer created.

The layer that you're currently working on is *highlighted* (it shows up in a different color) on your list.

To select a layer to work on, just click its entry on the list. However, finding the entry you want might be a little tricky. Even when you name your layers, it's hard to recall which is which. If you don't bother to name your layers, they're named *Layer1*, *Layer2*, and so on. But it's easy to see the contents of a layer; just point to the layer's list entry, and leave your pointer there totally still (no wiggling!) for a second. A small version of the layer's contents is displayed at the base of the pointer.

Which Layers Do I See?

It's often easier to work on your picture when you just work on a few of the layers and hide the rest. That way, you can work on the background without the other layers blocking your view, or you can work on the top layer without being distracted by the background.

Each entry on the layer list includes a little picture of eyeglasses. The eyeglasses indicate that this layer is currently visible. If you click on the glasses, the glasses become crossed out, indicating that the layer is invisible. Click there again to make them visible.

(Picking eyeglasses for this makes sense. When I take off my glasses, I can barely see a thing. When my mom takes off her glasses, she can barely see a thing. When my friend Clark takes off his glasses, he turns into Superman. Life isn't fair.)

Do the Layer Shuffle

To move a layer higher or lower in the stack, just drag the layer's button on the list. This looks like you're dragging a horizontal line between the list entries. The layer you're moving ends up wherever you release the line.

To delete a layer, right-click its list entry, and choose **Delete** from the list that appears. Poof, it's gone!

Layer Copier

To make a second copy of a layer in your image, right-click the layer, then choose **Duplicate** from the pop-up menu. The copy is added just above the original on the list.

To copy a layer from one image to another image, first open both images, so both windows are visible. Select the image you're copying from. Open up your layer palette, and drag the list entry for that layer from the palette onto the second image.

Merging Emergency

If you wind up with too many layers, and you want to combine several layers into one, right-click the layer list and choose **Merge**. The sub-menu gives you two choices:

➤ **Merge All (flatten)**   This command turns all the layers into a single layer.

➤ **Merge Visible**   This command combines only the layers on which the little eyeglasses symbol is not crossed out.

When you merge the layers, all the vector layers are converted into raster layers, and then the layers are pasted in order to make a single layer. This is an action you should only take when you're absolutely positive you don't want to work on the separate layers anymore.

Single-Layer Vision Plan

To view just one layer, right-click it on the list and select **View, Current Only** from the pop-up menu.

A Solid Background

The background cannot be moved from the bottom of the stack.

But if You Really Want to Move It...

Select the background layer; then choose **Layer, Promote to Layer**, and PSP will forget it is the background. Now you can move it.

That Stubborn Background

You can't slide the background around. Selecting the background and choosing **Layer, Promote to Layer** leaves you with a slidable version.

Laying the Layer Down and Sliding It Around

You've already seen how to move a layer up and down in a stack. But what about when you want to slide it side to side? When that giant tomato is blocking Harold-the-Husband's face and you want it blocking Harold-the-Kangaroo's face instead, what do you do?

First, deselect any currently selected areas by choosing **Selections, Select None** (shortcut: **Ctrl+D**). Any marquees should disappear.

 Next, select the **Mover** tool and point to a visible portion of the layer that you want to move. When you drag that, you find that you're dragging the whole layer. Don't worry if you drag a visible part of the layer off the edge of the image; Paint Shop Pro remembers all the contents of the layer. If you drag the layer in the other direction later, the hidden portion reappears.

The Least You Need to Know

➤ *Layers* are overlapping pieces that can be used to make up your image.

➤ To create a new raster layer, choose **Layers, New Raster Layer**.

➤ To see the layer palette, click **Toggle Layer Palette** (shortcut: **L**).

➤ To select a layer to work on, click the layer's name on the layer palette.

➤ To hide a layer, click the eyeglass button on the layer's list entry.

➤ You can rearrange the layer pile by dragging a layer's list entry up or down the list.

GRRR...

Chapter 8

Vector Frankenstein: The Science of Making Vector Objects

In This Chapter

➤ Understanding vectors

➤ Making lines and curves

➤ Making shapes

➤ Rearranging vector objects

When your monitor displays an image, it's actually displaying a gridwork of pixels, with a color set for each pixel. When the computer prints the image on a printer, it's printed as a gridwork of pixels. Up until now, you've been reading about editing *raster* images, images that the computer stores by remembering which color goes in each pixel. That's the obvious way for the computer to store the image information, but (oddly enough) it's not the only way.

Vhat Are Vectors and Vhy Do Ve Vant 'em?

Vector objects are portions of your image that Paint Shop Pro keeps track of by remembering them as a series of points (called *nodes*), with lines and curves that connect points. Whenever the program needs to display those objects, it plots out those lines and curves, and converts the shapes into a pixel grid so that they can be displayed. (This makes vector objects similar to TV sitcoms, which are plotted with plot points, plot twists, and plenty of straight lines, but still end up on your screen as a grid of dots.)

They Couldn't Mix at All

Early computer art programs were either *paint* programs (raster art) or *draw* programs (vector art). That terminology is still with us, even though now there are many programs that mix the two.

Paint Shop Pro treats vector object images so differently from raster object images that the two can't even live on the same layer. They just don't get along.

Vectors Grow Up Well

Let's say you have a cute little raster drawing of a duck that is 100 pixels by 100 pixels. You like it so much that you want to make it bigger, to expand it to 300 by 300 (which you can do with the **Image, Resize** command). Suddenly, your duck ain't so cute any more. It looks all blocky with pointy edges. Why? Because when Paint Shop Pro doesn't know how a duck looks. All it knows is what color was in each pixel. When you made your picture three times as wide and three times as high, the program just took the color from each pixel and expanded it to fill nine pixels. Suddenly, the too-small-to-notice individual dots that made up the original picture are huge squares, easily visible.

If you draw the duck using vector objects, however, it expands nicely. As you can see in Figure 8.1, when you expand a curved vector line, you just get a larger curved line. Paint Shop Pro replots the line, pixel by pixel. You can blow it up as far as you want, and the curve is replotted precisely, down to the nice little pixel.

Figure 8.1

The raster-drawn bunny ear expands to be pointy and painful, but the vector bunny ear stays smooth and soft!

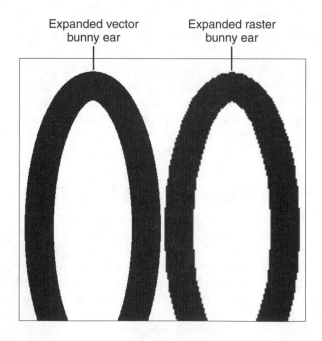

Expanded vector bunny ear

Expanded raster bunny ear

Vectors Vary Very Well

If you draw a squiggle on a raster layer, and later decide it's not quite right, you can undo all the steps you've done since and try it again. You have to be very sure that the line is *just right* before you move on to doing other work with your image—or before you give up and settle for less.

But if you draw a squiggle using a vector tool, Paint Shop Pro sees it as a series of points (called *nodes*) and the curves (called *segments*) that connect it. At any time, you can take that almost-right squiggle and simply adjust the nodes and segments until it's bang-on!

Vectors: The Naturally Stackable Snack

If you draw a square overlapping a circle on a raster layer, and then decide you want the circle in front, you're out of luck. PSP doesn't know that it has a square and a circle; it thinks it has a bunch of dots. (Of course, you could have rearranged them easily if you had put the square and the circle on separate layers, but we don't always have the foresight to realize that we might change our mind.)

Facing the same situation with vectors is no problem. You can restack and rearrange vector objects all you want, just like layers. You can slide them around and back and forth with no problem.

The Draw Tool: Lines on the Loose

 The **Draw** tool is your first line of defense when it comes to creating lines, curves, and irregular or original shapes. (For standard shapes, use the Preset Shape tool.) Select the tool, and the first tab of the Draw Tool Options palette (seen in Figure 8.2) offers you the **Create as Vector** option. That's right, this tool doesn't have to be a vector tool. You can use this tool on raster image and create some very nice lines and shapes—you just don't have the ability to change the line or shape later.

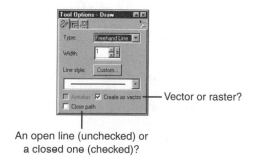

Vector or raster?

An open line (unchecked) or a closed one (checked)?

Figure 8.2

Choose Draw, and you can draw from these choices.

The **Type** drop-down list offers you four different styles of drawing. It's like having four drawing tools in one. That's even better than those pens that write in four different colors!

Straight Lines: Who Was That Lady I Saw You with Last Night?

Choose **Single Line** on the Type drop-down list, and you have a very simple tool for making straight lines. Point to where you want the line to begin, and then drag to where you want the line to end.

Right Angles

Hold down **Shift** while dragging to create lines precisely horizontal, vertical, or at 45 degree angles.

The key options to use with the Single Line tool are **Width** (which sets the width of your line, in pixels) and **Antialias** (which prevents visible jaggies when you're drawing in 16-million-color mode or in greyscale).

The Point of Point to Point

Choose **Point to Point Line** from the **Type** drop-down list to create a series of connected points (called *nodes*), or smooth curves or shapes that include those nodes.

Closing Up Shape Shop

If you didn't have the Close path option selected, you can still close off your path. Press **Shift+Ctrl+C** after placing your last node, and the path will close.

The easiest thing to make with this tool is a connected series of line segments, such as a triangle. Simply click where you want each node along the edge. PSP connects those dots as you draw them (displaying a square to show you the exact placement of each node). After you've added the last node, click anywhere outside of the image window (or press **Ctrl+Q**). If you have the **Close path** option checked on the Tool Options palette, PSP will add one more line segment, connecting your last node to your first one.

Paint Shop Pro traces the line you created with the Active Stroke Style, and fills in the area within the line with the Active Fill Style. If you don't want to create a filled area, before drawing make certain that your fill style is set to No (point to the Active Fill Style panel, hold down the left mouse button, and select the international **No** symbol from the toolbar that appears). Similarly, if you want a solid shape with no outline, keep the Active Fill Style but select the No symbol for your Active Stroke Style.

Curves Are Just Lines with Bad Posture

Using Point To Point to draw a curved line instead of a straight one is simple. Instead of clicking each node along the curve, click the first node. For each later point, aim at where you want the node to be, then drag away from that node. This tells Paint Shop Pro that you're making a *curved segment node*. When you drag, you're dragging an arrowhead of an arrow that goes through the node, as seen in Figure 8.3. By moving the location of the arrowhead, you're changing the shape of the curve into that node. When the curve looks good, release the mouse button and go to work on the next node.

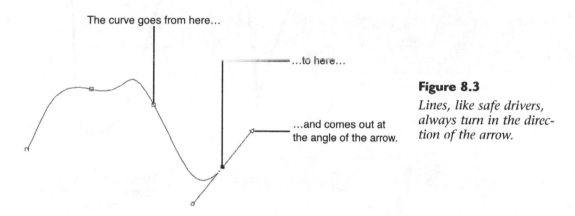

The curve goes from here...

...to here...

...and comes out at the angle of the arrow.

Figure 8.3

Lines, like safe drivers, always turn in the direction of the arrow.

Any line segment going from a curve segment node to another node (even if it's a *straight segment node*, the single-click type of node) is a curve, as you can see in Figure 8.4. The line coming out of the curve segment node is at the angle of the arrow, as well. If you want to create a point where two curves meet at an angle (such as the dip in a top of the valentine heart), use a curve segment node as the start of the first curve, then a straight segment node where the curves meet, then another curve segment node at the end of the second curve.

Curved segment node   Curved segment node

Figure 8.4

If you want to create an angle between two curves, you need a straight segment node.

Straight segment node   Same shape, with a curved segment node instead of a straight one

Freehand: It Sure Doesn't Look Like Vectors

Choose **Freehand Line** from the Type drop-down list in the Draw Tool Options palette, and you can use the Draw tool to quickly scribble, just as you can with a brush. PSP is actually watching your squiggle and figuring out how to build it out of vectors.

The Science of Art

How Does It Do That?

The program converts your drawing to a vector by setting nodes at various points along your doodle. The Curve Tracking setting on the second tab of the Tool Options palette lets you choose how frequently nodes are set. A higher number means more nodes, which is more precise (but also means a slower processing and bigger files in the end).

As you draw, you leave behind either a single straight line (if you're using a very small width setting) or a series of rectangles (if using a larger width, as seen in Figure 8.5). Only when you complete your squiggle and release the mouse button does PSP fill in the colors.

Figure 8.5

The Freehand Line tool waits for me to release the button before filling in my friendly greeting.

Bèzier Curves: More Bezy Than Other Curves

Another way to draw curved lines can be chosen by choosing **Bezier Curve** from the Type drop-down list. I'm not really fond of this method; I find it a bit cumbersome, but not everyone agrees with me. (Some people swear by Bèzier curves; I just swear at them.)

To draw your curve, follow these steps:

1. Drag a line from the start of your curve to the end of your curve, as shown in Figure 8.6.

2. Click a point that the curve should be aimed toward when coming from the start node (where you started your drag). If you drag this target instead of just clicking it, Paint Shop Pro shows you how this point affects the path of the curve. Release the mouse button when you're happy with the path.

3. Similarly, click or drag a point in the direction that the curve should enter the end-point from.

Give it a try. Bèzier curves (like Brussels sprouts) ain't for everyone, but some folks love 'em.

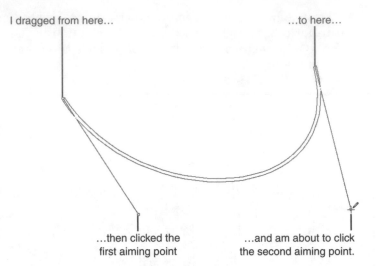

I dragged from here...   ...to here...

...then clicked the
first aiming point

...and am about to click
the second aiming point.

Figure 8.6

A Bézier curve in progress.

Dots, Dashes, and Pointy Ends: Styling Your Lines

Smooth, even lines are nice, but they're not the only thing out there. Click the **Line style** drop-down list on the first tab of the Tool Options palette, and you'll find a range of dotted lines, dashed lines, fuzzy and spiky lines, and even lines with arrowheads on the end. As you can see in figure 8.7, using one of these line styles can give your line a certain verve.

Figure 8.7

Some line styles look downright dangerous.

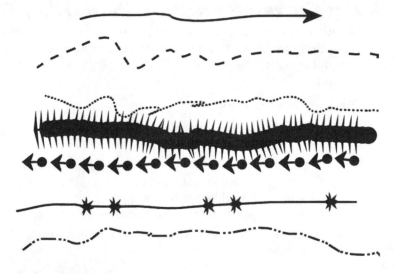

Remember to reselect **#1 Solid** from the drop-down list if you want to return to drawing smooth, even lines. A few dotted lines are fine, but too many wacky lines get hard on the eyes.

If you want to create your own line styles, you can. I'll show you how in Chapter 18, "Upgrading Shapes."

Miters: Going Smoothly Through the Corners

The second tab of the Draw Tool Options palette (see Figure 8.8) is very concerned with the pointyness of your objects. Aren't pointy objects a concern to everyone?

Click the **Join** drop-down list to adjust the sharpness of the corners on your shapes. As you see in Figure 8.9, choosing **Bevel** gives you a smooth cut off the edge of the corner, **Round** gives you nice curved corners, and **Miter** gives you square corners.

Tricks 'n' Tips

Shapely Styles

The same Line Style drop-down list can be found on the Preset Shape dialog box, letting you used a designed line as the stroke of your shape.

Figure 8.8

Many people set limits to make a point. Here, you set limits to avoid making a point.

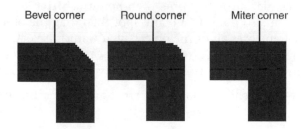

Bevel corner   Round corner   Miter corner

Figure 8.9

So the Miter corner said to the corner next to him, "Where did you get that nice smooth edge?" The reply came back, "You know that place 'round the corner?" To which the Miter retorted, "Hey, if I knew 'round the corner', I wouldn't have needed to ask!"

When two thick lines come together at a shallow angle in a miter corner, the point can end up being quite long. If the point gets too long, Paint Shop Pro automatically chops it off and bevels it. You can use the **Miter limit** option to adjust the limit (higher numbers for longer points), but you'll probably never have to change this figure.

The Shape of Vectors to Come

 The **Preset Shape** tool, discussed in Chapter 4, "The First Coat of Paint," can be used to create vector objects. Just put a check in the **Create as Vector** check box on the Tool Options palette.

Shapes are something you should usually create as vector objects, rather than in raster form. They lend themselves to that sort of fine-tuning.

Arrangements and Marriages

One of the nice things about vector objects is that you can arrange them and rearrange them easily. If you have a little time, you can fine-tune the placement of each object. (If you have a lot of time, you can sort the objects by size, color, and alphabetical order!)

Selecting Objects: The Click That Picks

 Click the **Object Selector** button if you want to select objects. I admit, few people really *want* to select vector objects. I've never heard of anyone waking up in the morning and looking forward to the day because there's *vector object selection to be done!* But if you're going to be moving, restacking, deleting, or copying objects, then there is selection to be done.

Click the visible portion of any object to select the object. (Be careful with objects that are just outlines; it might be tempting to click inside the outline, but you have to click the outline itself!)

To select multiple objects at once, select the first one, then hold the **Shift** key down while selecting the others. You can also point to a blank spot then drag the object selector to make a rectangle that encloses all of the objects you want to select. Selecting vector objects is not limited to the current layer. You can select objects from any layer at any time, and even select objects from different layers simultaneously.

A selected object can be copied to the clipboard (**Ctrl+C**), cut and placed on the clipboard (**Ctrl+X**), or simply deleted (press **Delete**).

Handling with Care

A rectangular border appears around the object (or group of objects) you select, as seen in Figure 8.10. Ten smaller squares appear at points on or around the border. These are *handles.*

When you point to any one of these handles, you can drag it to change the object:

➤ Dragging the handle on the center of the top or bottom edge of the border makes the object taller or shorter.

➤ Dragging the handle on the center of the left or right edge of the border makes the object wider or thinner.

➤ Dragging a corner handle changes both the height and the width of the object.

➤ Dragging the center handle moves the object.

➤ Dragging the handle that's to the right of the center rotates the object around the center.

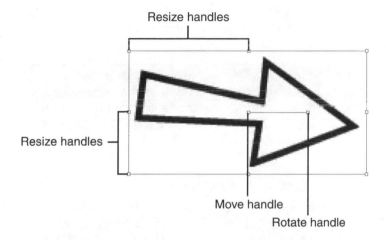

Resize handles

Resize handles

Move handle

Rotate handle

Figure 8.10

Handles are easy things to pick up on!

When you resize an object, the line thickness does not change. This means that your object might end up looking a little odd. A thick line on a small object looks very different from the same line on a large object.

You can do a lot of other editing with vector objects. You can drag their nodes and change their appearances. There's so much that can be done with that sort of editing that it gets its own chapter: Chapter 18, "Upgrading Shapes."

Tricks 'n' Tips

Making the Line Fine

Double-click an object to get the Vector Properties dialog box, in which you can change the line width, color, cap style, and more.

Things to Do with 57 Objects

When multiple objects are selected, there are a number of things you can do that you can't (or wouldn't want to) do with one object. For instance, you can

➤ Tell Paint Shop Pro to consider all the objects as one single bigger object, by choosing **Objects, Group**. (You can always be the Yoko Ono of the object world by breaking up the group later: **Objects, Ungroup**.)

➤ Line up the objects so that they meet at the top, or bottom, or side, or share the same center, by using the commands on the **Objects, Align** submenu. (And that last joke about Yoko wasn't fair. She didn't really break up the Beatles.

91

People were looking for someone to blame, and she was weird enough to make a convincing scapegoat.)

➤ Space the objects evenly from one another, using the commands on the **Objects, Distribution** submenu. (The **Horizontal** commands spaces them across, the **Vertical** commands spaces them up and down. The other part of the command descriptors—**Center**, **Top**, **Bottom**, **Left**, or **Right**—indicate what part of the objects are being checked to make certain of even distribution.)

➤ Resize them to the same height or width, using the **Objects**, **Make Same Size** submenu. (Remember, the first object you select is the guide for the size of the other objects. Also, remember, *don't blame Yoko!*)

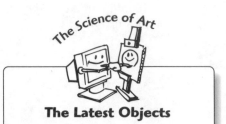

The Latest Objects

Most of the commands on the Objects menu are new in Paint Shop Pro version 7.0. Early revisions didn't even have an Objects menu.

Line Up with Ease

Turn on the grid (**View, Grid**) and choose **View, Snap to Grid**, and any objects you move are instantly lined up against the nearest grid line. (Double-click a ruler to get the **Grid and Guide Properties** dialog where you can pick which edge of the item adheres to the grid.)

Many of these commands, and several others to boot, can be reached by right-clicking the selected objects. They're also available via buttons on the second tab of the Object Selector Tool Options palette.

Stack Cracker

Objects can overlap other objects. Whenever you add a new object, Paint Shop Pro thinks of it as being in front of the other objects (even if it doesn't overlap them; PSP thinks of all the objects on a layer as being in a stack). The best way to rearrange the stack should look very familiar; it's basically the same way you rearrange layers.

To reorder the stack, open the Layer Palette (remember: if you don't see it, just press **L** and it appears). Next to the list entry for the current layer is a little plus sign (**+**). Click that plus sign, and the list expands to show all of the objects on the current layer, as seen in Figure 8.11. The currently selected object is then named in bold type.

The objects are listed in the order that they appear on the stack. The first object on the list is at the top of the stack, and the second one is second, and so on down.

Point to any entry on that list and let the pointer hover. An image appears, showing that object and where it is on the layer. When you're sure you're pointing to the object that you want to move, drag its list entry up or down the list. (You can even drag it past the list for this layer, to drop it down on another layer. It might not be as easy as falling off a log, but it is as easy as dropping an object!)

Open/close list ——

Objects on layer ——

Figure 8.11

Here's a list of objects, so you don't have to look so listless!

Vectors, Feh! I Want Raster!

There will be times that you want to take a vector layer and turn it into a raster layer. This takes a snapshot of what your vector layer looks like, and turns it into a big array of pixels. It's not something you want to do casually, because after you switch you aren't able to use all those great vector-editing tools. However, you should gain the ability to do the sort of individual pixel tweaking that makes raster work so much fun.

When you're sure you want to do this, just choose **Layers**, **Convert To Raster**. Alert little elves working inside your PC rush to document what every pixel will be.

The Least You Need to Know

➤ Vector objects are made up of editable lines, shapes, and nodes.

➤ The **Draw** tool has four types, including the **Single Line** type, with which you drag straight lines into place.

➤ With the **Point to Point Line** type, you click angle points and drag curve points for a line path.

➤ The **Freehand Line** type lets you draw whatever squiggle you want. Paint Shop Pro plots the nodes needed to make that squiggle.

➤ The **Object Selector** is used to select individual or multiple objects for moving, reshaping, and other activities.

➤ Click the plus sign next to the vector layer's entry on the layer palette, and a rearrangable list of objects on that layer appears.

Chapter 9

Getting Images In

> **In This Chapter**
>
> ➤ Load images from the hard disk
>
> ➤ Use images from other programs
>
> ➤ Scan in images
>
> ➤ Transfer images from a digital camera

You might be the sort of person who starts every drawing from a fresh, blank canvas, works on it once, and then never wants to see it again. I don't know if such people exist; but if they do, and you're one of them, you can skip this chapter.

If you're the sort of person who wants to work on photographs, to rework images you've already worked on, and to bring in images from other programs, you should read this chapter.

And if you're the sort of person who wants to make a generous gift of a million dollars to a long-suffering computer book writer, you should write me at nat@MillionsOnTheInternet.com.

Browsing for Brilliance

Your hard disk has a lot of images on it. Even if you've never saved any images to the hard disk, the programs that you run often come with images for their own uses. And if you *have* saved images to your hard disk, they should still be there—unless you've been hit with one of those dreaded little computer elves that like to erase all your work while you're asleep.

I Just Used That File

The bottom of the **File** menu lists the files you worked on most recently. Choose a file from that list to open it.

If you've ever used a word processor, a spreadsheet, or any other sort of editing program, you're probably used to using an Open command to open up old files. Paint Shop Pro has one of those, as well (**File, Open**; shortcut: **Ctrl+O**), and it works just like the Open command you're used to. But if you go that route, you're missing out on a better way of opening files.

Choose **File, Browse** (shortcut: **Ctrl+B**). You'll get a browser like you see in Figure 9.1, except with different pictures—unless you've sent your elves over to copy things from my hard disk. Oh, those little elfin sneaks!

Double-click to display sub-folders

Sub-folders appear beneath folders

Figure 9.1

The Browse window shows you all the pretty pictures on your hard disk...and all the ugly ones, as well!

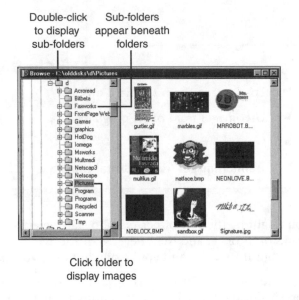

Click folder to display images

The Browse window has two panes. The left pane displays a list of disks and folders on your system. Double-click any disk or folder, and the list expands to show all the sub-folders within that folder. Single-click any folder, and it becomes the current folder.

The right pane is where the magic takes place. Here, you see all the image files in the currently selected folder. This isn't just a list of filenames, it actually shows a small version of the image in each file. By seeing the image, you can tell quickly if that `life.psp` file contains a picture of *Life* magazine, Life cereal, or Life, the board game for ages 10 to adult.

To open a file, just double-click it.

Trouser Bricks...er... Browser Tricks

The browser has a number of cool tricks built in, letting you do more than just simply open files:

➤ Point to any image and let your pointer rest there for a second. A little box appears with the file size, the image dimensions, and other bits of information.

➤ Right-click any file image, and a menu of commands pops up. You can use this to delete your file, rename it, get further information on it, and more!

➤ Right-click any blank area in the right pane, and another list of commands pops up. This includes **Sort** (which lets you organize the files by name, size, age, and other attributes), **Select** (which lets you select multiple files based on a set of criteria), and **Find Name** (which helps you locate files based on the file name).

➤ Drag an image from the right pane onto any open image window. Suddenly, the image you dragged appears as a new layer on your open image.

➤ Drag an image from the right pane onto a folder in the left pane, and that image is moved to the folder you dropped it into (unless the folder is on a different disk, in which case you end up making a copy, ending up with two files). If you want to make a copy to a different folder on the same disk, hold down **Ctrl** while dragging.

You can select more than one image for dragging. To select a series of images, click the first image, and then hold down **Shift** while clicking on the last image. To select multiple individual images, hold down **Ctrl** while clicking on each image.

Foreign Files

The browser can display image files that weren't created with Paint Shop Pro. It can display dozens of different file types, almost any type of image file you're likely to have. And PSP can work with any file you see in the browser.

Frivolous Files?

When you browse any hard disk directory with the browser, it creates a new file in that directory named pspbrwse.jbf. This file stores the thumbnails for the images in that directory; the next time your browse to that directory, PSP will read this file instead of having to read all of the unchanged graphic files. Feel free to delete the pspbrwse.jbf files; the only effect will be that it will take the browser longer to display the contents of that directory next time you visit it.

Taking Pictures: Swiping Images from Other Programs

Usually, when you want to open an image from another program, you use the other program to save the file to disk and then use Paint Shop Pro to open it. After all, PSP understands so many different file formats that it probably understands the other programs files. Even if it doesn't understand the other program's *native* file format (the format that the other program usually wants to save its document in), most graphics programs have a **File, Save As** command or a **File, Export** command that you can use to save the file as a *GIF* (Graphic Interchange Format), *JPEG* (Joint Photographic Experts Group), *TIFF* (Tagged Image File Format), or *BMP* (bitmap) file, all of which Paint Shop Pro can read.

Sometimes, however, you're using a program that really isn't intended as an image-creating program. But just because it doesn't want to give you images doesn't mean that you don't want to take them. You're not going to let a silly little program boss you around, are you?

Be a Master Paster

The first thing you should try is to use the **Copy** command of the program from which you want to copy the image. This should copy whatever you've selected onto the Windows clipboard. Then, flip over to Paint Shop Pro and choose **Edit, Paste, As New Image** (shortcut: **Ctrl+V**). This should create a new image of the selected item.

Notice that I said *should*. It doesn't always work. After using the other program's copy command, you might find that PSP's paste commands are grayed out. Obviously, those evil computer-fouling elves have been at it again. If this happens:

1. Start your word processor.
2. Use your word processor's Paste command (**Edit, Paste** or **Ctrl+V**) to paste the item into your word processor.
3. Reselect the material in your word processor, then copy it from there (**Edit, Copy** or **Ctrl+C**).
4. Head back over to Paint Shop Pro, and try the **Edit, Paste** command again. It should work this time.

(Then again, you usually run into this problem if you copy something with text in it. Pasting is not the best way to handle text. You should use the Text tool, which is described in Chapter 19, "Text Tricks.")

Coping with the Uncopiable

But what if the program from which you want to copy doesn't even have a Copy command? What if you try to copy an image from your favorite game, or a snapshot from a video streaming across the Internet? It sure sounds like you're stuck. Sounds like you're stuck higher and drier than a desert vulture on free pretzel day.

Trust in Paint Shop Pro. It can outsmart that program. It can create an image out of almost anything that appears on your computer screen.

Choose **File, Import, Screen Capture, Setup**. The dialog box seen in Figure 9.2 appears. This is your control for turning any screen image into a PSP image.

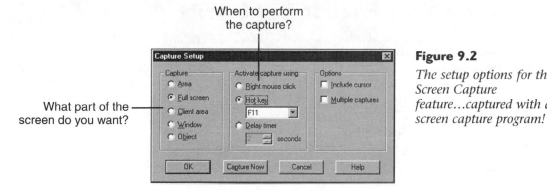

When to perform the capture?

What part of the screen do you want?

Figure 9.2

The setup options for the Screen Capture feature...captured with a screen capture program!

The best option to select for the **Capture** setting is **Full Screen**. That way, you don't have to keep changing this setting. You always get the full screen, and you can just crop it down to what you want.

You can use the **Activate capture using** option to select what you want to use as a trigger for letting PSP know when to take the shot. When you tell PSP to start capturing screens, it gets out of the way and then waits for

➤ You right-clicking (the **Right mouse click** option), or...

➤ You pressing one of the function keys, possibly combined with **Shift**, **Ctrl**, or **Alt** (the **Hot key** option), or...

➤ A pre-set amount of time to pass by (the **Delay timer** option). This is limited to one minute or less.

The **Include cursor** option includes the pointer as part of the shot. The **Multiple captures** option can be used with the right-click or hot key options to let you capture a series of images without having to return to Paint Shop Pro after each one.

Click **OK** to accept the settings you've selected.

Snapping the Shot

 After you have the screen capture settings in place, you can start the capture process by clicking **Start Capture** or pressing **Shift+C**. Paint Shop Pro reduces its window, and waits for the trigger (the right-click, the hot key, or the time delay).

When the trigger goes off, alert little *good* elves inside your computer rush to copy every pixel of the screen, and put it up as an image in a new window in PSP. After the capture, PSP reopens automatically, unless you selected the multiple captures option (in which case, just click the **Jasc Paint Shop Pro** button on the Windows task bar when you're done).

Scannerize Your Friends and Family

A *scanner* is a device that can take a flat item (a photograph, a magazine cover, a typed page, or a squished evil elf) and create a computer image of it. If you have photographs sitting around that you want to put on your computer, a scanner is what you need. Basic scanners start at well under $100, although if you're creating items to be commercially printed, you want a better scanner for more exact color reproduction. (Stop by www.MillionsOnTheInternet.com, where I've put some links to some good deals on scanners.)

Is That Mark TWAIN or Choo-Choo TWAIN?

We computer geeks come up with a lot of standards, and we like to give them weird names like Kermit, XINU (short for *XINU Is Not Unix*), and Mozilla. The geeks who came up with the standard software interface between your computer and your scanner apparently wanted to rebel against this practice, so they named it *Toolbox Without An Interesting Name*, or TWAIN for short. Frankly, that's the most interesting name of the bunch!

If you have a scanner set up and installed, you can scan images directly into Paint Shop Pro. Just choose **File, Import, TWAIN, Acquire**. PSP starts your scanner controller program. I can't tell you how to use that; each scanner comes with its own program. They all let you do the same things (select the area to scan, the resolution to scan at, and whether the image should be color, grayscale, or black and white). Set up whatever you have to set up, and click whatever you have to click to get your scanner to scan.

When the scanning is done, check Photo Shop Pro to make sure your image arrived okay. After you've done this, close the scanner control program. (PSP doesn't let you work on the image while that program is still open.)

DC Power: Digital Cameras Rule!

Digital cameras are great. There's no need to buy film and pay for developing any-more; all you have to do is buy a digital camera and transfer images directly to your computer for printing and processing. Of course, you have to spend a fair chunk of change to get a digital camera that takes better pictures than a $5 disposable film camera. Still, digital cameras are getting better all the time, and are often quite convenient.

Paint Shop Pro is very friendly with digital cameras. Not only can it import images from the camera, it can also be used to manage the images stored in the camera. That way, you can delete the ones you don't need, or save others straight to disk. However, that all assumes that you've set up PSP to work with your digital camera in the first place.

If you have a Kodak camera, you're in luck. Paint Shop Pro ships with built-in support for their models. Otherwise, you have to surf over to http://www.jasc.com/dcsdl.asp where you can download the Direct Digital Camera Support software for other brands. Download and then run this program; you now have the proper drivers installed for most digital cameras available.

After you've installed the drivers, connect your camera to your computer using whatever form of connection the camera maker provided. Next, choose **File, Import, Digital Camera, Configure**. The dialog box seen in Figure 9.3 appears.

Why Not Include All The Drivers?

New cameras come out too fast. By sending you to their Web site for the drivers, they can make sure that you get the latest set of drivers. They already support over 100 different models; it's likely that they have yours.

Choose your camera from the **Camera Type** drop-down list (PSP supports over 100 different camera types). Make sure both **Communication Port** and **Baud Rate** are set to **Auto**. Click **OK**, and Paint Shop Pro takes care of the rest of the details of setting it up.

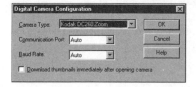

Figure 9.3

Komplete kwik kamera konfiguration.

If Your Camera Is Not Supported...

Choose **File, Import, TWAIN, Select Source**. If your camera is listed in the dialog box that appears, click it and then click **Select**. Now you'll be able to import your images using **File, Import, TWAIN, Acquire**.

Shoot the Shots In

Choose **File, Import, Digital Camera, Access** to start PSP's digital camera control feature. When you have it open, click the Forward and Back arrow buttons to look through the images stored on your camera. After you get past all the images that you don't want (beautiful sunsets and playful puppies) and find the photo that you do want (your snobbish Uncle Horatio standing in line for Wrestlemania—high-quality blackmail material!), click **Open in PSP**.

You can open as many shots as you want. (If you want to open every shot in the camera, including Uncle Horatio buying a hot dog and Uncle Horatio wearing a big foam hand at the wrestling match, click **Open All in PSP**.) When you have imported all the ones you need, click **OK**.

The Least You Need to Know

➤ Choose **File, Browse** (shortcut: **Ctrl+B**) to open your image file browser.

➤ In the browser, double-click a folder to see sub-folders; click a folder to list the images in those folders; and double-click an image to open it.

➤ You can import images from other programs by using the other program's **Cut** or **Copy** command, then using PSP's **File, Paste, As New Image** command.

 ➤ Click **Start Capture** to hide PSP and capture the screen image of another program.

➤ Choose **File, Import, TWAIN, Acquire** to run your scanner and scan images directly into PSP.

➤ If you use a non–Kodak digital camera, you have to go to www.jasc.com to download support software so that PSP can read images directly from your camera.

STOP!!
GETTING
THEM OUT!!
NOT
THROWING.

Chapter 10

Getting Images Out

In This Chapter

➤ Save your Image

➤ Choose a file format

➤ Print your image

➤ Print multiple images on a page

Maybe you don't like to keep your images around. Maybe you think your art should be fleeting and disappear, never to be seen again. If so, you don't need Paint Shop Pro—you need an Etch A Sketch. (And be sure to purchase my next book, *The Complete Idiot's Guide to Etch A Sketch!*)

Saving Your File for a Rainy Day

The basics of saving your PSP files are the same as saving a word processor file or a spreadsheet, if you've ever done either of those. The standard commands are

➤ Choose **File, Save** (shortcut: **Ctrl+S**) to save the image under the same name and format that it had when you loaded it. If this is a new image, a dialog box opens in which you can type in the name and select the file format and location.

➤ Choose **File, Save As** (shortcut: **F12**) and a dialog box opens asking you to type in the name and select the file format and location. If you open a file named Fred and use Save As to save it as Barney, then the next time you do a Save it will be saved as Barney, not Fred. This is handy for keeping a copy of your file with some changes, without wiping out the original.

To those standard options, Paint Shop Pro adds a third:

➤ Choose **File, Save Copy As** (shortcut: **Ctrl+F12**) and a dialog box opens in which you type the name and select the file format and location. Even if you save it under a new name (Barney), the next time you do a Save command the original file (Fred) will be the one that was updated. This is handy for saving intermediary steps while building a file.

Selecting a file location works the same with PSP as it does with most programs. You can use the **Save in** drop-down list to select a disk or network location to store your file on. Double-click any folder icon to maneuver into that folder.

File Formats: Fabulous Friends, Fearsome Foes

The choice of file formats, which you make from the **Save as type** drop-down list on the Save dialog box, is very important. I cannot overstress how important it is. If the ancient Atlanteans had chosen the right file format, they would still be with us today.

Star Dot What?

The item in parenthesis at the end of the "Save as type" entries is the file extension that goes with type of file. So, if you save a file named hot with a type that lists its extension as (*.dog), then hot.dog will be the file's full name.

The right file format to choose to save your file in is **Paint Shop Pro Image (*.psp)**. You should always save a copy of your image in this format. Why? Because the other formats won't hold the data about all your layers and vectors. Most graphic file formats are made to store simple, flat raster images. If you were to save a file in one of those formats, then reload it later to work on it some more, you couldn't edit your vectors or layers anymore. It would all have become one big raster picture.

Having said that, you may want to save your file in another format as well. That way, you can open your file with another program that doesn't read Paint Shop Pro files (most don't), or share your file with other folks.

Antique Paint Shop Pro Formats

If you're sharing your file with someone who uses an earlier version of Paint Shop Pro, you'll have to take some care. Although revision 7 can read any file created with earlier revisions, the reverse is not true. After selecting **Paint Shop Pro Image** from the Save As Type drop-down list, click **Options**. From the dialog box that appears, you can choose **Save as PSP 5 compatible file** or **Save as PSP 6 compatible file**.

After you've saved a copy for the earlier-version user, go through the Save As process again and enter a different filename (or a different file location) so that you don't overwrite the file you just saved. Click **Option** again and choose **Save as PSP 7 compatible file**. Why? Two reasons:

Autosave Your Autobutt

Choose **File, Preferences, Autosave Settings** to have your image automatically saved every few minutes, in case your computer crashes.

➤ As you can see in Figure 10.1, the revision 5 and 6 file formats don't support all of revision 7's new features. You want to make sure that you save a version that is exactly like the one that you designed, and that would be the revision 7 version.

➤ When you choose an earlier PSP file format, Paint Shop Pro assumes that you always want to save in that format. Even if you aren't using any of the new features in the file you just saved, the next file you create might have those features. If you went ahead and clicked Save and didn't think to click **Options** and check the format revision, it would save your file under the earlier format. The next time you loaded your image, it would be missing all those features.

File saved in
PSP 7 format

Figure 10.1

Save your picture in an older PSP file format and it may not be your picture any more.

Same file,
PSP 6 format

105

Always checking the revision is a pain in the neck. Really, the best answer is to talk to your friends who use old versions of Paint Shop Pro and hound them into upgrading. It's the twenty-first century, and here they are using twentieth-century graphics programs. They're a whole century behind!

PCX: Pretty, Compact, Xchangable

If you do need to work with your image in another program, your best bet is to choose **Zsoft Paintbrush (*.pcx)**. It will capture the colors of your image exactly, it uses disk space efficiently, and it's a format that *almost* any graphics program can understand. The only downside is that the PCX format doesn't support having transparent areas on your image. (The **Windows or OS/2 bitmap (*.bmp)** format is actually accepted by a few more programs, but it creates much larger files, which eat up your disk space and can be slow to transfer around.)

GIF: Good Idea For-the-Web

The *CompuServe Graphics Interchange Format* (GIF) is a popular format on the Web. All the Web browsers support it. It creates nicely small files (very important for Web work) and it does support transparency (making it possible to create images that do not look rectangular).

Mass Conversion

PSP easily converts bunches of images from one file format to another. Choose **File, Batch Conversion**, then select the files, the format to convert them to, and a directory to store the converted files.

The down side? It can only handle up to 256 different colors per image (although it does reproduce those precisely). That's more than enough for doing logos, buttons, and other simple Web features, but not enough to make photos look good. The GIF format has so many features that PSP has a special export routine to help you make the most of it. See Chapter 24, "Working Wonder on the World Wide Web," to learn more details about it.

JPEG: Just Partially Eroded Graphics

The *Joint Photographic Experts Group* (JPEG) format is designed to compress your image into small files. The problem is that it doesn't re-create your image exactly. It varies the colors of individual pixels somewhat.

How bad does a JPEG image look? That depends on how much you compress it. Select JPEG as the type, then click **Options** on the Save dialog box and you can choose how much to compress it. If you set the compression low, you'll get very good-looking pictures. If you set the compression high, you'll get much smaller files, but your pictures will look pretty rough (see Figure 10.2). (There's a nice export command that makes it easier to choose the amount of compression; this command is explained in Chapter 28, "Photo Finish.")

Don't use JPEG for transferring images to other graphics programs. What you're most likely to use it for is putting photographs on the Web. The only two formats you can count on Web browsers understanding are GIF and JPEG (although many also support *Portable Network Graphics*, or *PNG*).

Save It to Someone Else

You can easily email your picture file to anyone. First, save the file. Next, choose **File, Send**. Your email program will open, and the file will already be attached.

Original image

After fairly strong
JPEG conversion

Figure 10.2

Pity the poor compressed girl. She looks fuzzier, and her cone looks crusty around the edges.

Printing Worth the Paper Its Printed On

Back in the 1980s, we were taught that the advent of computers and networks would bring about the *paperless office*, where all work was done electronically and far fewer trees would have to die. What nobody counted on was that computers would let us do such wonderful things with paper. The modern printer can put out a picture that's almost twice as good as any picture you could make with a typewriter.

Don't Get Upset—Get Setup

The first step in printing is to set up your page. Choose **File, Page Setup**, and the dialog box seen in Figure 10.3 appears. The items you have to set are

➤ *Paper Size* (which is self-explanatory) and *Source*(if your printer has multiple paper bins to choose from).

➤ *Orientation*—choose whether the image is on paper in the normal up-and-down way (which artists call *portrait*) or if it's sideways (*landscape*).

➤ *Position*—the image will print at the top of the page, unless you choose the **Center on page** option. You can also set the page margins.

➤ *Scale*—your image has a *natural size* in inches, even if you've been working in pixels. PSP has a setting for your image as to how many pixels make up an inch. The *Scale* is how big it prints as a percentage of the image's natural size. Scale it up or shrink it down as much as you want—or just check the **Fit To Page** option and your image will be printed as big as it can be and still fit on the page.

➤ *Color, Greyscale or CMYK*—you can choose to print in color, or save that costly color ink and print in greyscale. (The CMYK separations option is for people preparing for commercial printing; see Chapter 31, "Digital Laundry Day: Separating Colors.")

➤ *Negative*—prints a reverse-color image, while clicking Background will let you choose a color to fill all the nonimage space.

When this is all set up, click **OK**. You won't have to return to this dialog box for every page you print, just when you want to change the existing settings.

Figure 10.3

Pick the setup that will make them sit up and take notice!

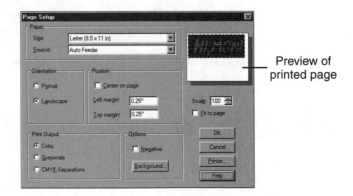

Preview of printed page

Paint Print

Click **Print** (shortcut: **Ctrl+P**) to open the Print dialog box. There you'll find a quartet of check box options that you can use to add *crop marks* (markings outside the edge of the image, useful if the printout is going to be pasted up into a page layout), *registration marks* (useful for making sure that the colors are properly aligned), and a *title* (the filename, unless you choose **View, Image Information** and enter an image title on the **Creator Information** tab). You'll even find **Properties**, a button you click if you want to change your printer's configuration.

But the most important thing is the **OK** button. Click that, and the magic begins—assuming you have a printer, of course.

Print a Plethora of Pictures

To print more than one open image on a page, choose **File, Print Multiple Images**. A layout screen appears, like the one in Figure 10.4.

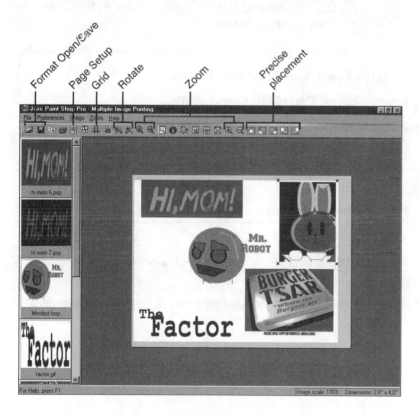

Figure 10.4

You can print a page with many images, or with no images—although it would be quicker to not print at all.

At the left side of the screen is a scrollable list showing all your currently open images. Just drag the images you want onto the page. You can place them as you want. To delete an image from the page, just double-click it.

You can resize any image on your page. Just click it, then drag the resize handles.

Include Files from the Disk

Before you choose **File, Print Multiple Images**, open the Browser (**File, Browse**) and select the files you want.

There are a plethora of commands in the Multiple Image Printing controls to help you hone your layout. The **File** menu has commands for saving your layout to be reused later. The **Preferences** menu gives you access to a grid (to help you line up your images) and borders. On the **Image** menu are commands to rotate the image, or to place them precisely in a corner or the center of the page. The **Zoom** menu gives you access to close-ups of the page.

 When you have everything in place, click **Print** and the page will be sent right out to your printing machine.

The Least You Need to Know

➤ Choose **File, Save** (shortcut: **Ctrl+S**) to save your file.

➤ Be sure to save at least one copy of your file in Paint Shop Pro revision 7 format.

➤ Save the file in the PCX file format to have a raster version of the image you can edit with other programs.

➤ Choose **File, Page Setup** to plan the arrangement of your page.

➤ Choose **File, Print** (**Ctrl+P**) to print your file.

➤ Choose **File, Print Multiple Images** to get a layout window for putting more than one image on the page.

Part III
Painting Outside the Lines

You've already learned the basics of the painting tools. Now it's time to crank it up a notch and learn the full power of these tools. Learn to use brilliant, break-through brushes. Find out about the fantastic frills of fabulous fills. Get a handle on deformations, filters, and special effects, and learn to become a master raster crafter and a pixel perfectionist!

Chapter 11

Fun with Fills

In This Chapter

➤ Fill areas with a repeating pattern or image

➤ Create your own patterns

➤ Give your image a texture

➤ Fill with designs that fade from one color to the next

Up until now I've been showing you various ways to add solid colors to your pictures. Solid colors are fine. They're the meat-and-potatoes of the art world (or, given that so many artists are vegetarians, perhaps they are the tofu and potatoes).

But one can only have so much meat and potatoes before getting desperate for something else. In this chapter, I show you the all-the-toppings pizza and the rocky road ice cream of the art world.

One warning, however: Everything in this chapter is meant solely for 16 million color or greyscale images. When you limit your colors, you really limit the toys you get to play with.

Paintin' with a Pattern

Nature doesn't like solid colors. It likes variances in color that create patterns like wood grain, marble, and sandy beaches.

Science fiction doesn't like solid colors either. It prefers bizarre oozing lumps of colors and grids full of odd blinky lights.

Paint Shop Pro provides a way to create such things using a feature called *patterns*. A *pattern* is an image that is used to fill in an area. It can be a picture of wood grain or of oozing lumps of color.

The pattern image might not be big enough to fill the area you're working with, but patterns are designed to be *repeatable*. This means that when you place two copies of the image right next to each other (either side-to-side or top-to-bottom), there is no visible seam where the two copies touch. When you use a pattern, PSP repeats the image as many times as it takes to fill the space you provide. In a way, it's more like putting up wallpaper than it is like painting.

Pattern-Putting Pieces

 Patterns are most commonly used with the Flood Fill tool. You can quickly fill any odd shape you already have by using this tool.

  Patterns can also be used with the Draw and Preset Shape tools. You can use the pattern for the fill (the most common usage), the stroke outline (a less common usage), or even use different patterns for both (a very uncommon usage, so it's a quick way to make your image look weird, if that's what you want).

Ever-Widening Pattern

Earlier versions of Paint Shop Pro used patterns on only Flood Fills, so you couldn't have any patterns on vector layers. Thanks to version 7, you can have your vectors and your patterns too!

Pattern Pickin'

If you want to use a pattern, move the pointer to the Stroke or Fill Active Style area on the Color palette (remember, the Stroke Active Style area sets the outline of drawn objects and what you paint when you drag brushes, while the Fill Style Area sets the inside of objects and what you get when you right-drag a brush). Keep your mouse button pressed down for a full second and you see the row of buttons depicted in Figure 11.1.

Click the **Pattern** button. The color in the Stroke or Outline style area changes into a pattern—although odds are that it's not the pattern you want. Click the style area and, instead of the color selector that you're used to, a Pattern dialog box pops up. It includes a drop-down list showing a nice big picture of the current pattern. Click this, and a scrollable display of available patterns appears, as seen in Figure 11.2.

Figure 11.1

Drag to choose how color-ful you want to get.

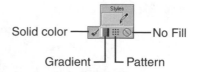

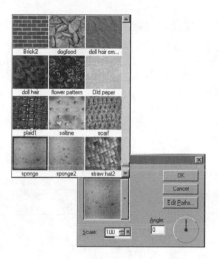

Figure 11.2
Peter Piper picked a peck of pretty patterns.

Scroll through the list, find the pattern you want, and click it. Click **OK**, and you're ready to fill, draw a shape, or use a brush with the pattern you've selected. Use any tool to draw as you normally would, and wherever the Stroke color (or Fill color, if that's what you changed) normally appears, you get the pattern instead!

Your Own Personal Pattern

You can create your own pattern, either by drawing something fresh or by selecting something

Tilt It

Drag the handle next to the **Angle** field on the Pattern dialog box to rotate your pattern.

that already exists in one of your images. To do this, you need to have two images open: an image that contains a pattern that you want to use, and the image into which you want to put the pattern. Then

1. On the image with the pattern, use a selection tool to select a rectangular area of the pattern. (If you don't select anything, your entire image becomes the pattern.)
2. Click the menu bar of the image that you want to put the pattern into.
3. Bring up the Pattern dialog box as described in the previous section.
4. Click the drop-down list of patterns, and scroll to the top of the list. The area you selected in step 1 is now available as a pattern!

Making Your Pattern Repeatable

The problem with selecting a bit from one of your images to use as a pattern is that the portion you select is probably not repeatable. If you have a beautiful picture of the surface of a calm lake, for example, the right edge of your selection might be darker than the left, or there might be a gleam of light that runs right through the top edge. If you use a selection like this as a pattern, you'll see a visible line wherever one repetition of the pattern ends and the next begins, like the one you see in Figure 11.3.

Figure 11.3

Some patterns, like some rumors, should not be repeated. The repetitions cause visible clashes.

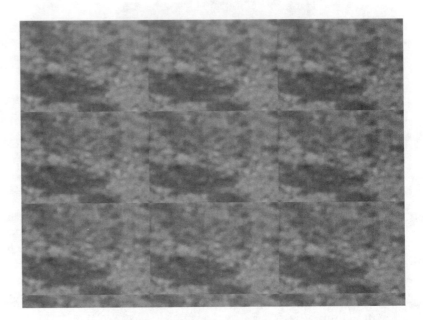

Pattern Permutation

Use the **Scale** field on the Pattern dialog box to increase or decrease the size of the pattern. A word of caution: Using a pattern at a greatly increased scale will usually cause a grainy appearance.

Paint Shop Pro has a trick that fixes this in many cases. Now, this trick works only if you're dealing with a selection from a larger image, and none of the edges of your selection are close to the edges of your image.

Make your selection, then choose **Selections, Convert to Seamless Pattern**. A new image window opens, displaying a more-repeatable version of the selection.

Saving Your Pattern

If you've made a pattern that you really like, you can add it to your standard pattern list so that you can use it anytime. First, you need to know where your pattern files are stored on your system. With a pattern selected for one of the Active Style areas, click that area. When the Pattern dialog box appears, click **Edit Paths**. A File Locations dialog box appears, showing you the directory (or directories) in which your patterns are stored.

Next, you need your pattern in an image all its own. If you've been using a selection as a pattern, use the **Edit, Copy** command (shortcut: **Ctrl+C**) followed by the **Edit, Paste, As New Image** command (shortcut: **Ctrl+V**) to put a copy in an image of its own.

Finally, use the **File, Save Copy As** command (shortcut: **Ctrl+F12**) to save your image. Put the image in your main patterns folder. Give your image a good, descriptive name. Most importantly, click the **Save as Type** drop-down list and choose **Windows or OS/2 Bitmap (*.bmp)**. Click **Save**. From now on, your own pattern is on your pattern list!

Gradients: Fading with Great Radiance

Ah, the sunset. You look at the sky, seeing how the orange of the horizon goes through a range of colors as it fades into the purple of the on-coming night sky. You might look at it and say, "That's beautiful," but an experienced computer artist looks at that and says, "That's a *gradient*!"

A *gradient* is a fade from one color to another, and possibly on to still more colors. Drawing gradients is handy when you want to draw something glowing, or shining, or a tilted object that gets darker in the distance. Gradients work with all of the drawing tools.

Choosing the Gradient

Setting your fill to a gradient works pretty much the same way as setting your fill to a pattern. First, point to the Stroke or Fill Active Style area on the color palette. Hold down the mouse button, and the row of buttons appears, as you saw in Figure 11.1. Click the **Gradient** button. A gradient appears on the color area, but it probably doesn't contain the colors that you want.

Click the color area, and a gradient dialog box opens up, as seen in Figure 11.4. Click the drop-down list, and up pops a scrollable display of gradients, each with its own name.

> *Seventh Heaven*
>
> **Expanding Glows**
>
> Version 7 is the first version of PSP that lets you use gradients with brushes.

Control handle   Gradient drop-down list

Figure 11.4

Grab a groovy gradient from the Gradient dialog box.

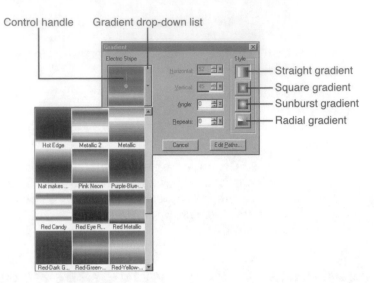

Straight gradient
Square gradient
Sunburst gradient
Radial gradient

Click the gradient color pattern that you want. It becomes the currently selected one. Now you have to select how that gradient flows, using the buttons on the right side of the dialog box:

➤ **Straight Gradient** will put the color in parallel lines, generally fading from one color at the top of the fill to the bottom of the fill. This is the type of gradient (which, with the other types, you can see in Figure 11.5) you'll probably use most often.

Figure 11.5

Four gradients, no waiting.

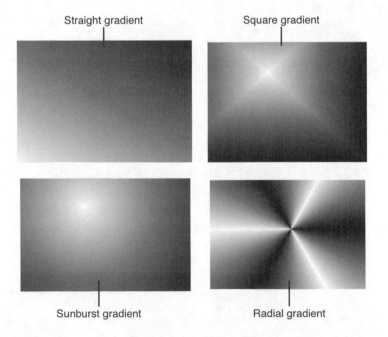

Straight gradient   Square gradient

Sunburst gradient   Radial gradient

➤ **Square Gradient** starts with one color in the middle and then builds to other colors in an ever-expanding series of squares.

➤ **Sunburst Gradient** starts with one color in the middle and builds out in ever-expanding circles. You're likely to use this option frequently.

➤ **Radial Gradient** sets a center point, sticks out a single color in the nine o'clock direction, and then runs the color variations counterclockwise.

Gradient Adjustments-R-Us

What the control handle on the center of the picture of the gradient on the Gradient dialog box does depends on the sort of gradient you have.

Stupid Psychedelic Fun

Click the **Square** or **Sunburst Gradient** button, and then click the gradient drop-down list. When it opens, drag the scroll box up and down quickly. This doesn't do anything for your drawing, but it looks *really cool* while you do it.

If you have a straight gradient, the handle is a dot with a line coming out of it. Drag the line around the center handle, and you rotate the gradient. This way, you can make a side-to-side gradient, a gradient at a tilted angle, or reverse the direction of the gradient so that the top color is on the bottom and vice-versa.

For any other gradient type, the handle is a crosshairs. Dragging the crosshairs moves where the center of gradient goes. Using this you can create fills where the center of the circles, squares, or rotation is not at the center of your drawn object.

The other fine-tuning you might want to do is adjusting the figure in the Repeats field. Normally (with Repeats set to zero), the color flows once along the range. Set Repeats to 1, and the color in your gradient flows from the start color to the end color, then back again. Increase the value further, and you increase the number of times the color runs back and forth through the range.

You probably don't want to use radial gradients with Repeats set to 0, because it creates a harsh-looking line where the end of the gradient meets the start. Radial gradients work best with Repeats set to an odd number. (If you have Radial Gradients selected, and drag the slider at the bottom of the Repeats field back and forth quickly, you see a hypnotic effect!)

119

St. Neidarg: Backward Gradients

To quickly switch the order of colors on your gradient, put a check in the **Invert gradient** checkbox on the Gradient dialog box.

After you've made all your adjustments, click **OK**. Your gradient is now pictured in your Stroke or Fill Active area, and you can use your current tool to put it on the page.

Build Your Own Gradient and Save!

The gradients that come with PSP are nice, no doubt about it. However, you're frequently going to want a gradient with a specific look that the preset gradients just don't provide.

Setting up a simple one-color-to-another gradient is easy. On the Available Colors area of the Color palette, click the color you want to start with, and right-click the color you want to end with. Open the Gradient dialog box, and from the top of the gradient drop-down list, choose the gradient named **#1 Foreground-Background**. This gradient, instead of having fixed colors, uses the colors you selected and fades between them.

Build Your Own Gradient the Harder Way

That easy-to-make gradient feature is nice, but it's limited. If you look through the gradients that come with PSP, you'll see that many don't just fade smoothly from one color to another. Some go through several colors, or change colors abruptly. For example, take a look at the gradient named **Sunset** on the gradient drop-down list. It fades slowly from blue to yellow, goes quickly through a range of oranges and purples, and then it fades gently from middle blue to dark blue and stays an even amount of dark blue for about a quarter of the image. If you tried to build this by just picking the first color and the last color, you'd end up with a fade from blue to dark blue, and that's a lousy sunset.

To build a fancy gradient, you have to put a little more elbow grease into it—though not *much* more. Open the Gradient dialog box and click **Edit**. Up pops the dialog box seen in Figure 11.6.

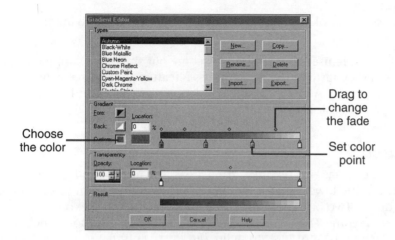

Figure 11.6
Here you find all the ingredients to make gradients.

To make your own gradient, follow these steps:

1. Click **New**.
2. Enter a name for your gradient, and then press **Enter**.
3. Click the set color point under the left end of the gradient bar.
4. Click the **Custom** button, and then click the color area next to the button. Using the color selector, choose the color you want to start your gradient.
5. Click the set color point under the right end of the gradient bar, and repeat step 4 to select the color that ends your gradient.
6. To set another color point on your gradient, click directly below that spot on the gradient. Repeat step 4 to set the color for this point. You can add as many points as you want.
7. To change how quickly the color fades from one point into the next, try dragging the little diamond above the gradient bar, between the two color points.
8. Click **OK**. Your new gradient is added to the list of Gradient types.

Put a Little Texture in Your Life

Hang out at an art supply store in the paper section sometime, and you'll quickly see people you think are absolutely nuts. They go through the different paper stocks and feel them, run their fingers over them, and tilt them against the light so that they can see the surface.

Some of these folks are looking for the smoothest possible paper so that they get clean, sharp, flat drawings. Others, however, are looking for a certain roughness to the paper. This might sound odd, but there really is a point to it. When you draw lightly on textured paper, it catches the pencil or charcoal in interesting ways, creating shading and character. The same holds true for paint and canvas. The artist who is looking for rougher paper is looking to embrace her tools and media, giving the work a natural feel.

Drawing on a computer, you're used to seeing things come out smooth. Computer bits have no texture (and they taste lousy). But PSP has a feature that makes your drawings appear to have texture. And cooler still, it works with brushes and fills and drawn objects and shapes, so basically all your tools can feel the texture.

Be a Texture Selector

Paint Shop Pro's color palette has two texture setting areas, the upper one for the stroke (or foreground) and the lower one for the fill (or background). Point to one of these areas, and drag down. Two buttons appear. One has a picture of a texture, which means it turns on texture. The other has the international *no* symbol, which means it turns off the texture. It's not hard to figure out.

Texture Trading

Swap the Fill texture for the Stroke texture (and vice versa) by clicking the double-headed arrow between the two texture areas.

If you select **Texture**, a picture of the current texture shows up in the setting area. Click this, and a texture dialog box appears. Click the pictured texture, and a scrollable display of greyscale textures appears. Some look like standard drawing surfaces, others look like brick walls and crumpled paper, and some even look like twigs and grass. Pick the texture you like, and click **OK**. Paint away, and the texture will show up in whatever you add to your picture, as you can see in Figure 11.7.

Figure 11.7
A little texture.

The Least You Need to Know

➤ To turn on patterns, click on the Stroke or Fill Active Style areas on the color palette, and then press down the third button from the left.

➤ Choose your pattern by clicking on the style area, and then choosing the pattern from the Pattern dialog box that appears.

➤ To turn on gradients, click on the Stroke or Fill Active Style areas on the color palette, and then press down the second button from the left.

➤ Click the style area to get the Gradient dialog box, where you can select the gradient, the angle, and the gradient style.

➤ To turn on textures, click on the Fill or Stroke Texture areas on the color palette, and then press down the left button.

➤ Pick your texture by clicking the texture area, and then choosing the texture from the drop-down list on the Texture dialog box.

Chapter 12

Fuller Brush Knowledge

In This Chapter

➤ Use translucent brushes

➤ Making soft and fuzzy brushes

➤ Draw straight lines with brushes

➤ Make your own brush shapes

By now, you probably have a good handle on using brushes. (If you don't have a handle on your brush, then you just have bristles in your hand.) You can draw a nice solid stroke and pick your brush width and color. Those are the basics. You've probably noticed that the tool option palettes for brush tools have other settings that you're not using yet. It's time to learn about those and a few other tricks, and move on from good brushing to brushing with greatness.

Clear Talk About Opacity

You have seen the opacity setting on many tools, not just brush tools. The opacity feature applies to fills, shapes, lines, and more. It's probably used most often with brushes, which is why I'm talking about it here, but you should remember this information when you're reading other sections as well. In fact, you should photocopy this section and stick copies in the other chapters. Better yet, go buy more copies of this book, cut these pages out of those copies, and stick them in the other chapters of this copy! (This message brought to you by The Fund To Get the Author a New Car.)

Opacity is the measurement of how difficult it is to see through something. A brick wall is completely *opaque* to everyone but Superman; we can't see through it at all. That would be 100% opacity. A perfect glass window is completely transparent to everyone but Daredevil, the blind superhero. You can see everything through it perfectly, so it has zero opacity. Sunglasses would have a fairly low opacity, since you can still see everything through them but it all looks tinted green. Stained glass windows have a high opacity, but less than 100%; you can still make out light and vague shapes through them.

Are You Tinting or Painting?

Normally when you're painting, you want to see exactly the color you're painting, wherever you're painting it. That's an opacity setting of 100. If you're working in any mode other than 16-million-color or greyscale mode, that's the only option you have.

If you set the **Opacity** field on the Tool Options palette below 100, and you paint over another color on the same layer, then the color you see is a mixture of the color that was there and the color you're painting with. The lower the opacity level, the less the color you're painting with will show, as you can see in Figure 12.1.

Figure 12.1

The problem with setting your opacity too low is all too clear.

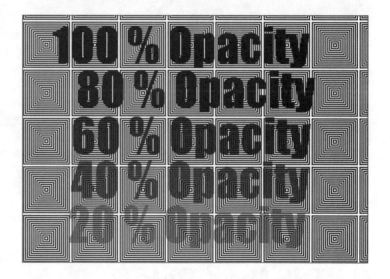

If you're painting on a transparent part of a layer, painting with less than 100% opacity makes the area translucent. Anything on a layer below the current one will be tinted by the color you're brushing with. The higher the opacity value, the heavier the tint.

Brushing Up

The **Build Up Brush** check box selects what happens when your non-opaque brush line crosses over itself. Use the brush to write an **8** onto your image with an opacity setting of 20. If you don't have the Build Up Brush option checked, the entire **8** is uniform in color. If you have it checked, however, the place where the lines cross in the center will be more opaque. This is because you've painted two translucent layers on top of one another.

Please note that this option only effects what you do with a single stroke. If you write the letter **X**, for example, you will always need to use two strokes, so the area where the strokes cross will be more opaque than the rest of the letter.

Brushing Inconsistently

So far, your entire brush line has been consistent, even if it hasn't been opaque. There are two settings on your brush's Tool Options palette that let you set your brush to be inconsistent, with parts that are more solid and parts that are less—much like real brushes.

Tricks 'n' Tips

Constant Opacity

To have a consistent opacity in an item with multiple strokes, draw it on its own layer at 100% opacity. Then lower the opacity of the whole layer, as explained in Chapter 20, "Egging On Layers."

Adjust the **Hardness** value below 100, and the edges of your brush will be less opaque then the center. The lower the Hardness value, the softer the edges. Because this feature is based on opacity, it only works with 16-million-color or greyscale mode.

The Science of Art

The Airbrush Is the Paint Brush

When you're working in 16-million-color or greyscale mode, the Airbrush tool achieves its effect simply by using a low hardness value. Set the airbrush's hardness to 100, and it will work just like the paint brush. Or, if you lower the paint brush's hardness, it will work just like the airbrush, except that if you stay in one point with the mouse button pushed down, the paint won't build up. (In lower-color modes, the airbrush uses a different trick to achieve the soft effect.)

Lower the **Density** below 100, and holes begin to appear in your brush. This setting drops pixels from your brush in order to make less solid paint marks. The value is what percentage of dots are actually used; bring the setting down to 1, and even a large brush will have very few pixels. Because it's not dependent on opacity, you can use the Density setting in any color mode. You can also combine Density and Hardness settings for a range of effects, as shown in Figure 12.2.

Figure 12.2

A big round brush with different hardness and density settings.

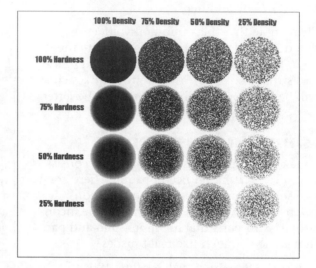

Chalk and Charcoal Without Messy Fingers

Paint Shop Pro offers premixed combinations of brush shape, hardness, and density, designed to simulate various natural drawing tools. Click the Brush icon on the upper-right of the main tab of the brush Tool Options palette. A drop-down list appears, offering you such tasty options as Paintbrush, Pen, Pencil, Marker, Crayon, Chalk, and Charcoal.

Fancy Brush Shapes

You've seen the list of brush shapes on the brush Tool Options palette. Round, square, slashes—pretty boring. Oh, they're fine if you want to make a line, but what if you want a really nice point decoration? They just won't cut it. Let's face it, those folks who made PSP didn't have any imagination.

Or did they?

They're really hiding their light under a bushel. Double-click the *picture* of a brush shape, and the Custom Brush dialog box seen in Figure 12.3 appears. Now this is more like it!

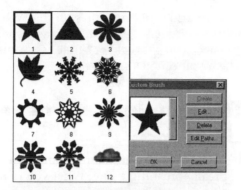

Figure 12.3

Fancy brushes—fancy that!

Click the button for the drop-down list and find the brush you want. Click it, then click **OK**, and you're ready to go!

The Real Custom Brush

The dialog box says that those brushes are custom, which is crazy. They come with the software! How *custom* can they be if everyone who buys the software gets the exact same ones?

Dagnabbit, we each deserve genuinely custom brushes. And if the software people aren't willing to give them to us, we'll have to make them ourselves! To do this

1. Create a new blank image.

2. Draw the shape you want for your custom brush.

3. Select the shape you drew. You need to select it closely, so you're probably best off using the Magic Wand.

4. Choose the Paint Brush tool.

5. On the Tool Option palette, double-click the brush shape display area.

6. On the Custom Brush dialog box that appears, click **Create**. Your brush will be added to the list.

Custom-Made for Other Folks

If someone else has some brushes that you'd like, let them give them to you. Any brushes they created are in their brush directory (listed on the Custom Brush dialog box), in a file called ubrush.jbr.

Copy your friend's ubrush.jbr into your own brush directory under a different name (so as not to wipe out the brushes you've created), and the brushes will be added to your brush list. The filename has to keep the .jbr extension.

Be Flush With Brushes

You can have three folders of brush files. Click **Edit Paths** on the Custom Brushes dialog box to select the folders.

Bigger Steps

If you need a step greater than 100, you'll have to fake it by making a custom brush that includes the brush shape as only a small part of a larger empty area.

You can also find brush files on the Web. The Jasc Software site has a page at www.jasc.com/resources.asp#stockart? that lists some sites where you can get brushes.

The Simple Steps of Setting Up Steps

When you brush a line onto your picture, you're not really brushing a line. What you're really doing is stamping the brush shape onto your picture, over and over.

How often does it stamp it? Ah, that's what the **Step** setting on the brush Tool Options palette is for. It tells how often to stamp the brush down as you drag your brush. It's measured in percentage of the width of the brush. Set it to 100 and each stamping of the brush will touch but not overlap the one before it. If you have a round brush, this will draw a row of circles. If you have a custom Elvis-shaped brush, you'll get a whole series of Elvii.

Set the value to 50, and each image stamped will overlap half of the one before it. Set the value to 1, and you'll have a smooth-edge line no matter what your brush shape is.

The Least You Need to Know

➤ The **Opacity** setting on brushes (and other tools) sets how transparent the color you put down will be.

➤ The **Hardness** setting varies the transparency at the edges of the brush.

➤ The **Density** setting adjusts how many pixels in the brush shape actually add paint.

➤ The **Step** setting adjusts how frequently the brush shape is stamped as you drag it.

➤ Double-click the brush image display to get the **Custom Brush** dialog, where you can select fancier brush shapes.

➤ Select an image area, and then click **Create** on the Custom Brush dialog to create your own brush.

Chapter 13

Pressure-Sensitive Tablets Cure the Pressures of the Mouse

In This Chapter

➤ What is a tablet

➤ Operating a tablet

➤ Varying line width

➤ Varying color and opacity

The mouse is a wonderful invention. (The computer mouse, I mean; about the only thing that regular mice give mankind is the inspiration for some hilarious cartoons.) It creates a great way of interacting with computers, allowing you to point and click at things rather than typing in arcane commands. They bring the power of computers to those of us who are too lazy to learn to type and too hypnotized by the screen to look down to the keyboard.

But as a drawing tool, a mouse is strictly for the birds. (My cat just looked up, hungrily.)

Open a new Paint Shop Pro window and try signing your name using the mouse. It takes a while, and ends up looking all jerky and rough, right? And this is your name, which you've practically got memorized. Using a pen and paper, you can dash off your signature in two seconds, and it looks just like you're signature is supposed to look (which, in my case, is Nal $errrii, oddly enough).

Take One Tablet

A *tablet* is a device designed to let you draw smoothly on the computer. It's a special flat surface that you connect to your computer. The tablet comes with a stylus that you drag across the tablet just like you drag a pen across a piece of paper. The tablet controls your screen pointer, moving the pointer to follow the path you move the stylus in. When you're using it with Paint Shop Pro, you can write with your stylus on a tablet and see the paint brush writing the exact same thing onscreen.

Over-the-Counter Tablets: Buying One

A lot of people think that tablets are expensive. There's a reason for that: They used to be. In addition to their high price, they also had some reliability problems. And because they were expensive, they were seen as a specialty item, and few stores carried them.

Times have changed.

These days, with a little bit of looking, you can find tablets that start at under $50. They can be made more cheaply now because they've also simplified the technology—which makes them more reliable. They're also quite light, weighing about the same as a clipboard. You can lean back in your favorite chair, tablet in one hand and stylus in the other, and draw away.

Any good computer store should have at least one affordable tablet on hand (or you can find them online, via www.MillionsOnTheInternet.com). I paid about 90 bucks for mine (one of the lower-end models made by Wacom, the big name in tablets), and it substantially improved my ability to draw on my computer. If you're serious about computer art, you really should look into getting a tablet.

Pointing and Dragging, Tablet Style

Every tablet comes with its own configuration software, with which you can vary how the tablet works. Most tablets come with reasonable default settings, which reflect how most people use their tablets.

The tablet has a rectangular drawing area, which matches the parts of your screen. Move your pen to the upper left of the tablet, and the pointer goes to the upper left of your screen. Move your pen to the center of the tablet, and the pointer goes to the center of your screen. And so on.

If you want to move the pointer without doing anything, just hold the pen a little above the surface of the tablet as you move it (some folks call this *hovering*). Don't actually touch the pen to the tablet.

To click on something, point to it, then quickly tap the stylus against the tablet. To drag, first point to where you want to start the drag. Press the stylus down, and then move the stylus across the tablet.

Is It ESP?

It seems almost psychic that the tablet knows where you're holding the pen even if it isn't quite touching the tablet. Actually, the tablet itself doesn't have any touch-sensitivity. It uses a radio system to detect where your pen is. A sensor in the pen tip recognizes when the pen is actually pressed against something, and sends that information by radio to the tablet.

So, for example, if you want to use the Paint Brush tool to paint something in Paint Shop Pro, you

1. Hover the stylus over the Paint Brush button.
2. Tap the button to click it.
3. Hover the stylus over your image.
4. Press the stylus against your tablet and start drawing.

This may sound complicated, and it may feel a little complicated the first time you do it, but by the third time it feels quite natural when you do it.

Other Tablet Features

Some tablets have a special function grid across the top, with a series of programmable *hot spots*. You can program these hot spots to link them to program features. For example, you can set up one hot spot so that when you click it, your tool switches to the Paint Brush tool, and another so that clicking it will save your file to disk, and a third so that quickly opens a spreadsheet so that you can hide your doodles when the boss comes.

Some styluses have an *eraser* on the butt end. Turn your stylus upside-down, and Paint Shop Pro will switch to the Eraser tool, letting you wipe away your errors. Return the stylus to right-side up, and you're back to the tool you had before—free to make totally new errors.

USB? I C!

Some tablets plug into your PC's serial port, whereas others plug into the USB port. If your PC has a USB port (and almost all desktops sold since 1998 do), then get the USB version. You're less likely to have to unplug something else to plug it in (and if you do, it's less of pain to unplug a USB device, since you don't need to turn off the PC power to do it safely). Plus, a USB tablet is more likely to be compatible with your next computer, which may not have a serial port.

Styles from the Stylus: Nifty PSP Features

Paint Shop Pro is specifically designed to support *pressure-sensitive* tablets, which detect not only where the stylus is pressed, but also how hard. Any tablet you're likely to buy will be pressure-sensitive. (Again, it's not the tablet that actually detects the pressure; it's the stylus.)

Click the right-most tab of any tool's Options palette, and you'll see the options displayed in Figure 13.1. These options tell Paint Shop Pro what effect pressing harder on the pen has.

Figure 13.1

Pick parameters to be permuted by pressing your pen!

Vary Opacity: Lay It on Thick (or Thin)

Choose **Vary Opacity**, and your brush tools can vary the weight of the paint. Press your stylus lightly against the tablet and just a fine mist of color comes out, barely tinting the color below it. The harder you press, the more opaque the paint. The upper limit to the opacity is the percentage you set on the first tab of the Tool Options palette. Set that to 100, and you can paint with totally solid color.

Remember that your stylus is a sensitive instrument. You don't have to ram it hard against the tablet to get that 100%. Think of it as a felt-tip pen; you can have

134

different effects with a felt-tip pen depending on how light you press it to the paper, but even for the heaviest effect you don't need to press very hard.

This feature only works in 16-million-color mode or in greyscale mode.

Don't Get Stuck

If you're done working with the tablet and going back to working with your mouse, don't just lay the stylus on the tablet. The tablet will continue to detect it, and you won't be able to move the pointer with the mouse.

Vary Color: The Radiance of Casual Gradients

Choose **Vary Color**, and a light touch on the stylus has you drawing in the Fill style. A heavy touch has you drawing in the Stroke style. Amounts of pressure in between create a color that mixes the stroke and fill style. Again, this feature only works in 16-million-color or greyscale mode.

Vary Width: Fine and Porcine Lines

Probably the most useful option for the traditional artist is **Vary Width**. Press delicately on the stylus and a fine line is created. Press more firmly and the line grows thicker. This works very much like traditional pens and brushes, where mashing down the nib gives you a wider point. As you can see in Figure 13.2, this gives you the ability to do a wide variety of different line widths without changing your options. You can vary width within the line or you can vary it from line to line.

Be a Copycat

Figure 13.2 shows an example of another feature of tablets: tracing. Most tablets have a clear overlay you can stick a photo under. Go over the lines of the photo with your stylus (as I did in this figure), and those lines are reproduced onscreen.

Figure 13.2

This sketch shows that you can get a range of line widths without changing your width options. It also shows that I'm not a great renderer.

The Vary Width option works in any color mode. The minimum width of your line is always one pixel; the maximum width is the width set in the first tab of the brush options.

These options aren't mutually exclusive. You can turn on all three options at once, or have none of them on at all.

The Least You Need to Know

➤ A tablet gives you the ability to draw with a pen-like stylus and have your drawing appear on screen.

➤ Tablets are inexpensive and widely available.

➤ The pressure-sensitive tablet options are on the last tab of any tool option palette.

➤ Choose **Vary Opacity** to paint translucent colors with a light touch, or opaque colors with a heavier touch.

➤ Choose **Vary Color** to paint the background color with a light touch, or the foreground color with a heavier touch.

➤ Choose **Vary Width** to paint thin lines with a light touch, or thick lines with a heavy touch.

Chapter 14

Picture Tubes

In This Chapter

➤ Quickly decorate your image with detailed features

➤ Make busy themed backgrounds

➤ Draw tracks and paths

➤ Create your own tubes

Sometimes you can't paint the forest for the trees. There are just too many of them, and they each want to be painted individually. If only there were a tub full of trees you could plunk down, putting a lot of trees where you want a thick copse, or occasional trees by the side of the road.

Well, you can't get a tub full of trees. You can get a *tube* filled with them, however, and that's just as good.

Picture Tubes Squirt Pictures Out

 Click **Picture Tubes**, and you'll have a new raster tool that will let you lay down interesting design elements and multiple similar-but-not-identical items very quickly. (This feature works only in 16-million-color and greyscale modes.)

On the Picture Tube Tools Options palette, click the button for the drop-down menu next to the display area. A scrollable display opens, showing all the different picture tubes available, each with a sample image from the tube and a title for that tube. Select one of these, then drag across your image. Suddenly, you're adding a lot to your

Tricks 'n' Tips

Too Few Toobs, er, Tubes?

The downloaded versions of Paint Shop Pro come with only a few tubes (CD-ROM versions have more). You can download tubes from www.jasc.com, among other places.

picture. If you selected a tube marked trees, for example, the path you dragged will have trees scattered across it. Select popcorn, and you'll have left a stream of popcorn.

Tube Types

If you're anything like me, right after you tried your first tube, you tried almost all of them. These are fun. As you may or may not have noticed, tubes tend to break down into three categories:

➤ *Object tubes* have pictures of several different but similar objects in them. These can be trees of various shapes and types, planes, candy corn, and so on.

➤ *Path tubes* are designed to paint a path, with arrows, footsteps, or some other sort of path marker. These are nifty, because the path actually points in the direction you drag the brush. Drag it upwards, and you paint a series of arrows pointing up. Drag to the right, and the arrows go to the right.

➤ *Design tubes* are the ones that always look boring when you're selecting tubes. They might look like a few dots or a little bit of glow. Don't ignore these. As you can see in Figure 14.1, when you drag them you can achieve some very interesting effects.

Figure 14.1

The boring picture tube elements on the left make the exciting designs on the right.

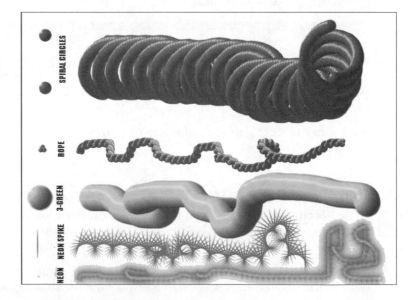

Tubing Downstream: Keeping It Easy

To make good, quick use of tubes, remember the following tips:

➤ Click once to get a single image from the picture tube, or drag to get a series of images.

➤ To get a line of various images from the tube, click one end of the line and then hold **Shift** while clicking the other end of the line. (Depending on the tube, the line might be very uneven.)

➤ If you're drawing on a field of objects, draw the ones that are farthest away (generally the highest on the page) first, then work your way forward (down the page).

As you see in Figure 14.2, you can throw together an image pretty quickly with wise use of brushes. To draw a picture of a 1940s picnic, I created a background with a standard gradient (Summer Field). I used the Summer Tree tube to add trees and an Old Cars tube to add the autos. The sun is actually an effect called Sunburst, which you'll read about in Chapter 16, "Special Effects"—it only took four mouse clicks to add it. I added the clouds last so that they block the sun slightly.

Fruitless Clicking?

If no picture appears when you click, you're using a path tube. Those have to be dragged before a picture will appear.

Figure 14.2

It's not an amazing picture, but it's pretty good for 90 seconds of work!

Total time it took to draw that picture? About a minute-and-a-half. Don't let anyone tell you that using Paint Shop Pro is no picnic!

Tuning the Tube

The settings on the Picture Tube Tool Options palette let you fine-tune the way the tube works and help you make the image you want (see Figure 14.3).

Figure 14.3

Don't let any sign stop you from changing your Picture Tube options.

On the first tab of options (seen in Figure 14.3), change the **Step** setting to change how frequently an image appears when you drag. As with the Step option on brush tools, this is measured as a percentage of the width of the brush. However, the width of a picture tube brush is hard to judge, because it's based on the way the images are stored. This field takes values ranging from 1 (the tube pictures overlap heavily) to 500 (you have to drag a lot for each picture you lay down).

Change the **Scale** figure to reduce or enlarge the images coming out of your picture tube. You can set values anywhere from 1% to 250%. Shrinking works better than enlarging. Enlarged picture tubes tend to have pointy edges that come from enlarging the pixels on a raster image.

De Fault of Default

Each tube has its own set of default option settings. Select the tube you want before setting your options or you'll just have to set them again.

On the second tab of the options, the **Placement mode** drop-down list selects the evenness of the distribution of pictures as you drag. Choose **Continuous**, and the images will come out exactly according to your Step setting. Choose **Random**, and it will vary the step a bit, putting out some images sooner and others later. The Random setting is good for creating natural-looking images. It's hard to make a convincing forest when all the trees are evenly spaced!

The second drop-down list on the second tab has enough settings that it deserves a subsection all its own.

A Subsection Just for the Selection Mode Drop-Down List

Each tube is made up of a number of pictures, in a certain order. For example, you might have a tube labeled Famous Things Not Made Of Cheese, with pictures of a ducky, a horsy, a bunny, and Sir Isaac Newton (inventor of both gravity and an enjoyable fig-based treat). Whenever you drag far enough or you click, another picture comes out of the tube. To decide which picture comes out, PSP checks the value in the **Selection Mode** drop-down list. You can set this value to:

➤ **Random**—every time a new picture comes out, it could be any one of them. You might get two duckies in a row, or you might put down a dozen images without seeing a ducky.

➤ **Incremental**—goes through all the images in order, and then repeats. Ducky, horsy, bunny, Sir Isaac, ducky, horsy...

➤ **Angular**—chooses the picture based on which direction you're dragging the mouse. Drag it upwards and you get a ducky. Drag to the right and you get a horsy. Drag down and you get a bunny. Drag to the left, and there's Sir Isaac. All path brushes depend on this setting. (Because this option is dependent on dragging, you won't be able to click pictures into place with it.)

➤ **Pressure**—an option just for people who use pressure-sensitive tablets. Press your stylus lightly when dragging, and you'll place a ducky. The harder you press, the farther down the list you go. (If you choose this option then draw with a mouse, you'll always get the last image in the tube: Sir Isaac.)

➤ **Velocity**—varies which picture is chosen based on how fast you're dragging. The slower you go, the farther down the list it takes the picture from. Drag quickly for a ducky, or drag very slowly (or just click) for Sir Isaac.

Find Your Inner Tube: Make Your Own Picture Tubes

Picture tubes might seem like advanced technological things that can be made only by picture tube monks that have been honing their craft for thousands of years. Actually, if you can use Paint Shop Pro, you can be a tuber too!

It's not that hard to do, but it does require some precision, so make sure you follow the instructions carefully.

Starting a Blank Image

You'll need to create a new image on which to build your picture tube. To get the proper blank image use the following steps:

1. Choose **File, Preferences, General Program Preferences**, and click the **Rulers and Units** tab on the resulting dialog box.

2. Choose **Pixels** from the **Units** drop-down list.

3. Set the **Horizontal Spacing** value to be a few pixels wider than the widest picture that will be in your tube. Set the **Vertical Spacing** value to be a few pixels more than the tallest picture. Click **OK**.

4. Click **New** to create a new image.

5. Calculate the dimensions for your image. Each picture will need its own cell, a section of your image as wide and as high as the values set in step 3. Let's say your settings are 50 pixels wide and 50 pixels high, and you're putting 12 pictures in your tube. You could set up your image to hold 4 rows of 3 cells apiece, making your image 150 wide and 200 high. Or you could set it up as a single row of 12 images, which would be 600 pixels wide and 50 pixels high.

6. In the **New Image** dialog box, select **Pixels** as your units, and enter the width and height you calculated. For **Background Color**, choose **Transparent**. For **Image Type**, choose **16.7 Million Colors**. Click **OK**.

7. Choose **View, Grid**.

Building Your Tube

The grid lines divide your image into the cells that make it up. Put one picture for your tube in each cell.

The order of the cells is important. As you see in Figure 14.4, the cells are numbered across each row. If you're planning to have the selection mode for this tube set to Random, it doesn't matter what order you put these images in. For Incremental mode, you should put them from first to last in the series. For Pressure mode, the cell for the lightest touch should go first, and the one with the heaviest touch will be last. For Velocity mode, the first cell's picture will be associated with the fastest mouse motion, and the last cell the slowest.

If you're designing a path tube, you're going to use Angular mode. Imagine there's a pizza around the pointer on the screen, and it's cut into as many pieces as you have cells. The first cell holds the picture that will come out of the tube if the pointer is dragged straight up into the top piece of pizza. The second cell is what you get if you drag towards the second piece of pizza, clockwise. Each of the following pictures is formed from dragging toward that piece of pizza, numbered clockwise.

Tricks 'n' Tips

Laziness Is Good

If you're designing a path, you'll probably have a series of very similar images. Don't keep trying to draw the same thing. Do what I did: draw it once as a vector item, then just copy and rotate the first drawing.

Cell 1   Cell 2...

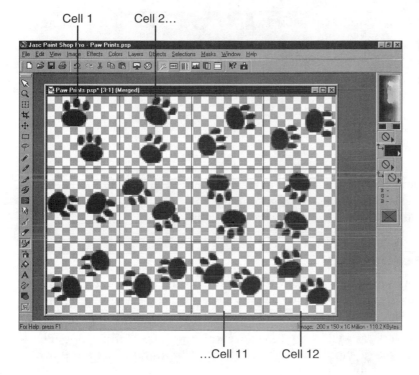

Figure 14.4
This tube will certainly make tracks!

...Cell 11   Cell 12

Saving Your Tube

After your image looks good, it's time to save it. It's not a tube until you make it a tube. To do this

1. First, click **Save** to store a copy of your file as a standard PSP file. (This isn't actually needed to make a tube, but doing this will let you make corrections if you discover a problem with the tube.)

2. Choose **Layers, Merge, Merge All (Flatten)** to turn your image into a single-layer raster image.

3. Choose **File, Export, Picture Tube**, which will open the dialog box seen in Figure 14.5.

4. Enter the number of columns in your cell grid into the **Cells across** field, and the number of rows in **Cells down**.

5. Enter the default options for your brush in the **Placement mode**, **Step size**, and **Selection mode** fields.

6. Type a name for your brush into the **Tube name** field, then click **OK**. Your tube will be created, and put in a directory with the rest of your tubes!

Figure 14.5

Set the options for your tube-to-be.

If you close your image file now, PSP will ask you if you want to save the changes. Choose **No**. Otherwise, you'll be overwriting the copy you saved in step 1 (which has all your layers and vectors) with the flattened raster version you created in step 2. It's better to keep the full version so that you can edit it later.

Put Your Tube to the Test

 After you're done, it's time to take the new tube for a test drive! Open a new image, click **Picture Tube**. On the Tool Options palette, click open the list of tubes. Your tube will be there, in alphabetical order, based on the name you gave it.

Draw away! I hope it works as well as my tube does in Figure 14.6. But if it doesn't, just open up the saved file (it should be quickly selectable from the **File** drop-down list), edit, and resave your tube.

Figure 14.6

Oh no! Some animal has walked all over my new image!

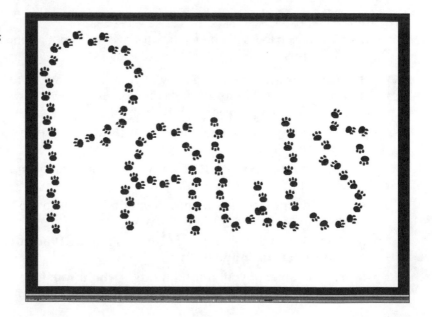

Taking the Tubes of Others

You can download tubes from various sources, or get tubes from friends (or archenemies). They have links to various tube sites at www.jasc.com. You can even buy tubes, generally as part of collections of graphic files.

You can recognize a tube file because it has the file extension .tub. To find out where your tube files go, choose **File, Preferences, File Locations**. On the **Tubes** tab, you'll find your tube directory listed. (You can also add two more directories to the list, so you'll have three directories of tubes. This can be handy for organizing different types of tubes.)

The Least You Need to Know

➤ Click **Picture Tube** to be able to paint with a series of predesigned pictures.

➤ Change the **Step** setting to alter the spacing between pictures.

➤ Change the **Scale** option to change the size of the pictures.

➤ To create your own picture tube, build an image with evenly spaced cells, one picture per cell.

➤ To turn that image into a picture tube, choose **File, Export, Tube**.

➤ Add downloaded picture tube files (extension: .tub) to the directory that's displayed when you choose **File, Preferences, File Locations** and choose the **Tubes** tab.

Chapter 15

Deformation Information

In This Chapter

➤ Resize selections

➤ Tilt and skew selections

➤ Rotate selections

➤ Tilt, skew, and rotate layers

So you've designed this great-looking magazine cover for the magazine you work for, *Dust Collector's Monthly*. You're expecting your boss to lavish you with praise and tell you to take the rest of the day off. You're half right. She thinks the cover's great—so great that she wants to run a new ad for the magazine, one showing this cover plastered on the wall of the museum. She already has the picture of a museum wall that she wants you to add it to. Great, you think, just a quick copy-and-paste job. Should just take a couple of minutes.

Then she shows you the picture. The museum wall is at an angle! It has perspective. This means you'll have to redraw the entire thing onto the photo, meaning hours of work and no going home until 10 p.m., right?

That's what you should tell your boss, anyway. Get her to cough up some overtime pay. Actually, putting that picture into place will only take a couple minutes.

Deform Your Picture: It's Better Than It Sounds

 You use the **Deformation** tool to resize layers and areas, to skew them, and to have perspective effects. *Perspective* is an artist term for viewing items at an angle so that parts of the object are farther away and thus look smaller.

Deformation Reduction

Previous versions of Paint Shop Pro had advanced deformations to do curved warping of your image. These features still exist; they've just been renamed. You can find them on the **Effects, Geometric Effects** submenu.

Deformation Situation?

How can you tell if your current selection is deformable? Just check to see if the **Deformation** button is available. If it is, deform away!

The Deformation tool works on raster selections and layers. This isn't to say that you can't deform vector selections—when you select a vector object, you automatically have access to all the deformation features.

The Deformable Versus the Undeformable

The bad news is, there are some types of raster areas you cannot deform. The good news is, you can change any of those areas into a type that you can deform, and then do the deformation.

For example, you can deform any layer except the background. Paint Shop Pro thinks of any nontransparent background as a special layer, immune to some of the commands that afflict ordinary layers. To tell PSP that you think the background isn't so special, right-click the **Background** entry on the layer palette, and then choose **Promote To Layer**.

Similarly, you can't transform just any selection, you can only transform *floating* selections—selections that have been detached from the layer surface. But a quick press of **Ctrl+F** will turn any selection into a floating selection.

Finally, deforming only works on 16-million-color or greyscale images. If you're using a lower color mode, choose **Colors, Increase Color Depth, 16 Million Colors**.

Doing the Deformation

 Click the **Deformation** button, and a rectangle with deformation handles appears around your selection (or around the whole layer, if nothing is selected). These may look familiar; they're exactly the same as the handles that appear around new and selected shapes, as seen in Chapter 8, "Vector Frankenstein: The Science of Making Vector Objects." These handles work like so:

➤ Dragging the center handle moves the selection.

➤ Dragging the handle to the right of the center rotates the selection around the center. Hold down **Shift** while dragging to rotate in exact 15-degree increments.

➤ Dragging the handle on the middle of the upper or lower edge changes the height of the selection. Similarly, the handles on the center of the right and left sides are dragged to change the width.

➤ Dragging the corner handles changes both the height and the width of the image. Right-dragging these corners makes certain you don't change the proportion between height and width.

The Tricks I Never Told You

There are a couple other tricks you can do with those handles, things I didn't mention earlier. These are the most powerful deformers.

➤ Hold down **Shift** while dragging the handle at the center of the top or bottom edge. This will perform a *horizontal skew* of the image. Think of it as if you grabbed a picture frame by the top and bottom edges, then moved your right hand to the right and your left hand to the left. What you end up with would be a skewed picture. (Note: Don't try this with your own framed painting, as you are likely to rip or break it. Instead, go to the museum and try it on one there. Don't worry, they have plenty of spares.)

➤ Holding down **Shift** while dragging the handle on the center of the left or right edge will perform a vertical skew, like grabbing both sides of a painting and moving one hand up, one hand down.

➤ Holding down **Shift** while dragging a corner handle performs a *corner skew*, stretching one corner up, down, or to the side. It leaves the other corners in place. (To move the corner both horizontally and vertically at once, hold down **Ctrl+Shift** while dragging.)

➤ Hold down **Ctrl** while dragging one of the corner handles to create perspective, which will look as though you're holding onto one edge of a picture frame and pushing the opposite edge away from you.

You can see the result of these various operations in Figure 15.1.

Tricks 'n' Tips

A Loose Skew

Holding down **Ctrl+Shift** while dragging the handle of the center on any edge to move the whole edge without changing its angle or size. This is only different from the usual skew controls if you do it on a selection that has already been skewed.

Figure 15.1

Elmer Fudd was wrong. The problem isn't with skwewy wabbits, it's with skewy wabbits!

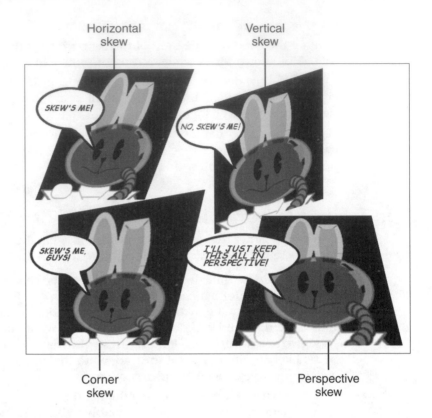

Done Deforming

When you're done making your deformations, click **Apply** on the Deformation Tool Options palette (or **Cancel** if you decide not to go through with the deformation). If you don't have the palette open, just click another tool button, and the deformation will take place.

If you're going to be performing several deformations on the same image area, try to do them all in one quick sequence. Don't apply one, go do some other work, and come back and do another. Every time you deform a raster image, it ends up blending some pixels of the image together in making the deformed image. This loses a little bit of detail. If you do it all at once, and then click **Apply**, you're really only going to lose a little data, kind of making a photocopy of a page. But if you do it repeatedly, it's like making a photocopy of a photocopy of a photocopy, and the results will become visibly degraded.

Perspective Perfection

If you're working with pasting things up on existing backgrounds, trying to put your selection into the right perspective to match something that is already there (such as

150

the magazine-cover-on-a-museum-wall example), you may find it a bit tricky. After all, it's hard to match an angle.

You're likely to find that doing the perspective drag is actually not the best way to match the background. Often, it's easiest to use the corner skew (**Shift+Ctrl** dragging the corner handles) to get the right placement.

If you're lucky enough to be covering up a rectangular object (such as replacing a painting on the museum wall with your magazine cover), just drag each corner of your selection so that it's right over the corner of what you're covering up, as shown in Figure 15.2.

Figure 15.2

The finest art deserves to be put into a frame.

A painting hanging on a wall is supposed to hang squarely, which means that its top and bottom edges are parallel to the lines where the wall meets the floor and ceiling. When viewed in perspective, the floor and ceiling lines aren't parallel; they'll be at an angle on your image. The angles of the top and bottom edge of the magazine cover will both be somewhere between the angle of the ceiling line and the angle of the floor line. If you hang the cover high on the wall, the top edge angle will be pretty close to the ceiling angle. The lower you put it, the closer to the floor angle it becomes.

The same goes for the angles of the magazine cover's sides. Looked at straight on, they would be parallel with the lines where this wall meets other walls. In perspective, the angles will be somewhere between the angle made with the next wall to the left and that of the next wall to the right.

Perspective That Ain't so Square

But what if your item isn't supposed to be square with the edges of what it's on. What if you're trying to create the image of a magazine cover thrown sloppily on a desk, for example?

Deformation By Number

Double-click the **Deformation** button, and the Deformation Settings dialog box opens. You can use this to deform by setting exact values for shearing, scaling, and others. (The X values are for horizontal adjustment, whereas the Y values are for vertical.)

The *easiest* way to do this is to violate the suggestion I made above that you don't deform things more than once. First, select the magazine cover and with the **Deformation** tool, rotate it to match the angle that the magazine would be at if you were looking straight down on the desk. Click **Apply**. Then click **Deformation** again and drag the corners to put it in perspective. Use the near and far edges of the desk as your guidelines for where to put the top and bottom edges of the deformation area, and the sides of the desk as guidelines for where to put your side edges.

This is all a little tricky, of course. You'll have to trust your eyeballs a lot to tell you when something is right or wrong.

The Least You Need to Know

➤ The **Deformation** tool works only on floating selections and nonbackground layers of 16-million-color or grayscale images.

➤ The **Deformation** tool creates editing handles on raster images that work the same as the editing handles on vector shapes.

➤ Drag a corner handle to resize the selection.

➤ Drag the handle to the right of center to rotate the selection.

➤ Hold down **Shift** while dragging an edge handle to skew the selection.

➤ Hold down **Ctrl** while dragging a corner handle to create perspective, or **Ctrl+Shift** to create a corner skew.

Chapter 16

Special Effects

In This Chapter

➤ Smooth and sharpen your image

➤ Warp your image

➤ Adjust your colors

➤ Create a look of special materials

You've got your image basically in shape, but it's a bit dull. It needs some zing, some pizzazz, some syzygy or some other z-heavy word. It needs some texture, some shine, and some *emotion*. Now's the time to reach for the **Effects** menu.

Getting Affection for Effects

An *effect* changes the look of your image without adding any new distinct shapes or features. Instead, it reworks the image you already have.

If that all sounds a bit vague, you're right. There are so many different effects available that any description that covers them all will be a bit vague. The best way to understand effects is to give them a try. So let's try...

Making Any Old Image an Old Image

To fool around with effects, you need to load up an image. Open up any image (not a blank new one). It needs to be in 16-million-color mode with a raster layer.

Effectively the Same

In previous versions of Paint Shop Pro, there were separate submenus for *effects*, *filters*, and *deformations*. Now they're all considered effects.

Make sure you have nothing selected (choose **Selection, Select None**) so that the effect alters the whole layer. Choose **Effects, Artistic Effects, Sepia**.

A dialog box appears. I'll get to some of the details of effects dialog boxes shortly, but for now just click **OK**. Violà! Your image is transformed into the muted brown tones of an old sepia-toned photo!

Click **Undo** (the experimenter's friend, shortcut: **Ctrl+Z**) to return your image to its original state.

Options That Affect Effects

When you choose an effect, you are likely to get a dialog box with its own set of options. Some effects have a *lot* of options. I could try to describe every single option in full; however, you would fall asleep trying to read through all those descriptions, and it would make this book so thick that it would need its own zip code.

Choose **Effects, Texture Effects, Tiles**. The dialog box in Figure 16.1 appears, except it shows up without space bunny images on it (unless the space bunnies have invaded your images, as well; in which case it's time to call the government's Space Bunny Prevention Hotline).

Figure 16.1

I wish chocolate chip cookies had as many chocolate chips as effects dialog boxes have options...

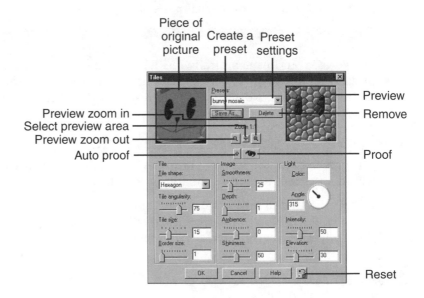

Preview: Your Future Is Told

When you open the dialog box, Paint Shop Pro takes a portion of your image (displayed in the upper left-hand area of the dialog box) and shows you what that area will look like after the effect is in place (in the upper right). You might have to wait a few seconds before the preview is properly displayed, particularly if you're using an old, steam-powered PC like I am. As you set the various options in the dialog box, the preview display is redrawn to match the new settings.

If you want the preview to show a different part of your image, point to the **Select Preview Area** button (indicated in Figure 16.1) and press and hold down your mouse button. A small picture of your layer or selection appears, with a rectangle indicating the area that is currently displayed. Drag this rectangle over the area you want displayed, and then release the mouse button.

To the right and left of the Select Preview Area button are zoom in and zoom out buttons. Click **Zoom In** to get a closer preview of what the effect does to each pixel. Use **Zoom Out** to see more of the image in the preview window. (Use Zoom Out lightly; the more image you display, the longer it takes to redraw the preview each time you change a setting.)

Click **Proof**, and the current settings are applied to your main image window. Don't worry, PSP hasn't actually made the transformation on your picture; if you click **Cancel** now, you can leave the dialog box without any transformation taking place.

If you press the **Auto Proof** button, Paint Shop Pro automatically proofs your settings in the main image window every time you make a change. After you turn on this feature, it stays turned on for every effect until you turn it off.

Setting the Settings

Each effect has its own group of settings. A lot of these settings are self-explanatory. In the Tile effect (which shows your images as if it's made up of a bunch of tiles), the **Tile Shape** drop-down list lets you pick the shape of the tiles! Pretty obvious, right?

More Colors Please

Remember, you can convert any image to 16-million-color mode by choosing **Colors, Increase Color Depth, 16 Million Colors**, and you can turn any image into a single flat raster layer by choosing **Layers, Merge, Merge All**.

Better Off Off

Unless you have a very fast processor, Auto Proof slows down working with your effect. Unless your display is set to a high resolution, most of your image is hidden behind the dialog box anyway!

But some settings are more obscure. Feel free to click the **Help** button to get a written description of what each setting is. There's a better way to see what the setting does: change it, and see how your preview window changes. This is a case where a picture is worth a thousand words (or, in metric terms, a kiloword).

Play Around

Don't be afraid to play around with the settings; you can always click **Reset** to return them to the effect's default.

Most of the settings on a dialog box are numerical values that you can change by either entering a new number or dragging a slider. When you have to choose a color, the currently selected color is displayed. Click the color to get the full PSP color selector, or right-click the color to choose from the colors you've been using recently.

The one setting tool you might not have run into before is the Angle setting, as you can see in the Light area of the Tiles dialog box. There, it's used to select the angle as which light strikes the tiles, setting which edges of the tiles are lit and which are in shadow, as seen in Figure 16.2. Just drag the pointer around the edge of the circle to set the angle at which you want light to come in.

Light coming from left

Figure 16.2

The direction of the lighting effect on the tiles makes a subtle but visible difference.

Light coming from upper right

Presenting Presets

When you create really cool image effects that have a large number of settings, save your settings to reuse them on other images. You can do this by clicking the **Save As** button in your effect's dialog box. Another dialog box appears with a field for a name for your setting. Type in a name, hit return, and your settings are saved.

You can call back your saved settings any time you open this effect, by clicking the **Preset** drop-down list. The name you entered appears on the list.

Even if you haven't saved any settings, click the **Preset** button anyway, and you might be pleasantly surprised. Some (not all) of the effects have predesigned presets. For example, on the Preset list for Tiles, you'll find Basketball (gives your image round dimples like a basketball) and Stained Glass (turn your image into a stained glass window)!

When you've got all your settings selected, click **OK** to apply them, or **Cancel** if you've had second thoughts about using the effect.

Name Value

Pick a name for your settings that will remind you what impact the settings had. For example, if you had a setting for the tile effect that made your tiles look shiny and sharp, name the setting **Shiny and Sharp**.

Upset About Your Preset?

Click **Delete** to remove the current preset from the effect's list.

One Hundred and One Effects (Give or Take Three)

The **Effects** menu has a series of submenus that group the effects by style. This makes it easy to find the effect you want, and it keeps them from having a single menu that's 100 items long. You can see examples of all these effects in the color section of this book.

Blur Menu

The choices on the **Blur** menu soften the look of your image, taking it a little out of focus or lighting it more softly. This is particularly useful when you're dealing with a computer-generated image that is not anti-aliased, and has a lot of visibly jaggies. By averaging the value of each pixel with those of the surrounding pixels, Paint Shop Pro takes the sharpness off the image.

If you just want to quickly adjust your picture, choose **Blur** or **Blur More** (to take the image slightly out of focus) or **Soften** or **Soften More** (to make it look like a softer light effect). None of these choices have any dialog boxes.

Tricks 'n' Tips

Settings or No Settings

If a menu command has **...** at the end, that means that there is a dialog box with settings.

The Science of Art

Think Sharp

Don't fall for the beginner's assumption that sharper is always better. *Sharp* sounds like such a positive term, but remember that it goes hand-in-hand with *harsh*, which is not so good.

Average and **Gaussian Blur** each have settings that you use to adjust the degree of blurring. **Motion Blur** is handy if your drawing shows objects that are supposed to be in motion. If you look at a photo of a moving car, the image is blurred at least slightly, because the car moves while the camera aperture is open. With Motion Blur, you can simulate that effect, setting the direction and speed of apparent motion.

Sharpen Menu

The effects on the **Sharpen** submenu do the opposite of those on the **Blur** submenu: They make the image seem more in-focus and make the work seem sharper. Neither the **Sharpen** nor **Sharpen More** choice has a dialog box. If you want more precise control over how much sharper and harsher the image seems, use the **Unsharp Mask** command (which, despite its name, is a sharpening command). These commands can really bring out the detail in your image, by increasing the contrast between adjacent colors.

Edge Menu

The effects on the **Edge** menu play with the edges of the pieces of your image, where one object meets another. **Dilate** gets rid of the darkness at the edges; **Erode** increases the darkness. **Enhance** and **Enhance More** are very similar to the Sharpen effect, although they produce more exaggerated results.

The **Find All**, **Find Horizontal**, **Find Vertical**, and **Trace Contour** commands turn your picture into an outline drawing. The outlines are colorful (unless you're working in greyscale mode, of course, in which case they're greyful).

Noise Menu

On the **Effects, Noise** menu are commands that adjust the stray specks on your image. These individual pixels don't quite match the color of the pixels beside them. **Despeckle** covers up these pixels by blurring together the pixels in an area of similar color. **Median Cut** has a similar effect, bringing the stray pixel into line by averaging it with the pixels around it. None of those choices have dialog boxes. **Add** actually increases the speckling of your image if you want it.

Decreased Noise, Decreased Colors

If you're planning to use **Color, Decrease Color Depth** to change your color mode, it's a good idea to run **Effects, Noise, Despeckle** first. Speckles are apt to be harsh in a reduced-color image, and they might tie up valuable spots on your limited color palette that could be better used on other colors.

There are dialog boxes for both the **Edge-Preserving Smooth** (which makes your picture look like an in-focus shot of less detailed, more blob-like objects) and **Median Filter** (which uses a different method to achieve a similar effect). **Texture Preserving Smooth** does a good job of losing the stray dots without making it look like your images are blobs. **Salt and Pepper Filter** can adjust your grainy look, integrating your specks into a more pleasing texture.

Enhance Photo Menu

The **Effects, Enhance Photo** menu has some keen tools designed specifically for making photos look better. Because of their specific use, I talk about them in Chapter 28, "Photo Finish."

3D Effects

The **Effects, 3D Effects** menu has effects that make parts of your image appear raised over or indented into the rest. This effect is achieved by creating highlights of light and shadow around the edge of your selection.

Choose **Buttonize**, and the edges of your selection become shaded so that they appear to rise away from the rest of your image. This effect is really designed for rectangular selections; it does not work properly on freehand selections, as you can see in Figure 16.3. However, this is the only 3D effect that can be applied to an entire layer. (Other 3D effects add shadows and light *outside* the edge of the selected area, and you can't add anything outside the edge of a layer.)

Figures 16.3

Try to buttonize a non-rectangular selection, and PSP will try to pretend it's rectangular. The result is a pointless mess.

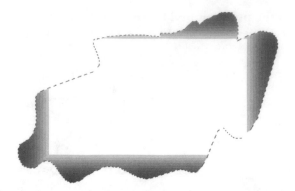

Choosing **Chisel** makes your selection look cut into the image (this looks best with rectangular selections). **Cutout** removes the selected area, leaving a hole in your picture looking into a blank area below, with a shadow being cast in the light through the hole. **Drop Shadow** makes the selection appear to hover over the rest of the image, casting a shadow on it. **Inner Bevel** and **Outer Bevel** create fancy raised edges inside and outside the selected area.

Artistic Effects

If you're not really an artist at heart, but you want to con people into believing otherwise, choose **Effects, Artistic Effects** and look at all that's offered there. Scan in a photo at high resolution, run it through the **Brush Strokes** effect, then email the resultant image off to some friends—they'll think you've spent hours making a painting, scanned it in, and sent it off.

Tricks 'n' Tips

Sooo Slooooow

Some effects can take a long time, particularly if you're working with a large image or have an old steam-powered PC like mine. If the effect is taking a long time and you want to give up, press **Esc** (the Escape key). This stops the effect, leaving your image unaltered.

You can also apply the look of other standard artistic media. Choose **Black Pencil**, **Charcoal**, **Colored Chalk**, **Colored Pencil**, or **Pencil**, and your image is redrawn as if you were working on paper with that drawing implement.

Other artistic effects make it look like your image is made of an odd substance (like **Chrome**, **Colored Foil**, or **Enamel**), or even under some odd substance like **Hot Wax Coating** (which makes the image bolder and darker).

Still other effects focus on emphasizing the outlines of the parts of your images in different ways. **Colored Edges** adds colored highlights to the edges in your picture. **Glowing Edges** transform your image into nothing but glowing, neon outlines—but that should not be confused with **Neon Glow**, which doesn't add outlines but does interesting tricks with your colors.

Contours flattens your colors, and adds lines to separate one color from the next. (It could serve as a good base for designing your own paint-by-numbers pictures!) **Topography** is similar to contours; only instead of outlining each color, each color appears to be on a different layer. This effect looks a lot like pictures that are made up of different colored construction paper pasted on top of each other.

The remaining two artistic effects make your pictures look old. **Sepia**, as shown earlier, turns your picture into the shades of brown of old photographs. **Aged Newspaper** makes your picture look like it was printed a long time ago, and left to fade. (Neither of these aging effects is available in greyscale mode.)

What's the Difference?

Both **Sepia** and **Aged Newspaper** change your image color in the same way. The latter command also blurs the image a bit, to emulate the effect of the newspaper ink slowly bleeding across the page.

Geometric Effects Menu

Geometric effects mess with the shape, rather than the color, of your image. This includes **Skew**, **Horizontal Perspective**, and **Vertical Perspective**, which work a lot like the Deformation tool you learned about in the last chapter. Your image can be bent to fit a **Circle** (so that it looks like you're seeing it through a crystal ball) or a **Pentagon**.

Many geometric effects make your image look like it's been painted on some flexible material that is being abused in the third dimension. You can **Warp**, **Punch**, or **Pinch** your image, or place it over a **Vertical** or **Horizontal Cylinder**. **Page Curl** makes your image look like it's turning up at a corner.

The **Twist** effect makes it look like you grabbed a spot on your image and twisted it like a knob, while the **CurlyQs** effect looks like you were twisting simultaneously with dozens of hands. **Spiky Halo** makes your image look as though it's been grabbed at the corners and stretched painfully.

Wave makes your image look like it's reflected in flowing water, and **Ripple** makes it look like it's reflected in a calm pond that someone just dropped a pebble in.

Strange, but True

A pixilated image is often easier to recognize if you squint at it.

Pictured Placement

Starting in PSP version 7, you can set certain effects settings by clicking or dragging within the left preview panel (the one with the unaltered picture) of the effect dialog box. For example, click in the left panel of the Sunburst dialog box to set the center of the sun.

The **Pixelate** effect makes your image look like it's of a very low resolution made up of very large pixels. Last but not least, **Wind** creates a blowy blur to your image.

Illumination Effects Menu

Sunburst gives you a burst of light with rays shooting out of it. This can simulate the sun or the lens flare that cameras pick up when exposed to bright light sources.

Lights darkens your image and puts spotlights on specific areas. You can set the placement, angle, strength, and color of up to five different light sources. Remember, however, that these are just lights on a flat picture. It can't figure out what objects are in your picture and cause them to cast shadows.

Reflection Effects Menu

Choose **Effects, Reflection Effects** when you want to repeat parts of the image within itself. **Feedback** overlaps a series of ever-smaller copies of your image. **Kaleidoscope** takes an angular slice from your image and repeats it in a circle; after using this, your image is pretty darned unrecognizable, but you end up with something cool. **Pattern** takes a square slice, reflects it, and repeats it. **Rotating Mirror** is like taking a mirror and putting it edge-down across your image.

Texture Effects Menu

Most computer art is clearly imitating art on paper. Most of your art looks like paper art, I bet, but that isn't written in stone. In fact, if you *want* your art written in stone, just choose **Effects, Texture Effects, Sandstone**, and it makes your image look like it was sandblasted into rock.

Other textures you can fake include **Polished Stone**, **Fine** and **Rough Leather**, **Sculpture**, **Soft Plastic Forms**, **Straw Wall**, and you've really never seen your own photo until you've seen it printed on **Fur**. Your image can look like it's made up of regular **Tiles** or as a **Mosaic** (either **Antique** or **Glass**).

TV or Not TV?

If you need part of your picture to look as if its an image on a TV screen, select that image portion, choose **Effects, Texture Effects, Blinds**. Choose the **Horizontal** option, set **Width** to 2, and **Opacity** to 75 or higher. This simulates an *interlace* effect, with alternating lines of light and dark image.

The **Blinds** and **Weave** effects both make your image look like it's projected onto slats, with warping and shading. **Emboss** (the only effect here without a dialog box) makes your image look pressed out of flat grey cardboard.

To make your image look like it's painted on textured paper, choose **Effects, Texture Effects, Texture** (sounds like I'm repeating myself, eh?). The textures you have to select from here are the same as the textures discussed in Chapter 11, "Fun with Fills."

Effective Inventing

You can create your own effects, even without knowing any programming. What you do have to have a grasp of, alas, is mathematics and logic. Even with that, you can't come up with any old effect you want; you can only come up with effects that alter each pixel based on the colors of the pixels within three pixels up-and-down and three side-to-side. Effects like blurs, sharpens, and embosses can be made this way, but you can't create advanced textures.

To find out how to do this, open the help system, click the **Index** tab, and look up Creating Filters.

Browsing Effects with Glee (and Your Mouse)

Sometimes you get in the mood for an effect, but you're not sure which one. That's when the Effect Browser dialog box seen in Figure 16.4 comes in handy.

Choose
an Effect

See the
Effect

Figure 16.4

The Effect Browser can show you what happens when you pinch a baby's face. Ouch!

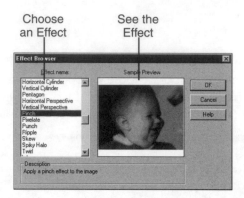

Choose **Effects, Effect Browser**, and the Effect Browser appears. On the left is a list of all the applicable effects. Click any one of these effects, and a rough version of that effect applied to your current selection appears to the right.

After you find the effect you want, click **OK**. If the effect has a dialog box, it appears. Otherwise, the effect is immediately applied. If you want to back out of applying any effect, just click **Cancel**.

The Least You Need to Know

➤ The **Effects** menu is laden with commands to transform your raster layers or selections, so long as they're in 16-million-color or greyscale mode.

➤ Most effects have dialog boxes with settings that fine-tune the effect.

➤ Dialog boxes with many settings include a **Save As** button that you use to save the settings you choose, and bring them back later using the **Presets** drop-down list.

➤ The **Effects, Blur, Blur** command is good at hiding the jaggies of computer-generated images.

➤ The commands on the **Effects, Artistic Effects** menu can make you look a lot more talented and hard working than you really are.

➤ Choose **Effects, Effect Browser** to quickly check out how various effects change your selection.

Chapter 17

Color Inspection, Correction, and Rejection

In This Chapter

➤ Make your image brighter or darker

➤ Match colors to the real world

➤ Limit your colors

➤ Master tinting, bleeding, and other neat color effects

Paint Shop Pro has a set of commands designed to adjust the colors of your selection. The fine folks at Paint Shop Pro Central don't consider these to be *effects*. They work on the same sorts of layers and selections as effects, and they have dialog boxes with the same features as effects dialog boxes, so they pass the duck test ("if it looks like an effect, walks like an effect, and quacks like an effect, it's an effect"). In fact, you should make sure you've read Chapter 16, "Special Effects," before reading this one, because it tells you how to use the dialog boxes with their preview features.

But you won't find these color adjustments in the Effect Browser, and you won't find them on the **Effects** menu. No, to find these, you have to delve into that deep well of mystery that men call "the **Colors** menu."

Wash That Color Away

Because it is easier to destroy than it is to build, let's take the easy route and learn about destroying your image colors. If you want a colorless image—pure black-and-white—choose **Colors, Adjust, Threshold**. This command turns all the brighter colors in the current selection into white, and turns all the darker colors black. Ah, but brighter and darker than what? You get to choose! By dragging the slider in the **Threshold** dialog box, you set the breaking point. Put the slider all the way to the left, and your whole selection turns black. Put it to the right, and your selection is all white. Odds are, you want it somewhere in the middle, so you get a bit of each.

Shades of Grey...or Blue or Green or Whatever

Pure black and white, while conveniently colorless, is harsh. It's not used very often; what we often consider to be black-and-white (old TV, old films, new furniture) usually includes shades of grey.

Grey All The Way

Choose **Colors, Grey Scale** and your entire image turns grey. Its color mode also changes to Greyscale mode.

Paint Shop Pro has a command to turn your selection grey, but it's been hidden by being named **Colorize**, and you can find on the **Colors** menu. Choose **Colorize** (shortcut: **Shift+L**) for a dialog box with **Hue** and **Saturation** settings. Keep Saturation set to 0, click **OK**, and your selection turns grey.

Ah, but what if you don't set saturation to 0? In this case, your image comes out not in shades of grey, but in shades of some other color. Adjust **Hue** to choose the color and use the **Saturation** slider to set the boldness of that color.

This lends itself to one of my favorite tricks, showing a photo with a focus on a certain area, which is done like so:

1. Select the area that you want to highlight.
2. Choose **Selections, Invert** (shortcut: **Shift+Ctrl+I**) so that everything *but* the area is selected.
3. Choose **Colors, Colorize** and set Saturation to 0.
4. Click **OK**.

The entire image is now in greyscale, except for the area you selected, which is in full color!

Color Tuner

Most of the time, the colors on your image are *pretty much* right. Oh, you might want to make your blues bluer, your whole image brighter, or you want Kelly green rather than bagel-that's-been-sitting-on-the-counter-for-two-weeks green. Paint Shop Pro has a range of commands for adjusting these colors. Some are easy to use, while some are tricky but let you do all sorts of different alterations.

Brightness and Contrast, Darkness, and Dimness

Choose **Colors, Adjust, Brightness/Contrast** (shortcut: **Shift+B**) to be able to make the following adjustments:

➤ Increase the **Brightness** setting to make the entire image brighter.

➤ Decrease the **Brightness** level to make the entire image darker.

➤ Increase the **Contrast** setting to make the bright parts brighter and the dark parts darker, making the image stand out more.

➤ Decrease the **Contrast** setting to make the bright parts dimmer and the dark parts lighter, washing out the image.

Reduce Reds, Grow Greens, and Blow Away the Blues

If your image appears tinted a certain color (which often happens with old photos, oddly lit photos, and cheap scanners), you can take that tint away. On the other hand, you can tint it more if you so desire.

Choose **Colors, Adjust, Red/Green/Blue** (shortcut: **Shift+U**). The Red/Green/Blue dialog box (seen in Figure 17.1) has three settings: one to adjust the amount of red in your selection, one for the amount of green, and one for the amount of blue. Slide a slider to the right to tint the selection with that color, or to the left to decrease the amount of that color in the mix.

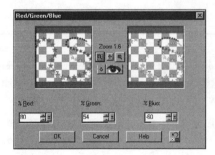

Figure 17.1

Just seeing Red/Green/ Blue makes me feel like a true American, looking at the flag through my sunglasses.

Grading on Curves

What if you don't want to change *all* the reds in your selection, but only some of them? What if you want to make the rich reds even richer and leave the dull reds alone? Or what if you want to darken all the dark areas while leaving the bright areas alone? Just when you're getting a hang of changing color tones, we start pitching you curves. And curves are just what you need.

Choose **Colors, Adjust, Curves**, and you get the Curves dialog box, as seen in Figure 17.2.

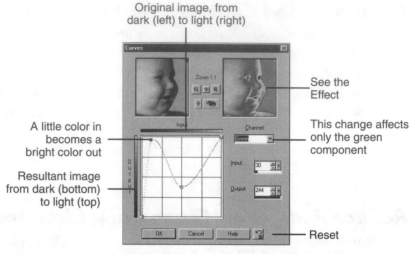

Original image, from
dark (left) to light (right)

Figure 17.2

The Curves command helps you subtly remix your colors and give your baby a healthy glow.

See the
Effect

This change affects
only the green
component

A little color in
becomes a
bright color out

Resultant image
from dark (bottom)
to light (top)

Reset

When you first open this dialog box, the line across the graph area is a simple diagonal line from the bottom left to the upper right. This line represents how the colors are going to change. Along the top of the graph, you see a gradient from dark to light. Let's say you want to find how a pixel that is 25% bright is going to fare in this color transformation. Find the matching brightness spot on the top bar, and then look straight down the graph until you see where the red line crosses under the point you selected. Point to that spot on the line, and look directly to the left. There is another gradient, showing how bright that pixel will be on the output.

If you do this check when the line is still a diagonal, you find that a 25% bright spot going in is a 25% bright spot going out. It doesn't change at all. That's what the diagonal line indicates. But in the example in Figure 17.1, the line isn't a diagonal, but an interesting curve. Go to the 25% brightness spot at the top, look straight down until you hit the line, and then look to the left; the output is 80% bright.

Seventh Heaven

Curves Are a New Spin

The Curves command is new in version 7.0. It gives you access to subtler effects than any color adjustment tool in previous versions.

So how did I change the diagonal line into that nice curve? I dragged parts of the line. Whenever you drag part of the line, a new node spot appears along the line, and the curve is shaped by connecting those nodes. You can also drag the endpoints of the line so that parts of the selection that were completely dark originally are given some light.

Four curves are available to you to set. Using the **Channel** drop-down list, you can choose **RGB** (changing the brightness of each pixel) or **Red**, **Green**, or **Blue** (changing just the brightness of just that component of each pixel). In the example, I adjust just the green component. So what's the effect of this particular curve? The areas that had a fair amount of green become a little bit greener, but it's the dark areas that really change. All the shadows on the baby's face turn a bright green. Cute little Ben ends up glowing like the nuclear-fed monster from a cheap science fiction movie. (I wish I could have published this picture in color. It looks *really cool!*)

Color Replacement

Tricks 'n' Tips

Reset, Don't Repeat

Whenever you use the **Curves** command, it automatically brings up the last curves you set. Usually, you'll want to rebuild the curves each time. Remember to click the **Reset** button to return all four curves to straight diagonals.

You've already seen how to use the Color Replacer tool to turn your grey skies blue, or your blueberries orange. The Color Replacer works very well with solid areas of color, and works pretty well with areas where the color is fairly consistent. It does have its limits, however. If you are trying to change someone's wrinkled pink blouse into a wrinkled blue blouse, for example, it's hard to capture the full range of shades within the blouse. Even if you do, you end up turning them all into the same color of blue, making the wrinkles disappear (and making the blouse look suspiciously like a flat slab of blue cardboard).

To change the colors on a complex subtle object

1. Select the area with the color as tightly as possible (remember, the Smart Edge option of the Freehand tool is great for selecting tricky areas).

2. Choose **Colors, Adjust, Hue Map**, and the Hue Map dialog box seen in Figure 17.3 opens.

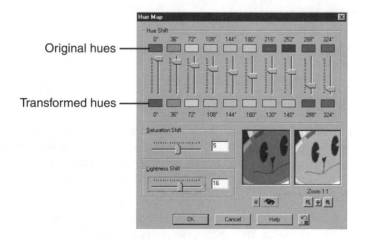

Original hues

Transformed hues

Figure 17.3

The Hue Map command helps you make a horse (or bunny) of a different color.

3. Find the color closest to the one that you want to change on the Original Hue list. Drag the slider below that color until the Transformed Hue matches the hue you're aiming for.

4. Click **OK**.

The colors close to the original hue you chose are transformed to the new hue, keeping all the light and dark variances.

Hue Map Tips (That's "Spit Pa Me Uh," Spelled Backward)

Some quick tips for dealing with the Hue Map controls:

➤ You're not limited to changing just one color at a time. You can change an ugly blue blouse with pink polka dots into an ugly pink blouse with blue polka dots by sliding two sliders.

➤ If the hue you're looking to change falls almost evenly between two adjacent hues on the Original Hue display, try adjusting both sliders about the same amount.

➤ If your selected area is not a rectangle, the preview window might show color changes occurring in areas outside of your selection. Don't worry; this is just a problem with the preview window. The change is restricted to inside your selection.

➤ You can use the Lightness and Saturation sliders to change the brightness and color richness. This works on the entire selection, not just on the colors you alter.

Cooler Color Creators

Sometimes, you want to do more than just tweak colors. You want to do radical and bizarre things, turn your sedate pictures into psychedelic maelstroms of bizarreness. Realism is a crutch for people who can't think of anything better.

Ooh, Pretty Colors

Choose **Colors, Negative Image**, and all your layer's colors are reversed like a film negative. Blacks turn white, blues become yellow, and it all looks spooky and weird. If you like this, you should try **Colors, Solarize**, which has the same effect but lets you adjust whether it effects all the colors on your layer or just some of them.

Choose **Colors, Posterize** (shortcut: **Shift+Z**) to reduce the number of colors in your image without actually changing color modes. If you reduce the **Levels** setting to 10 or below, you'll start to see some pretty weird effects. The lower the value, the weirder it gets!

Color Examples

Retouch Tools

Sharpen Emboss Smudge
Lighten RGB Darken RGB Soften

Push Dodge Burn

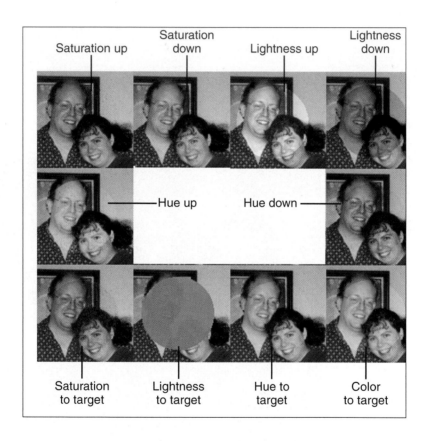

Saturation up

Saturation down

Lightness up

Lightness down

Hue up

Hue down

Saturation to target

Lightness to target

Hue to target

Color to target

Effects

Commands on the Effects, Blur Menu

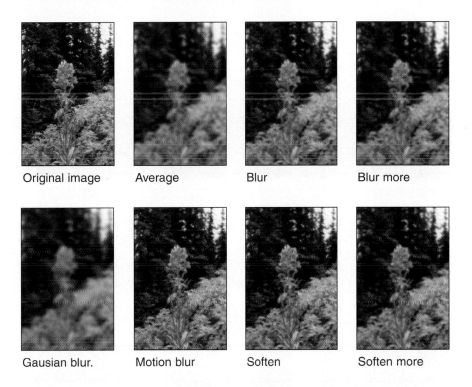

Original image   Average   Blur   Blur more

Gausian blur.   Motion blur   Soften   Soften more

Commands on the Effects, Sharpen Menu

Original image   Sharpen   Sharpen more   Unsharp mask

3

Commands on the Effects, Edge Menu

Original image

Dilate

Enhance

Enchance more

Erode

Find all

Find horizontal

Find vertical

Trace contours

4

Commands on the Effects, Noise Menu

Original pumpkin boy

Add

Despeckle

Edge preserving
smooth

Median cut

Median filter

Salt and pepper filter

Texture preserving
smooth

Commands on the Effects, Enhance Photo Menu

Original image

Automatic color balance

Automatic contrast enhancement

Automatic saturation enhancement

Deinterlace

JPEG artifact removal

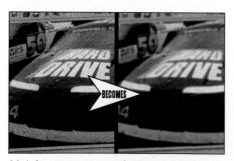

Moiré pattern removal

Automatic small scratch removall

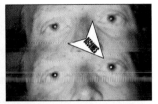

Clarify   Fade correction   Manual color   Red-eye removal
                                          correction

Commands on the Effects, 3D Effects Menu

Original   Buttonize   Chisel   Cutout
image—all
effects done
with the happy
face selected

Drop shadow   Inner bevel   Outer bevel

Commands on the Effects, Artistic Effects Menu

Original image

Aged newspaper

Black pencil

Brush strokes

Charcoal

Chrome

Colored chalk

Colored edges

Colored foil

Colored pencil

Contours

Enamel

Glowing edges

Hot wax coating

Neon glow

Pencil

Sepia

Topography

9

Commands on the Effects, Geometric Effects Menu

Original image

Circle

CurlyQs

Cylinder—horizontal

Cylinder—vertical

Page curl

Pentagon

Perspective—horizontal

Perspective—vertical

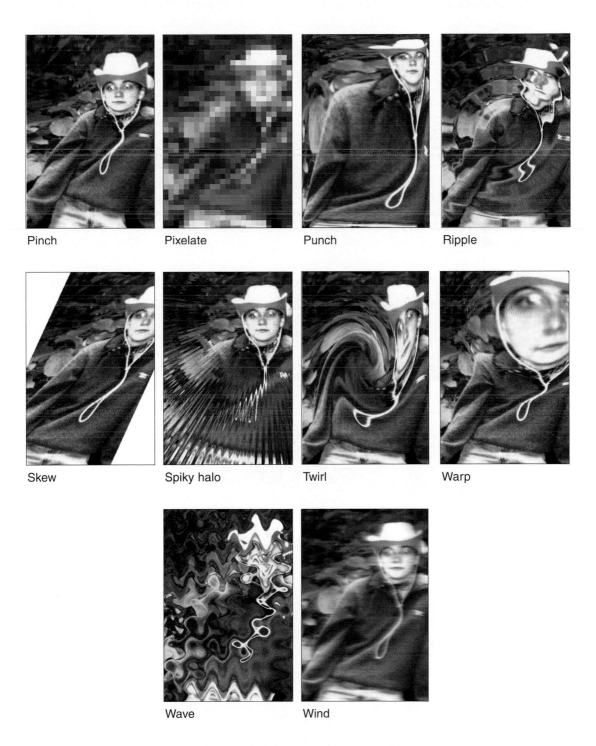

Pinch   Pixelate   Punch   Ripple

Skew   Spiky halo   Twirl   Warp

Wave   Wind

Commands on the Effects, Illumination Effects Menu

Original image

Sunburst

Lights

Commands on the Effects, Reflection Effects Menu

Original image

Feedback

Kaleidoscope

Pattern

Rotating mirror

Commands on the Effects, Texture Effects Menu

Original image

Blinds

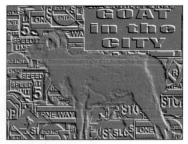

Emboss

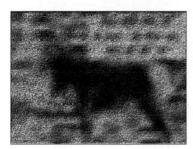

Fine leather

Fur

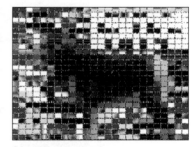

Mosaic—antique

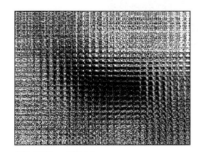

Mosaic—glass

Polished stone

Rough leather

13

Sandstone

Sculpture

Soft plastic forms

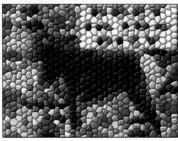

Straw wall

Texture

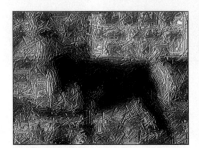

Tiles

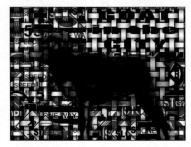

Weave

Adjustment Layers

I started with this drawing…

…and applied adjustments layer painted like this.

Brightness/contrast

Channel mixer

Color balance

Curves

Hue/saturation/lightness

Invert

Levels

Posterize

Threshold

Channel Mixer-Upper

Choose **Colors, Adjust, Channel Mixer** to get a genuine power-tool for abusing the colors in your selection (as seen in Figure 17.4). With this command, you can set the system to recalculate the red, green, and blue value of each pixel in the layer based on its existing red, green, and blue values.

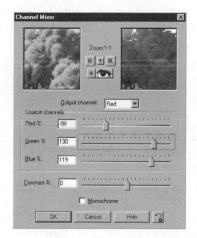

Figure 17.4

The Channel Mixer mixes your color values together, and mixes up your colors.

For example, choose **Red** from the **Output Channel** drop-down list. This indicates that you're setting the levels of red for each pixel in the transformed layer. If you set **Red%** to 50, **Green%** to 50, and **Blue%** to –20, then the redness of each pixel in the finished image is as rich as half (50 percent) of the redness from the original image plus half that of the green image, minus one fifth that of the blue image. Adjusting **Constant** makes the color grow richer (positive values) or duller (negative values) throughout the entire image. You can set similar calculations for the Blue and Green aspect of the pixels by choosing them in the **Output Channel** list before making your adjustment.

A Brand New Mixer

The Channel Mixer is new in Paint Shop Pro 7.

This all sounds like mathematical mumbo-jumbo, and it largely is. But what it really means is that by moving these sliders about, you radically change the color of each pixel, while keeping the shapes of your image. Experiment with this to see what I mean. This is a fun one to fool around with.

Other Color Tools

Paint Shop Pro has other color adjusting tools (and it's getting more all the time; version 7 has almost twice as many tools on the **Colors, Adjust** submenu as version 6 did). For the most part, you can do what you need to with the tools I've already discussed. These other tools are mainly used as different ways to get the same effects:

➤ **Color Balance**   adjusts the amount of red, green, and blue separately in the darker areas (*shadows*), lighter areas (*highlights*), and in-between areas (*midtones*).

➤ **Gamma Correction** (shortcut: **Shift+G**)   used to tint or remove tint, primarily by adjusting the mix of red, green, and blue on the midtones.

➤ **Highlight/Midtone/Shadow** (shortcut: **Shift+M**)   separately adjusts the brightness of the bright, mid, and dark sections of your image so that you can make your shadows darker and your sun sunnier.

➤ **Hue/Saturation/Lightness** (shortcut: **Shift+H**)   a tricky tool with which you can adjust the brightness and richness of each color in your selection, and make major and minor adjustments of hue.

➤ **Levels**   a somewhat less sophisticated tool for doing what Curves does.

The Least You Need to Know

➤ The color commands work a lot like the effects commands, including working only on raster selections and layers, and using preview effects in the dialog boxes.

➤ Choose **Color, Adjust, Threshold** to turn your selection or layer into harsh black-and-white, or use **Colors, Grey Scale** to turn it grey.

➤ To make your image brighter, dimmer, starker, or more washed out, choose **Colors, Adjust, Brightness/Contrast** (shortcut: **Shift+B**).

➤ Choose **Colors, Adjust, Curves** to have varying effects on areas, depending upon their brightness or the amounts of individual component colors.

➤ Use **Colors, Adjust, Hue Map** to replace one color with another on an item with variable lighting.

➤ The many other color adjustment commands can create bizarre and psychedelic color effects.

Part IV

Vector Victories and Layer Lay-Ups

Even if raster objects are the meat of your image, there are still plenty of things you can add to it. Adjustment layers that change the look of your image might be the cheese. Vector shapes that you scatter about are the pickles, and the vector text can add more spice than dijón mustard. Soon, your image is thicker and more luscious than a Dagwood sandwich. Soon I'm going to have to take a break—suddenly, I'm hungry...

Upgrading Shapes

The great thing about vector shapes is that you can always go back and change them: adjust their shapes, their colors, and the nature of their outlines. That's also what makes vectors such a pain in the neck: There's always the temptation to go make it just *that* much more perfect.

Node Editing

Every vector object is defined as a series of points (called *nodes*) and the lines that connect them (making up a *path*). Changing the shape of an object involves moving, adding, or removing nodes, as well as adjusting the shape of the path segment between the nodes.

Pick Your Nodes

 To get started on node editing, first use the **Object Selector** (shortcut: **Q**) to select the object that you want to edit. On the Object Selector Tool Options palette, click **Node Edit**. As you see in Figure 18.1, all the nodes show up as little squares, and your object becomes a thin black outline. The pointer becomes an arrow.

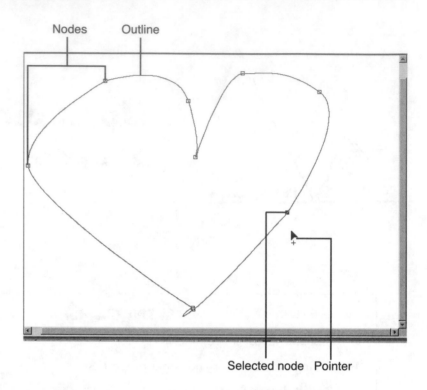

Figure 18.1

Editing nodes won't fix your broken heart, but it might correct a bent one!

You can move any node by simply dragging it into a new position. All your work is done on this outline version of your object. Only when you're doing editing and quit the editing mode is your object redrawn to match your new design.

You can select multiple nodes by holding down the **Shift** key as you click on them, or by pointing away from any nodes and then dragging a rectangle that holds all the nodes you've selected. You can drag any one node in a select group, and the other nodes follow along, as well.

Erode Your Nodes

If you want to simplify your object, you can delete nodes you've selected. There are two different ways of doing this, and each has a different effect:

➤ Press **Delete** (or right-click and choose **Edit, Delete** from the pop-up menu) and the node disappears, as do any line segments connecting to that node. Unless you're deleting an end point, this leaves a gap in your shape.

➤ Hold down **Ctrl** while clicking an already-selected node, and it disappears. A new line segment appears, connecting the two nodes that were adjacent to the one you deleted. This way, no gap is left.

Explode Your Nodes

If you want to add nodes to your shape, point to a place on the outline where you want to add the edge. Hold down **Ctrl**, and the word ADD appears beside the pointer.

Click this pointer on the line, and a new node is added where you've clicked. The new node is a curve node, so it has one of those arrows running through it showing the angle at which the curve is shaped. Drag the arrow to reshape the curve running through this node. (If you need some brushing-up on placing nodes and shaping curves, head back to Chapter 8, "Vector Frankenstein: The Science of Making Vector Objects").

Another Mode to Explode

Press **Ctrl+E** to get into *Drawing mode*, where you can draw a new line on your object using the click-for-corners, drag-for-curves method of Point-to-Point drawing tool. Press **Ctrl+E** again to return to Editing mode.

Taking a Different Angle

If you select a node, right-click, and choose **Node Type** from the pop-up menu, the submenu starts with four different node types:

➤ A *Symmetrical node* is the type of curve node that you make when you drag a node into place while drawing a line. You might have noticed that when you drag the arrowhead of the curve controller (which sets the steepness of the curve heading away from the node), the tail of the arrow also moves to the same distance away. This gives the curve coming into the node a similar steepness to the curve coming out of the node. That similarity makes this node symmetrical.

➤ An *Asymmetrical node* is one where the steepness coming in might not match the steepness going out (as seen in Figure 18.2). If you choose **Node Type, Asymmetric** from the pop-up menu (shortcut: **Shift+Ctrl+S**), you can drag the tail of the curve arrow, making the line from the tail to the node shorter or longer than the line from the node to the arrow. Dragging this tail sets the steepness of the curve.

➤ A *Cusp node* is a node where the line can turn at a sharp angle. (The corner nodes you clicked into place while drawing with the Point-To-Point tool are a type of cusp node.) If you have a curve node and choose **Node Type, Cusp** (shortcut:

Tracing Dick Tracy

Here's a good exercise for practicing fine-tuning shapes: Scan a picture from your favorite comic strip character, then create a vector layer and try to create as close a vector version of the character as you can, with as few nodes as possible.

Ctrl+X), you're able to drag the arrow and tail so that the arrow isn't even straight, but is broken at the node point, making curves that meet at an angle.

➤ A *Tangent node* is the opposite of a Cusp node; the line flows smoothly through the node, rather than coming to a corner. If you've turned a point into a cusp, you can turn it back into a Tangent node by choosing **Node Type, Smooth/Tangent** from the pop-up menu (shortcut: **Ctrl+T**).

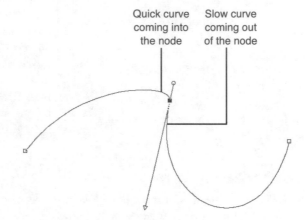

Quick curve coming into the node

Slow curve coming out of the node

Figure 18.2

Asymmetric nodes let you adjust the arrowhead and tail separately, creating a curve that suddenly changes steepness.

If you've drawn a curve node, and want the line coming into it to be a straight line rather than a curve (as seen in Figure 18.3), choose **Node Type, Line Before** from the pop-up menu (shortcut: **Ctrl+B**). If you want a curve going into the node but a straight line coming out of it, choose **Node Type, Line After** (shortcut: **Ctrl+F**).

Figure 18.3

Straight line going in, curve coming out.

Adding the Missing Link

If you drew a line or a squiggle, you can connect the ends easily. Select any node on the line. Right-click, and from the pop-up menu choose **Edit, Close** (shortcut: **Shift+Ctrl+C**).

If you want to connect the end points of two separate lines, you can do that as well. Select the end point on one line, and then hold down **Shift** while clicking the end point on the second line. From the pop-up menu, choose **Edit, Join Select** (shortcut: **Ctrl+J**).

You can also turn one path into two. Choose any node, and then choose **Edit, Break** from the pop-up menu (shortcut: **Ctrl+K**). The selected node is broken into two: one that ends one line, and the other that starts the next.

Ending Editing

When you're done editing nodes, choose **Quit Node Editing** from the pop-up menu, or just press **Ctrl+Q**. Your object can now be fully redrawn to match the node changes you've made, and you can go on to deal with other things, such as adding more objects, touching up pixels, or even eating donuts!

Properties: The Real E-State of Your Vector

Click **Properties** on the Object Selector Tool Options palette, and the Vector Properties dialog box (as seen on 60 Minutes, and in Figure 18.4) opens.

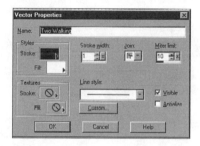

Figure 18.4

Vector Properties: All of your vector options in one place. It's like an option shopping mall!

This dialog box contains all of the options from the palette of the tool used to create the object. It also includes the options from the Color palette. Adjust any of these options here, and the object is corrected.

All Vectors Should Be Named "Eric"

The one option you can set in the Vector Properties dialog box that you couldn't set earlier is the *name* for your object. When you first open the Vector Properties, your object bears the name of the drawing tool that created it—but you can change it to whatever you want.

Tricks 'n' Tips

Shortcut to Your Properties

You can quickly open the Vector Properties dialog box by double-clicking any object with the Object Selector tool.

Now you're probably asking yourself, "Why would I want to give a vector object a name? After all, I never have to call the object for dinner. A vector object doesn't need to apply for a checking account, or receive junk mail. What would it do with a name?"

As you saw in Chapter 8, "Vector Frankenstein: The Science of Making Vector Objects," you can restack objects on the Layer palette by dragging items along the object list. Each item is listed by its name. Now, having your rectangles named "rectangle" is fine if you only have one rectangle and one ellipse. However, when you have a long list of different ellipses, it's hard to quickly find the one you want to work on. By giving each a unique name, you can better tell which ellipse is which, as Figure 18.5 shows.

Figure 18.5

If these vector objects had not been renamed, they would all be just ellipse.

Custom Styling for Your Lines

In Chapter 8, "Vector Frankenstein: The Science of Making Vector Objects," you learned how to choose a styled line so that an object's stroke is a dotted line, or a spiked line, or has arrows on the end. PSP provides a good set of line styles to choose from. But what if you need a special style, or are just too ornery to accept the styles handed to you?

Click **Custom** on the first tab of the Tool Options palette. A Styled Line dialog box appears as shown in Figure 18.6.

If you want to design your own line style, take the following steps:

1. First you need to set the length of the dashes that make up your line. The left end of the design area represents the start of the first dash. Click as far from the left edge as you want the length of the dash to be. Click a little more to the right to indicate the space between dashes. The Result display shows what your line looks like.

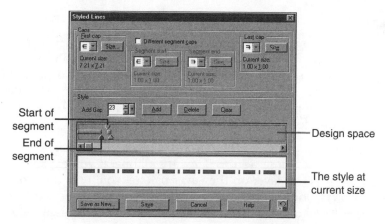

Start of segment

End of segment

Design space

The style at current size

Figure 18.6

Learn to use the Style Line Editor, and become The Line King!

2. If you want alternating dash lengths, click even farther to the right to set the length of the second dash, then a little more to the right to set the gap between the second dash and the next. You can repeat this for as many dashes as you want in your line design.

3. If you don't want the ends of your dashes to be flat, use the **First cap** and **Last cap** drop-down lists to select how you would like the ends to look. Here you'll find such useful choices as arrowhead ends and rounded ends—and such unlikely ends as fleur de lis and pineapple tops. Click the size button for each cap to set the size of the cap.

4. If you want the caps you've chosen to appear only on the very start and end of the line (rather than on each dash of the line), put a check in the **Different segment caps** check box. You can use the **Segment start** and **Segment end** controls to choose the caps for all the intermediate segments.

5. Click **Save as New** and a dialog box appears asking for a name for this line style. Type in a name. *Don't* just hit return to use the name that automatically appears in the dialog box; that name belongs to an existing line style, and you'll wipe out that style, never able to use it again.

6. Click **OK**, and the style is applied to the line around your object. The style you created will also be available on the Line style drop-down list, not just for this image but for every image you make.

Tricks 'n' Tips

Custom Is Common

You don't have to wait until after you've created your object to create a custom line style for it. The same **Custom** button is on the Tool Option palette for any tool that has line styling.

Group-De-Doo!

You can group several objects into a single larger object. This makes it easier to copy it, to move it, and to reuse it. To do this, use the Object Selector to select all the objects you want to group (either by holding down **Shift** while clicking on each one, or by dragging a rectangle around all the objects). When you do this, Paint Shop Pro shows a single outline with sizing handles around the entire set, letting you easily move, resize, or rotate these objects all at once.

Name Your Group

You can name your group by using the same method you use to name your shapes, using the group's Property dialog.

To make this group permanent, right-click it. Choose **Group**. Now it's all one. If you expand this layer on the Layer palette, you'll see the group on the list. Under the group, all the objects are individually listed, so you can still rearrange them separately.

To divorce this supposedly permanent group, right-click it and choose **Ungroup**.

Get Back the Shape You Had in High School

If you have a shape or group that you want to be able to reuse, you can make it one of your standard shapes, selectable with the Preset Shape tool. That's right: no longer will you be limited to the rectangle, star, and ellipse; you'll be able to use the squirmmel, the flibbertigibbet, and the Lord Peckinpah Junior.

Many Shapes in One File

If you select multiple shapes or groups before your Export Shape, PSP stores them all in one file. This can be quicker and makes it easier to share your shapes with others.

To do this, make sure that your shape or group has a good name. The name it has when you save it is the name that it has on the Preset Shape drop-down list. Use the Object Selector to select your shape or group. Right-click, and choose **Export Shape** from the pop-up menu. If a Warning dialog box appears, just click **OK**. Another dialog box asks for a name for your shape. Type in a name for a file (you should probably make it the same as your shape name), and then press **Enter**. Your shape is now saved!

It's No Shame to Share Your Shape

You can share your shape with others via email or by copying it onto disk. To find the file, choose **File, Preferences, File Locations**. On the **Shapes** tab of the resulting dialog box you will find the location of your Shapes directory. The file is in the directory named there, in a file with the name you had entered and the extension .jsl. Give that file to your friend, and have them copy it into their own Shapes directory. The next time they start Paint Shop Pro, they'll have those shapes at their disposal.

The Least You Need to Know

➤ To edit your vector object, select the object, and then click **Edit Nodes** on the Tool Option dialog box.

➤ Move a node by dragging it.

➤ Delete a node by pressing **Delete** (to leave a gap) or **Ctrl+M** (to leave no gap).

➤ Add a node by holding down **Ctrl** and clicking on the outline of the object.

➤ When you're done editing, press **Ctrl+Q** to leave the Edit Node mode.

➤ Click **Properties** on the Tool Options palette to change the selected object's colors, line thickness, and other standard options.

Chapter 19

Text Tricks

In This Chapter

➤ Add text to your image

➤ Wrap text around a shape

➤ Alter your text design

➤ Convert words into curves

A picture, we are told, is worth a thousand words. But what if the picture has a word on it? Is it then worth a thousand and one words? Or does the presence of the word bring down the value of the picture? Perhaps it's a multiplier: the more words you have, the more your picture is worth!

That's all too mathematical for me. No matter the value involved, putting words on a picture is often handy and is sometimes a necessity.

Putting Text in Context

 Click **Text**, and you find yourself wielding a flexible, fun tool for laying down words, letters, numbers, and even brief sentences. It's not really a good tool for putting in large blocks of text—a full paragraph, or more. Because PSP treats each letter as a complex shape, it takes a long time to create and adjust large amounts of text.

Text by the Ton

If you want to work with large amounts of text, you'll be better off copying your image into a desktop publishing program and adding text there.

Text Gets Better—Mostly

In older versions of PSP, text could only be solid colors. You couldn't use fills, gradients, patterns, or textures, the way you can with version 7. On the other hand, you could change the color of each letter, something you can no longer do.

Optional and Optimal Options

When you have the Text tool in hand, the first tab of your Tool Options palette has few options. You can choose a line width for the outline around the text with the **Width** field. Select a line style from the **Line style** drop list, or click **Custom** to create a dotted line in the same fashion described in Chapter 18, "Upgrading Shapes."

But those aren't the only options you need to set. In Paint Shop Pro, text is actually treated as a shape, although a very complex one. Before you can put in your letters, you need to pick the stroke and fill colors or pattern, using the standard Color palette controls.

Laying Down the Text

Click a blank area of your image. The Text Entry dialog box seen in Figure 19.1 appears.

The first choice you have to make is what type style you're going to use. Click the **Name** drop-down list, and take a look at the list of names of type faces. (Some people call type styles *fonts*, but serious type people get cranky when you do that; to them, to pick a font means picking the size, as well as the face.) Select the type face and size you want, and some letters in that font show up in the Sample Text area.

Figure 19.1

The Text Entry dialog box is like a word processor— a really crummy word processor.

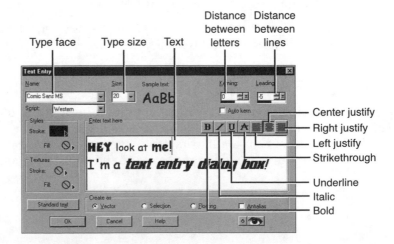

186

Type Style Secret?

If you have a lot of type styles on your system, it's hard to remember what they all look like, and trying them all takes too long. If you have a current version of WordPerfect or Microsoft Word, open that and click the **Fonts** drop-down list. This shows the name of every type style *in* that style, so you can quickly find the one you want.

Enter a type size in the **Size** field. Then start entering your text in the field mysteriously named **Enter Text Here**.

After entering your text, you can select portions of the text and click the **Bold**, **Italic**, **Underline**, or **Strikethrough** buttons to add emphasis. You can also change the type style or size of the selected area.

Use the **Kerning** field to adjust the spacing between letters, and use the **Leading** field to adjust spacing between lines of text. On both of these, zero is the standard setting. Setting a negative value decreases the spaces, and setting a positive value increases the space. If you set a large enough negative value, your letters overlap.

Working Blind

PSP doesn't show the effect of kerning and leading changes on the text. Click the **Preview** button to see the text on your image without closing the dialog box.

Where Do the Words Go?

The last choice you have to make is what form your text takes:

➤ Click **Vector**, and your text is created as a vector object. This is the choice you should go with, unless you have a specific reason to do otherwise. Creating your text as a vector keeps it correctible, resizable, and adjustable.

➤ Click **Floating** to create your text as a floating selection on a raster layer.

➤ Click **Selection**, and the program doesn't actually add text to your image. Instead, it creates a selection outline shaped like your text. This can be handy for doing various effects bounded within the shape of the text.

Tricks 'n' Tips

Smooth Writing

The **Antialias** option, so useful at keeping the text edge looking smooth at low resolutions, is even more important with small text. Text that would be too small to read with the option off can be readable with the option on.

After selecting one of those options at the bottom of the dialog box, click **OK**. Your text (or selection marquee) appears on your image.

Better Words: Updating Raster Text

If you chose the Floating option, your text is now a floating selection over your raster layer. You can drag this selection to reposition it, but you can't resize it or rotate it.

 If you don't like the size of the text after you see it in place, or if you want to make some other small adjustment, click **Undo** to make the selection go bye-bye. Then click with the Text tool again, and the Text Entry dialog box opens up with all of the text and settings still in place. It's time to try again!

Word Up: Improving Vector Text

When your vector text appears, it has the same resizing handles and rotation handles of any vector shape. As you saw in Chapter 18, you can use these to tilt, stretch, or shrink what you have, as seen in Figure 19.2.

 If you use the **Text** pointer to double-click your vector text, the Text Entry dialog box reopens. You can edit your text, change the font, and edit the spacing options. The only thing you can't change is that it's vector text; the Floating and Selection options are greyed out.

 On the other hand, if you use the **Object Selector** pointer to double-click the vector text, you get a Vector Properties dialog box, like the ones you saw in Chapter 18. Here you can change the stroke width, the line style, and the styles and textures that decorate the text.

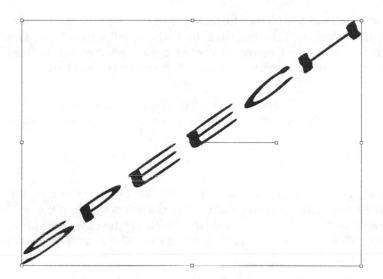

Figure 19.2
A long, uneven speech.

You can't change the name of the text object the way that you can with other vector objects; the name of the text object is always the same as the first line of the text. That's actually a very good way to name the text object, making it easy to quickly identify the object from the list of objects on the Layer palette—unless your text happens to be the word *rectangle*, in which case it could be very confusing!

Being Curvaceously Loquacious

The steps above are fine if you want to fit your text along a nice straight line, which is the way text usually appears. But what if you don't want that firm line there? What if you'd rather have the text meander (as seen in Figure 19.3), or wrap around in a circle, or do some other nifty trick? Try this:

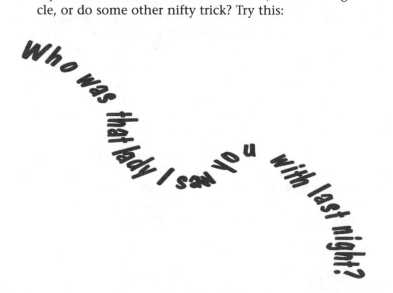

Figure 19.3
A famous comedic straight line gets put on a curved line.

1. Use either the Draw or Preset Shape tool to create the path that you want your text to follow. (In this example, I use the Draw tool with the Point-to-Point Line option.) Make sure you have the **Create as Vector** option selected on the Tool Option palette. Also, set the line width to at least 5; it makes the next step easier.

2. With the Text tool, point to the object you created. The pointer changes from its usual shape (a crosshairs with an upright A) to a different shape (a crosshairs with a tilted A and a curved line). Click the object.

3. The Text Entry dialog box appears. Fill it out as you usually do, and then click **OK**.

4. The text appears along the edge of the shape. If you created the text as a vector selection and it doesn't extend far enough along the shape's edge, drag the resize handles to enlarge it. If the text extends too far along the edge, or wraps around the object so that it overwrites itself, you can drag the resizing handles inward to shrink it down.

5. If you don't want the shape to remain visible, use the **Object Selector** to double-click it. In the Vector Properties dialog box that appears, set both Styles to **No Color** (the international no symbol).

Once you've put text on the shape, it's attached there. If you edit the nodes of the shape, the text will rearrange itself along its reshaped outline.

Giving Your Text Nodes

You can't node-edit vector text the way you can other vector objects. That doesn't mean that text doesn't have nodes, it's just that the nodes are built into the type style design.

Sometimes, you want your text to have nodes so that you can make little tweaks and changes to the letters. For example, consider Figure 19.4. The word zoom looks fine in its original text form, but I wanted to mess around with it. I wanted a pointier Z, and I wanted the Os to be solid, rather than having holes in their middles. There might well be a type face out there that matches my needs, but I'm a do-it-myself kind of guy (or, when it comes to car repair, a try-to-do-it-myself-then-shell-out-$900-to-get-the-mechanic-to-fix-not-only-the-original-problem-but-also-the-things-that-I-broke-when-I-was-trying-to-fix-the-original-problem kind of guy).

To convert your text into a vector shape made up of editable nodes, choose **Objects, Convert Text to Curves**. On the submenu that appears, you have two choices: **As Single Shape** and **As Character Shapes**. The first choice turns your entire text object into one single vector object; the second turns each letter into its own vector object. As you can see in Figure 19.4, this difference is important:

Original text object

Converted as a
single shape

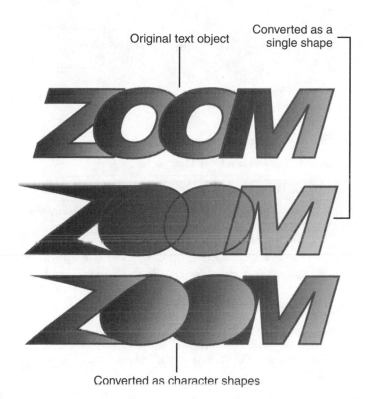

Figure 19.4
*The way you convert
your text to shapes is
important.*

Converted as character shapes

➤ Take a look at the gradient fade. In the
single shape, the fade goes across the
entire shape. When the text is broken
down as characters, however, the gradient
is restarted with each character. (It's interesting to note that the fade is restarted in
each character in the text object; internally, PSP is treating each letter as a different object, and that effects fades,
patterns, and textures.)

➤ When the text is a single object, no letters are on top or on bottom. Because of
this, the full stroke of each letter is visible, even when that stroke overlaps
another letter. (Note that this is only a
concern when your kerning value is set
low enough that the letters overlap.)

Tricks 'n' Tips

Get It Ryght?

Be sure to check your spelling
before converting your text to
shapes. After the conversion, you
are no longer able to use the special text-editing features (adding
letters, changing type faces, and so
on).

➤ In a text object, the first letter is always on the bottom and the last letter is
always on the top. When the text is converted to separate character objects, you
can use the standard object stacking controls to change which objects are on

191

top. In the figure, I reordered the letters so that the Z was on top and the M was on the bottom. (Again, this is only a concern when your letters overlap, or if you want to have some other object overlap some of the letters.)

Converting text to curves is very handy when you want to design a company logo, something that is covered in Chapter 29, "Leggo My Logo."

The Least You Need to Know

➤ To add text to your page, click **Text,** and then click your image.

➤ The Text Entry dialog box works a lot like a simple word processor, letting you type in your text and set its type style, size, and bold and italic features.

➤ It's usually best to create text as a vector object, using the **Vector** option on the Text Entry dialog box. This makes it possible to edit and correct the text later.

➤ Text uses the stroke and fill style settings on the Color palette, as well as the line width and style options on the Text Tool Options palette.

➤ To put text on a curve, first draw the curve as a vector object, and then click the **Text** tool on that object.

➤ To edit the nodes of a text object, you first have to convert it into a vector shape. To do that, choose **Objects, Convert Text to Curves** and pick one of the two options on the submenu.

Chapter 20

Egging On Layers

In This Chapter

➤ Renaming and grouping layers

➤ Making a layer translucent

➤ Creating special merging effects

➤ Preventing painting on transparent areas

Layers have a number of nifty tricks and underused talents. When needed, they can do amazing jump shots, lay-ups, and slam dunks, running their opponents up and down the boards.

No, wait, that's the Lakers. Layers can do some pretty neat things too, but they can't make jump shots (unless they're *basketballp layers*, of course!)

It's Time to Play "Name That Layer"

Every layer has a name. When you first make a new layer, it's given an innovative name like *Layer 3* or *Layer 72*. This name is very convenient for the program (just like it was for my mother, when she called her kids Thing 1, Thing 2, Thing 3, and Thing 4), but it can make things difficult on you. You had a chance to enter a different name for the layer when you created it, but it's easy to just hit return and let the system's name stay. It's only after you have 37 different layers and have trouble remembering what's on each that you realize you need to give each layer a clear name.

Replacing Rename

PSP version 7 is the first version that includes the Rename command on the pop-up menu from the palette. In previous versions, you had to use the main program menu to access this command.

To rename a layer, just right-click its entry on the layer palette, and pick **Rename** from the pop-up menu. The entry turns into a field where you can type the layer's name.

Transparency Lock: Locking Up Nothing

As you can see in Figure 20.1, at the far right of each entry on the layer palette's Appearance tab is a little lock icon. This is the *transparency lock*, a feature that only works on raster layers. Normally, the icon is crossed out, meaning the lock is not in place. Click the icon, and the cross out disappears, and the lock is in place.

Figure 20.1

The right side of the Layer palette has eerie and mysterious powers.

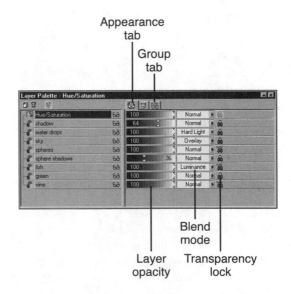

When you lock your transparency, you can't draw on the transparent portions of your layer. This way, if you just want to touch up the one object you have on the layer, you don't have to worry about straying outside the lines.

Paint Shop Pro Paper Dolls

Create a background of a person in a swimsuit, and then create layers with different pieces of clothing on them. Show your kids how to make layers visible, and they can pick and choose what clothes the character is wearing. Plus, if you transparency-lock the clothing layers, the kids can paint new patterns on the clothes without worrying about going outside the lines!

The transparency lock also locks in the opacity level of all the areas. If you have a blob drawn in 50% opaque blue, and you try painting over it with 100% opaque red, you'll end up with a blob that's 50% opaque red. And isn't that what we all really want?

Locking Out the Eraser

 The Eraser tool works differently on a layer than it does on the background. Instead of painting in the background color, the Eraser tool lowers the opacity of what you erase. Set the eraser's opacity to 100%, and it will turn anything you erase transparent. Set a lower opacity (say, 80%) and the eraser brings the opacity level of what you erase down that much from 100 (20%).

Since the transparency lock prevents any change to opacity, it renders the eraser utterly powerless. It is the eraser's kryptonite.

Layer Opacity: Clearly Useful

The sliders on the Appearance tab of the Layers palette set the opacity of the layer. Usually, you'll leave this set to 100%. Slide it down to 50% and the layer's image is half transparent, letting half the image below bleed through, as you can see in Figure 20.2.

If individual pixels of your drawing are less than 100% opaque to begin with, the slider setting works as a multiplier. If you have a blob that's 80% opaque, and you set the slider to 50%, suddenly that blob appears to be 40% opaque.

Figure 20.2

The ghost goat haunts Venice Beach, showing markedly good taste in hangouts.

Trace Tricks

If you're tracing an item on a lower layer, or trying to accurately line something up with the picture on a lower layer, set your current layer to 50% opacity, so you can see the lower layer. Once you have everything in place, you can bring the opacity back up to 100%.

If you're trying to make a translucent raster item, you should try painting it as a solid item on a new layer, then adjusting the layer transparency. This makes it much easier to adjust the transparency of the item layer, and it allows you the option of making the object solid again by setting the slider back to 100%. In general, it's easier to fine-tune an opaque drawing than one with a lower opacity.

Being Normal Is Not the Only Way to Blend In

To the right of the Layer Opacity slider you'll see the word *Normal*. In the art world, that word's considered practically obscene! Click on it, and you'll see a list of alternatives to your layer being normal. These are *Blend modes*, and they affect the way that this layer's image alters the appearance of the layers below it. Blend modes can be selected for both raster and vector layers.

Blend Modes: Chop, Purée, Liquify...

The Blend modes you get to choose from are

➤ *Normal* shows the color you painted as part of the image.

➤ *Darken* only shows the pixels from the current layer if they are darker than the colors below it. *Lighten* is the opposite of Darken, only showing current-layer pixels if they are lighter than the colors below.

➤ *Hue* shows the hue of everything on the current layer, but with the saturation and luminance of the layers below. Similarly, *Saturation* changes only the saturation (color richness), not the hue or the luminance. *Luminance* changes just the brightness, not the hue or the saturation.

➤ *Color* shows the hue and saturation of the current layer with the luminance of the layers below.

➤ *Multiply* creates darker colors that combine the current color on this layer with the colors below. *Screen* also combines this layer's color with the color below, but ends up with a lighter color. *Overlay* checks the darkness of each pixel of the image below; if it's a dark pixel, it uses the Multiple Effect, while light pixels get the Screen treatment. *Hard Light* is like Overlay, only it makes its decision based on the lightness or darkness of the pixel on the current layer, rather than the image below.

➤ *Dissolve* looks like *Normal* when you have opacity set to 100%. Slide the opacity slider to the left in Dissolve mode, and some of the pixels of this layer disappear entirely. In effect, it makes the objects on this level less opaque by making them out of scattered dots.

➤ *Difference* compares the pixel of the current image with the pixel from the image below, subtracts the darker one from the lighter one, and shows the result. This creates some weird color effects. *Exclusion* creates a similar but somewhat gentler effect.

➤ *Dodge* lightens the image below; the lighter the image on this layer, the lighter the layer below becomes. *Burn* has the opposite effect, with dark areas on this layer making the image from below darker. *Soft Light* uses the Dodge effect on this layer's lighter areas and the Burn effect on darker areas.

The Blend Ranger: Hi-Ho Greyscale, Away!

With all blend modes except Dissolve, the farther to the left you set the Layer Opacity slider, the less effect each pixel has on the image. But what if you don't want every pixel to have the same degree of effect? You can set it so that only very red pixels or not-very-green pixels have an effect, or that lighter pixels have less effect than darker pixels, or vice versa. You can create ranges of color that have effect.

To set these ranges, right-click on the layer's entry in the layer option palette, and choose **Properties**. On the Layer Properties dialog box that appears, click **Blend Ranges** tab. You'll get the controls seen in Figure 20.3.

Figure 20.3

Don't blend pixels that are too dark or too light, just blend pixels that are just right!

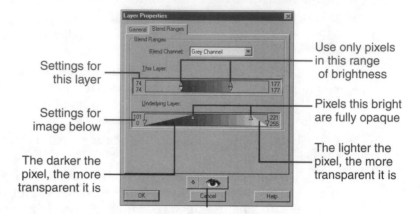

Settings for this layer

Settings for image below

The darker the pixel, the more transparent it is

Use only pixels in this range of brightness

Pixels this bright are fully opaque

The lighter the pixel, the more transparent it is

To set this, first use the **Blend Channel** drop-down list to choose whether you want your pixels separated based on the brightness (Grey Channel) or the amount of red, green, or blue in the pixel.

Why Wait?

If you create your new layer by choosing one of the New Layer commands on the Layer menu, or by clicking the **Create layer** button on the layer palette, the Layer Properties dialog opens automatically. Click on the **Blend Ranges** tab and set your ranges right away, rather than having to bring back the dialog box later.

There are two sets of range controls, one for how much to weigh the pixels on the current layer, and the other for the weight of the pixels built up from the layers below this one. Each set has four little arrow handles you can drag, putting it into position ranging from left (lowest brightness or color setting) to right (highest):

➤ Drag the upper-left arrow to the darkest point that you want to be 100% opaque.

➤ Drag the lower-left arrow to the darkest point that you want to have any opacity at all. Darkness levels between the lower- and upper-left arrows will have some but not complete opacity.

➤ Drag the upper-right arrow to the brightest point that you want to be 100% opaque.

➤ Drag the lower-right arrow to the brightest point that you want to have any opacity at all.

Because it's tricky to see the effect these changes will have, you will probably want to rely heavily on the **Proof** button to show you how your changes will look on your finished image. Once you've achieved your desired effect, click **OK**.

Gather Ye Layers Together

Layers are often designed to work together. You may have a single visual item built up of several layers. If you have a pool ball in your image, the ball may be on one layer, the shadow it leaves on a layer beneath, and the layer above may use one of the Blend modes to put a reflective glint on the ball.

Then you decide that you want to move the ball a little to the left—and then spend the next 15 minutes trying to line up the shadow layer and the shine layer with the ball again. There's got to be a better way. (On the other hand, there also has to be a worse way, so you're not doing too badly.)

Click the **Group** tab on the Layer palette. You'll find an entry for each layer, each marked **None**. That means that these layers aren't part of any group, that if you move one layer it doesn't move any others.

Click one of these entries, and the **None** turns into a **1**. That means that this layer is part of group 1. If you move this layer, then all the other layers in group 1 will move along with it. Of course, you don't actually have any other group 1 layers yet, but click the entry for another layer and you will.

Click repeatedly on the entry, and the group number will cycle through all the possible group numbers (which equals the number of layers in the image). After that, the value loops back to **None**, and the layer becomes a lone wolf again.

The Quicker Flipper-Backer

Right-clicking the group number decreases its value by 1.

The Least You Need to Know

➤ Rename a layer by right-clicking its entry on the palette, choosing **Rename**, and typing the name.

➤ Clicking the **Transparency Lock** icon on a layer's palette entry turns on the lock, which prevents you from painting on the layer's clear areas.

➤ The Layer Opacity slider on the Appearance tab of the Layer palette lets you adjust the layer between being transparent, translucent, and opaque.

➤ The Blend Mode menus on the Appearance tab let you select how the colors on this layer alter the appearance of the layers below this one.

➤ Right-click the Layer palette entry, choose **Properties**, and click the **Blend Ranges** tab to set which colors on your layer are opaque.

➤ On the Layer palette's Group tab, click a layer's entry to set its group number. All the layers with the same number will move together as a group.

Chapter 21

Playing Hide-and-Seek with Masks

> **In This Chapter**
>
> ➤ Hide portions of a layer
>
> ➤ Make portions of a layer less transparent
>
> ➤ Change a layer's mask
>
> ➤ Load and save a mask

We all have something to hide. I, for example, am carefully hiding what I was doing in Dubuque, Iowa, on December 3rd 1987, and how I ended up with all those penguins in my car. You, most likely, have different things to hide. (I'd hate to think there was more than one load of penguins in Iowa on that day.)

If you have something to hide on one of your layers, then you want to use a Paint Shop Pro feature called *masks*.

What Is a Mask?

A *mask* is a greyscale raster design that you attach to a single layer of your image. Wherever the mask is black, that part of the layer is hidden, revealing the layers beneath. Wherever the mask is white, the layer shows up. And wherever the mask is a shade of gray, the layer shows up as semi-opaque. The lighter the grey, the more opaque the mask is.

The mask feature works with both raster and vector layers (although the mask itself is a raster item, set up as a grid of pixels). It only works with 16-million-color and greyscale modes.

Why a Mask?

There are a number of other ways to eliminate part of a layer's image. And that's the big problem: those methods actually eliminate part of the image. If you decide later that you want part of the layer back, you're plumb out of luck. If you're using a mask to hide part of the layer, the drawing is still there. Just change your mask, and suddenly the missing portion of the image reappears.

Masks are also reusable. If you come up with a mask in the shape of James K. Polk, eleventh President of the United States, you can use it to crop every image you make into that shape.

Mask–Maker, Mask–Maker, Make Me a Mask

To create a mask for a layer, select the layer you want on the Layer palette. Right-click the **Create Mask** button on the Layer palette, as shown in Figure 21.1.

Figure 21.1

The little mask icons are all frowning. It's the mask of tragedy!

Create mask   Mask tab   This layer has a mask

Mask disabled
Mask enabled
Mask unlinked
Mask linked

Tricks 'n' Tips

Mask in a Moment

Clicking **Create Mask** creates a Hide All mask. Holding **Shift** while clicking creates a Show All mask.

The menu that appears has five choices. If you choose **Hide All**, the mask hides the entire layer. That would seem to make the layer useless. If you choose **Show All**, you get a mask that doesn't hide anything, which also sounds like a useless mask. These options are useful, however, because you can work with the mask, hiding more or fewer areas, after you create it.

The next two options are greyed out unless you have an area of the image selected. **Hide Selection** hides the selected area while revealing the rest of your layer. **Show Selection** has an opposite effect, hiding everything *but* the selected area.

From Image: It's French for "Cheese," Right?

The fifth and final choice on the **Create Mask** menu is a bit trickier. Choose **From Image** to create a mask based on any currently open image window, using the dialog box seen in Figure 21.2.

Figure 21.2

You can use any other picture as your layer's mask.

Click the **Source Window** drop-down list and choose the window holding the image out of which you want to make a mask. You can then choose if you want to make the mask based on

➤ A greyscale version of the image (**Source Luminance**).

➤ The visible areas of the image so that the transparent areas of the source image create hidden areas on the current layer and everything else is visible (**Any Non-Zero Value**).

➤ The opacity of the image so that transparent areas of source image create hidden areas on the current layer, semi-opaque areas on the source create semi-opaque on the masked layer, and opaque areas on the source create opaque areas on the masked layer (**Source Opacity**).

➤ The exact opposite of any of the above options, masking the areas that option would hide and hiding the areas that option would mask. To do this, select the option then click **Invert Mask Data**.

Who Was That Mask–Editing Man?

To change the contents of the current layer's mask, choose **Masks, View Mask** (shortcut: **Ctrl+Alt+V**). The mask shows up as a red sheen over your image. The reddest areas are the areas that are masked out. Pink areas of the mask signify the parts of your image that are translucent. Areas that aren't tinted red at all are unmasked.

Choose **Masks, Edit** (shortcut: **Ctrl+K**) to use any of the standard paint tools to change the mask. Brush tools, the Text tool, Flood fills—anything that works in greyscale mode—does a fine job of adding to or subtracting from the mask. Just remember that painting your mask with white unhides areas, painting with black hides areas, and painting with grey values makes the area translucent.

When you're done editing, choose **Masks, Edit** again to leave Mask Editing mode. Choosing **Masks, View Mask** a second time removes the mask from view.

Painting Invisible Masks

You don't actually need to be viewing the mask to paint it. Sometimes it's easier to see how you're changing the mask by seeing what gets hidden or revealed as you paint.

Masks Off!

You can turn off a layer's mask by clicking on the Layer palette's **Mask** tab and clicking the little mask icon on that layer's entry. When you do this, the icon appears crossed out.

Ala-KsaM

To reverse which parts of a mask are hidden, choose **Masks, Invert** when you're not in mask editing mode.

Turning off the mask does not get rid of it. You can bring it back into effect by clicking the mask icon again. (If you do want to get rid of a mask, select the layer and choose **Mask, Delete**.)

Recycling a Mask

You can save the current layer's mask to a file by choosing **Masks, Save to Disk**. A standard file browser appears, which you can use to enter a name for the file and to select a folder in which to store it.

When you're working on a layer and you want to reuse a saved mask, choose **Masks, Load From Disk**. Use the file browser that appears to select the mask file you want. (All mask files end with a .msk extension.)

The Masking Link

When you move your layer (or flip it, mirror it, or rotate it), the mask moves with it. You don't necessarily want that to happen.

Figure 21.3

Alaska in a mask-a.

For example, consider Figure 21.3, in which a photo of Alaska is masked with the text shape Alaska. What if I decided to show a little less of those clear Alaskan rivers and more of the vast Alaskan sky? You'd want to move the layer down, while leaving the mask where it is.

To do this, go to the Layers palette and choose the Masks tab. Click the little link icon on the current layer's entry. The icon becomes crossed out. Now you can move the layer without the mask moving at all.

The Least You Need to Know

➤ Create a mask for the current layer by right-clicking the **Create Mask** button on the Layer palette and selecting one of the five options there.

➤ To see your mask as a red tint, choose **Masks, View Mask** (shortcut: **Ctrl+Alt+V**). Repeat that command to make the mask invisible.

➤ To go into mask-editing mode, choose **Masks, Edit** (shortcut: **Ctrl+K**). You can then work on your mask with any raster tools.

➤ You can turn on and off your mask by clicking the mask icon on the Mask tab of the Layer palette.

➤ Save your mask by choosing **Masks, Save To Disk.**

➤ Reuse a saved mask by choosing **Masks, Load From Disk.**

Chapter 22

The Alpha Channel: All Alphas, All the Time

In This Chapter

➤ Store a selection shape with your image

➤ Reuse those stored selection shapes

➤ Store unused masks with your image

➤ Copy masks from layer to layer

There are a lot of channels involved in using Paint Shop Pro. Oh, not as many channels as you get with one of those satellite TV dishes that I was hoping my sister would buy me, but about as many channels as I can pick up with the 2.3" TV that she bought me instead.

Channel is the term that PSP uses for how it stores the information that makes up your picture. Each layer of a 16-million-color picture has three channels: the *red channel* stores the information about the amount of red in each pixel, the *green channel* records how much green is in each pixel, and the *blue channel*—obviously—shows reruns of old New York Knicks basketball games. If your layer isn't fully opaque, then you get another channel that stores how much opacity is in each pixel. If the layer has a mask, that gets a channel of its own.

There is one additional channel that doesn't apply to a specific layer and doesn't effect any visible pixels. That's the *alpha channel*.

What Is an Alpha Channel?

The *alpha channels* (named after Fred Alpha, who on a bet invented the lettering system that we all use today, hence the term *alphabet*) are your image's glove compartment. It's where you stash things that your image isn't actually using at the moment, but you want to keep close at hand in case you need them. Alpha channels can store the shapes of selections from your image, and they can store masks. Each item you store takes up one alpha channel, but an image can have as many alpha channels as you want.

When you save your image using the Paint Shop Pro file format, the alpha channels are saved with it. (If you save your image in TIFF format, the alpha channels are saved but the names of these channels are lost. If you save in PNG or TGA format, the first alpha channel is saved with it. In any other format, your alpha channel information is lost.)

Stuffing Selections into Alpha Channels

To store the shape of the current selection in an alpha channel, choose **Selections, Save to Alpha Channel**. The dialog box that appears is shown in Figure 22.1.

Figure 22.1

Click a channel name to see a preview of the image. It's like an alpha channel TV Guide!

Other alpha channels already in this image

Preveiw of selection shape

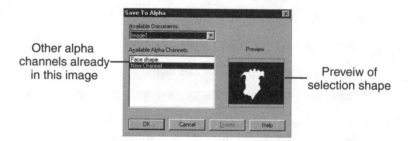

Click **OK**, and a dialog box appears, asking you for a name for the selection. You can type in a name if you want, but unless you're using alpha channels an awful lot, you're best off just hitting **Enter**. Paint Shop automatically names your alpha channel Selection #0 or Selection #1 or some similarly innovative name. That's okay; you never really need to rely on the name to choose a channel. Anytime you need to load anything from an alpha channel, you're able to see what all the image's channels look like.

Flipping Through the Channels

When you want to reuse a selection shape that you stored as an alpha channel, choose **Selections, Load From Alpha Channel**. The Load From Alpha dialog box appears. It looks just like the Save To Alpha dialog box, except it has the words Load From on it rather than the words Save To.

Click an entry in the **Available Alpha Channels** list, and an image of that selection shows up in the Preview area. The selected area shows up in white; the unselected area is black. Click through the list until you find the alpha channel you're looking for.

After you've located it, click **OK**. The selection marquee appears on your image.

Snatching Channels from Other Files

Let's say you have a selection shaped like an outline of a '57 Chevy in a file where you were drawing an old diner. Now you're touching up a photo of your mother, and you want to use the outline with this picture. (Why? So you can airbrush a tattoo of a '57 Chevy onto her upper arm, of course!) Here's how you can go about that:

1. Open both images.
2. Click the title bar of your mother's image, to make it the current image.
3. Choose **Selections, Load from Alpha Channel**.
4. Click the **Available Documents** drop-down list. The filenames of both images appear on the list. Select the filename of the diner image.
5. Select the 1957 Chevy outline from the **Available Alpha Channels** list.
6. Click **OK**.

The marquee will now show the shape of the 1957 Chevy on your mother's image. (Remember, by using the Mover tool you can right-drag the selection area to the exact spot on your mother's image where you want to place the tattoo.)

Halloween Layaway: Saving Masks

To save a mask in the current alpha channel, first select the layer with that mask. Choose **Masks, Save to Alpha Channel**. (If that's grayed out, the current layer doesn't have a mask.)

The rest of the procedure is the same as saving a selection: Click **OK**, type in a name if you want, and hit **Enter**.

By saving a mask to the alpha channel, you'll always have it around. This makes it easy to reuse that mask with another layer or another image.

Backmasking: Getting Your Mask Back

To load a mask out of an alpha channel, first select the layer that you want to use the mask with. Next, choose **Masks, Load from Alpha Channel**.

If you already have a mask on the current channel, Paint Shop Pro (correctly) warns you that loading this new mask replaces the mask you already have, and asks if you

Masking a Selection

The alpha channel doesn't keep track of what type of image you stored there. Because of this, a selection you stored can be loaded as a mask, and vice versa!

Removing Your Mask Isn't Enough

If you copy a mask to the alpha channel, that channel stays there even if you delete the original mask by using the **Masks, Delete** command or flattening your image.

really mean to do this. Of course you do! (If you don't want to see this warning again, put a check in the **Don't warn about this anymore** check box.)

Select the mask from the alpha channel list in the same way that you choose a selection from that list. It's the same list, with masks and selections listed together. You can also use the **Available Documents** drop-down list to select another image from which to choose the mask—but remember this only works if the mask you want had been saved as an alpha channel.

Flush Out Your Channels

After you're done making changes to your image and you're sure you will never again need the alpha channels you saved, you might want to clear them out. After all, the alpha channel information does take up space on your hard disk—and more importantly, it makes your file bigger and can slow down emailing the file to someone.

To clear out all the alpha channels

1. Choose **Selections, Load from Alpha Channel**. (Actually, any alpha channel command works, but this is one that isn't grayed out.)
2. Click the first entry on the **Available Alpha Channels** list.
3. Click **Delete.**
4. Paint Shop Pro asks if you're sure you want to delete this. Click **Yes.**
5. Repeat steps 3 and 4 for all the channels on the list.
6. Click **Cancel.** This cancels just the Load From Alpha Channel command. It doesn't undo your deletions.

The Least You Need to Know

➤ Alpha channels are used to store selection shapes and map designs in the image file without altering the look of the image.

➤ To store the current selection shape in the alpha channel, choose **Selections, Save to Alpha Channel**.

➤ To turn an alpha channel into a selection shape, choose **Selections, Load from Alpha Channel**.

➤ To store the current layer's mask in the alpha channel, choose **Masks, Save to Alpha Channel**.

➤ To turn an alpha channel into a mask, choose **Masks, Load from Alpha Channel**.

➤ With the dialog box of a Load From Alpha Channel command, you can use the masks from any currently open image (by using the **Available Documents** drop-down list) and see the contents of each alpha channel in the document. (Just click the alpha channel name, and a picture of it appears in the Preview display.)

211

Chapter 23

Layers of Adjustment

In This Chapter

➤ Adjust brightness and contrast on all or part of your image

➤ Eliminate or warp colors on parts of your image

➤ Correct the color balance of areas of your image

➤ Easily undo these effects

So far, you've learned about raster layers and vector layers. Perhaps you thought those are all the layers there are. But no! There are also *adjustment layers*. That's right, we've been holding out on you, and saving the best for last!

Well, not the best, actually. You need raster layers or vector layers to have an image at all. Adjustment layers don't actually make an image, they just adjust how it looks.

What Are Adjustment Layers?

An adjustment layer is kind of like a tinted glass windshield on the car that adjusts the appearance of the color of things. When you look at a flying airplane through the tinted top edge of the windshield, the plane's color looks dark to you. The plane isn't really that dark, of course; if you were to remove the windshield, you'd see that the color was the same as always. It just looks different when the windshield is in place. (Note: Neither Que Books nor its affiliated companies nor the author nor the author's cat will be liable for any damages caused by removing the windshield from a moving car in order to test this hypothesis.)

When you add an adjustment layer on top of other layers, you change the way those lower layers appear. You aren't actually changing the content of those layers.

On a normal tinted windshield, different parts of the windshield have different effects on the color of what you see. Most of the windshield is perfectly clear, and has no effect on your view of the outside. Only the top edge is tinted. Even the tinted part is not tinted evenly; it fades so that the further down you go, the less effect the tint has. An adjustment layer is like that; you can create areas where the adjustment has no effect or only partial effect.

Like Masks, but Only Kinda

If you've worked with masks (as described in Chapter 21, "Playing Hide-and-seek with Masks"), you know that you work with a mask as you work with a greyscale object; wherever it's painted black, the layer is masked. Wherever you paint the mask white, the layer is unmasked. Wherever you paint the mask a shade of gray, the mask has a partial effect. The darker the gray, the more the effect.

Adjustment layers also work like that, although the colors are reversed. They are greyscale layers that you can paint with any of the standard raster tools. When you create an adjustment layer by using one of the **Layers, New Adjustment Layer** commands, the area within the current selection is painted white, and the adjustment applies completely to the entire selection. (If you don't have anything selected, the effect hits the entire image.) When you paint parts of the adjustment layer gray or black, you create areas where the layer has less or no effect.

No-Adjustment Layer

Often, you want an adjustment layer to not effect most of the image, but only the spots you select. To do this, create the adjustment layer, and then use the **Flood Fill** tool to fill the entire layer with black. Now you can just paint white on the areas where you want an effect.

The main way an adjustment layer differs from a mask is in what it effects. A mask is part of a layer, having a direct effect only on that layer. An adjustment layer, on the other hand, is a complete layer in itself, and it has an effect on the appearance of every layer below it.

Why These Adjustments Look Familiar

There are nine different types of adjustment layers. These adjustments are Brightness/Contrast, Channel Mixer, Color Balance, Curves, Hue/Saturation/Lightness, Invert, Levels, Posterize, and Threshold.

Extraordinary Examples

Look at the last two pages of the color section of this book, and you'll see examples of the effect of every type of adjustment layer.

If those nine terms all look familiar, then you've been reading the book and paying close attention (yea!). Every single one is the same as a command on the **Colors** menu (mostly on the **Colors, Adjust** submenu). The adjustment layers have the same effect on the appearance of the image below as those Color commands had on the current selection or layer. Even the dialog box you get from each Adjustment Layer command has the same controls as the dialog boxes from those Color commands. As such, you can check back to Chapter 17, "Color Inspection, Correction, and Rejection" to remind yourself what each does. Meanwhile, I'll sneak out for a quick donut and a few hours of donut-removing exercise.

Sunglasses On: We're Looking Closely at Brightness

If you want to make your image brighter, dimmer, or change the brightness level between the bright and dim parts, choose **Layers, New Adjustment Layer, Brightness/Contrast.** A dialog box appears with two sliders, which you use to set how much you want to adjust the brightness and contrast (see Figure 23.1). Leave a slider at zero to have no effect on that value. Slide it to the right if you want to increase the brightness or contrast. Moving a slider to the left indicates that you want to decrease that setting.

The settings you pick control the maximum effect the adjustment layer will have (and it has its maximum effect wherever you paint white on it). For example, when you set Brightness to +10, wherever your layer is painted white, the brightness of the image below the mask is increased by 10 %. Where you paint your adjustment layer a medium gray, the image below is 5% brighter. Where you paint your image black, the image is the same brightness as without the adjustment layer.

Figure 23.1

The Brightness/Contrast settings are on the Layer Properties dialog box for the adjustment layer.

Be a Layer Looker

When you paint your adjustment layer, you don't actually see the greyscale object you're creating. Instead, you immediately see the effect that it has on the image. But what if you want to see this greyscale pattern you created? Simply point for a second to the adjustment layer's entry on the Layer palette, and a small version of the pattern appears.

A Bright Way to Make Shadows

Brightness/Contrast adjustment layers are good for creating areas of shadow or of light on an image. If the items that are casting shadows are on a separate raster layer from the rest of the image, you can do a really good job with shadows. To do this

1. Create a new raster layer (**Layers, New Raster Layer**) and on it draw the image that will be casting the shadow. In the example seen in Figure 23.2, the object in question is the rabbit.

 2. Use the **Freehand** selection lasso with the **Smart Edge** option to select the item that will be casting the shadow.

3. Choose **Layers, New Adjustment Layer, Brightness/Contrast**.

4. Set a negative **Brightness** value (the more negative, the darker the shadow). Click **OK**.

5. A shadow appears directly over the object you selected. Use the **Deform** tool (discussed in Chapter 15, "Deformation Information") to skew the shadow so that it looks like it's hitting the flat surface that the shadow-casting object is on, as seen in Figure 23.2.

6. On the Layer palette, drag the Brightness/Contrast layer down the list, placing it right below the layer that has the object casting the shadow.

Figure 23.2

A quickly drawn rabbit casts a quickly made shadow.

If the object that you want to cast a shadow with isn't on its own layer, just select it, copy it, and then choose **Edit, Paste, Paste as New Layer** (shortcut: **Ctrl+L**) to place it on its own layer. (You might need to use the Move tool to move the layer so that the copy is right over the original.) After this, proceed starting at step 2 in the numbered instructions.

Adjusting Adjustments

Changing the amount of contrast—or the setting of the curves or any of the other variables that you set—for any of the layers is easy. You don't have to redo the entire layer.

Instead, go to the Layer palette (shortcut: **L**) and find the entry for this adjustment layer. Right-click the entry, and choose **Properties** from the pop-up menu. The Layer Properties dialog box opens, and the **Adjustments** tab is already selected. Just change your settings, click **OK**, and you're good to go.

Invert Is a Rebel

The Invert adjustment layer is different; if you open the Layer Properties dialog box, it opens to the General tab. That's because an Invert adjustment doesn't have any variables, so there's nothing to change!

217

They Are Still Layers

You can use all of the standard Layer palette tools on the adjustment layers. To quickly turn off the effect of an adjustment layer, just click the eyeglasses icon on its Layer palette entry. You can also group adjustment layers with other layers. If you flatten your image, the effect that the adjustment layers had is built into the final image.

The only thing that you cannot do with an adjustment layer that you can do with raster and vector layers is give it a mask.

The Least You Need to Know

➤ An adjustment layer changes the appearance of layers below it without changing the actual information on those layers.

➤ Each adjustment layer is a greyscale raster image on which you can use all the normal raster painting tools. Where this image is white, the adjustment takes effect. Where it's black, there is no effect. If it's gray, there is a partial effect.

➤ To add an adjustment layer to your image, choose **Layers, New Adjustment Layer**, and select the time of layer from the submenu.

➤ The adjustment layers have the same visual effect as commands on the **Colors** menu or the **Colors, Adjust** menu, and the dialog boxes for setting the adjustment options work the same, as well.

➤ To view the greyscale image of an adjustment layer, point to the layer's entry on the Layer palette.

➤ The Layer palette can be used for moving adjustment layers within the layer pile, or in any other way this palette is used—*except* adding masks.

Part V
Painting the World Wide Web

The World Wide Web has definitely spread across the world. And it certainly is wide. Oh, and it's also Webulous—and that's not even a word! But the technology certainly has grown since its early days, when the Web pages were poorly punctuated text pages about some college student's favorite Mexican wrestler. Now, thanks to advancing technology and programs like Paint Shop Pro, it's filled with poorly written—but gorgeously illustrated—stories about Mexican wrestlers!

Working Wonder on the World Wide Web

There are no images on the Web.

I understand why you think that there are a lot of images on the Web. After all, on the Web you can see everything from little designed buttons to full-color shots of people wearing impractically small amounts of clothing. But you see, those aren't images because when you put a picture or design on the Web, it's not called an *image*. It's called a *graphic*.

This language is falling apart at the seams.

The Wonderful World of Web Graphics

Part of what makes the Web so interesting and useful is that Web browsers can display both text and graphics on the same page. That way, you not only get text to read, you also get annoying animations and confusing background images that make reading more of a challenge.

Theoretically, the Web can handle any of a huge number of graphics formats. However, browser designers have chosen to support just a select few. As such, the vast majority of graphics on the Web use one of two file formats.

PNGing

Most modern Web browsers can also understand graphics in the *Portable Network Graphics* (or *PNG*) format, which PSP does support. However, this newer format has not caught on with Web designers.

The *JPEG* (*Joint Photographic Experts Group*) format is designed for rectangular, full-color still images. It's biggest strength is its variable compression rate; the more you compress your image, the quicker the image is to download, but also the worse your picture looks. Its weaknesses are that it's a *lossy* compression scheme (it doesn't reproduce your image exactly) and that it doesn't support transparency, so the image will appear rectangular. JPEG files are good for storing photographic images or computer-generated images with a wide range of subtle colors, but they aren't so good for images with large areas of flat color.

The *GIF* (*Graphics Interchange Format*) format can handle still or animated images of any shape (non-rectangular images are stored as rectangles with transparent areas). Its primary weakness is that it's limited to 256 different colors per image, which makes it ill suited for large photographic color images. GIF has a *lossless* compression scheme, which means that you can't vary the amount of compression, but that it will re-create a 256-color image precisely. The compression scheme works well with areas of consistent color. GIF is used for almost all non-photographic images on the Web.

Some Practical Limits

It's very easy to forget about the realities of the Web when you're designing a Web site on your high-powered PC with all the latest software and your ultra-large monitor, checking your design by loading it from your fast hard drive.

Out there in the land of Web users, people are dialing up using modems that handle only 6,000 bytes of data per second when everything is flowing totally smoothly—which it rarely is. Someone using a slower modem to view a Web page might only be getting 1000 bytes per second. Trying to view a page full of graphics at that speed is like trying to suck a delicious chicken-and-waffle dinner using only a straw; it takes a long time to actually get anything, and by the time you do, the excitement is gone. If you make Web users wait to view your page, they're just as likely to leave and head somewhere less frustrating.

Another dose of reality is that not everyone is using high-resolution screens that support the full depth of color. Plenty of people out there surf the Web with older computers, or non-PC devices that have limited graphics capability. The simpler you make your graphics, the more likely those graphics will be viewable on those less-capable platforms.

The Science of Art

The Case Against Graphics

People used to worry about making sure that their Web sites were accessible to people who could only get the text, not the graphics. The biggest reason for this was that the only Web access for some users was a program called *Lynx*, which could only directly handle text. In those days of lower modem speeds, non-graphical terminals, and limited access to the Internet, using Lynx was often necessary. Some people think that because those limits are a thing of the past, everyone who matters now has easy access to Web graphics. Anyone surfing the Web without graphics must be a poor and unimportant neophyte, and thus there's no problem with making graphics vital in using their Web page.

The truth is much different. The advancing technology might have left Lynx largely in the dust, but the cutting-edge of Web technology is accessing the Web through hand-held devices, whether it's a personal organizer or a Web-enabled cell phone, neither of which are graphically powerful. In addition, some folks are browsing the Web using audio tools (mostly visually impaired folks who have no other option). If your site design is graphics-intensive, you should consider carefully whether people can actually access it without graphics. Most Web browsers have a no-graphics option; try checking your site with the graphics turned off and see how difficult it is. If your site can't be used with the graphics turned off, it's time to redesign your site.

Page Grease: Keeping Your Pages Fast

To keep your pages fast, keep the following goals in mind:

➤ **Use fewer images**—This can be good anyway. Too many images, particularly fancy images, make your page look busy and hard to read.

➤ **Use smaller images**—If you have a PC designed for artistic design, you might have a very high-resolution monitor and might tend to make images that take up more pixels than necessary. Most people are viewing with screens that are

800 or even 640 pixels wide. You don't need a lot of pixels for the image to be visible on their screens. Make the images just big enough for them to be clear.

➤ **Compress your JPEG files**—There's an instinct to make sure that your image is reproduced as wonderfully as possible, and that means keeping compression down. Generally, however, you can pick a middle level of compression and get a fine image at about half the file size. You might notice the difference in quality, but the Web page viewer probably won't care.

➤ **Keep your GIF files simple**—The size of a GIF file depends largely on the number of colors you use and how frequently you change the colors. Avoiding gradients and antialiasing can help a lot.

➤ **Reuse your images**—Odds are that your Web site is more than a single page. If you reuse images such as your logos or buttons from page to page, these images are only downloaded to the user's computer once. Sometimes, this means building what looks like a single image out of several images. For example, if each page has a title in a marble frame, the frame can be made up of four images (one for each edge of the frame) plus one image with the name of the page for the center. That way, for each subsequent page only the center image is new. (Plus, you might be able to use the same image for the right and left edges, for further savings.)

Limited Color Range

Many people surf the Web with devices (including some PCs) that don't support the full range of color. If your Web pages are more colorful than their system can support, their system will probably adapt your image by *dithering* (alternating dots of two different colors to simulate the color you choose). This does not lend to a good-looking image, as you can see in Figure 24.1.

Figure 24.1

Even a cute baby looks less cute after dithering.

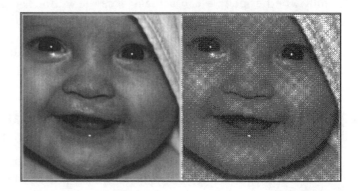

There is no getting around this limitation for quality color photographic images. However, if you're working on original graphics, you can deal easily with this by planning ahead. The best way to deal with it is to limit how many colors you use.

Instead of designing your image in 16-million-color mode, create your graphic as a 256-color image.

The Myth of Correct Color

Despite the precision with which colors are described, different computers reproduce the same graphics differently. Many graphics are visibly lighter on Macintosh computers than on PCs. As such, if choosing between a color that looks a little too dark and one that's a little too light, pick the one that's too dark.

PSP's default 256-color palette is called the *Web-safe palette*. This palette actually contains only 216 different colors. Although the 16-million-color palette is made up for all possible combinations of 256 different levels of red, green, blue, the Web safe palette uses all possible combinations of six different levels of red, green, and blue. As such, you might not always get the exact color you want, but you should be able to get one that's close enough.

The Clear Route to Transparency

Building a non-rectangular image with Paint Shop Pro is easy. When creating a new image, you start in 16-million-color mode and choose **Transparent** for your background. Anything you don't paint on stays clear, so creating something that's not rectangular is easy.

Unfortunately, it gets a little more complex when dealing with Web graphics. If you're creating a GIF, you should be creating it in 256-color mode, which does not support transparency. And if you're creating a JPEG, the image file won't support transparency. There are ways to deal with both of these problems, if you prepare.

Non-Rectangular JPEGs

Because you can't create transparent areas on a JPEG, you can fake it by creating areas that are the same color as the background of your Web page. This only works if your Web page has a solid color background rather than a patterned background.

If you're creating an image for an existing Web page, open the page's HTML file in a text editor. Near the top, you should find a line that starts with <BODY. On that line, you should see the term BGCOLOR= followed by a string of letters and numbers that

225

look something like "#F357B7". That string of the number sign and six letters and numbers is the way that HTML stores a color.

You can use this color with any of PSP's tools. The standard color selector (the one you get when you click a color panel, as shown in Figure 24.2) includes an **HTML Code** field. Enter the string (including the #) into that field, and your color will be set!

Figure 24.2

The HTML Code: It's not just for sending secret HTML messages.

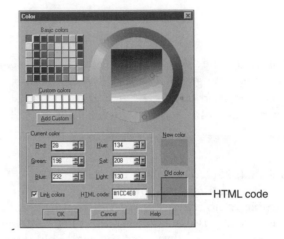

HTML code

If you're drawing the picture first and will be building the Web page later, you'll have to decide what color the Web page will be. Use that color to fill in the parts that should seem transparent. (You're probably best off starting with it as your background color when creating your image.) Then, when it's time to create your Web page, you can use the Dropper to select the color from the image, and then click your Active Stroke Style panel to bring up the Color selector. The HTML code for that color will be in the HTML Code field. You can enter that code into whatever program you're using as a Web page creator. (The exact way you enter it depends on what Web page creation program you're using, but you should be aware that some programs require the # whereas others require that you don't use it.)

GIF Transparency

The way that a GIF file handles transparency is that it treats it as one of the colors of its palette. If you have a 256-color GIF file with transparency, it has 255 colors and one transparent color.

When you're creating your GIF graphic, set aside one color for your transparent color. That shouldn't be hard; if you're using the Web-safe palette, you have 41 slots on your palette set to black. Choose **Colors, Edit Palette**. A display of all the colors in your palette appears. Double-click the last black entry and use the color selector that appears to set this palette entry to some color that you're not planning to actually use

226

in your graphic. Then use the Flood Fill tool to fill your image background with this special color. Build your image, leaving that special color wherever you want your image to be transparent.

You can tell PSP to treat that color as your transparent color when you save your GIF file. I explain how to save a copy of your graphic as a GIF file in a section that I like to call:

I Explain How to Save a Copy of Your Graphic as a GIF File

If you're working on a multilayered image, save a copy in PSP format. Saving your image as a GIF flattens it, leaving you with a single raster layer; you'll want the PSP file if you want to make adjustments or corrections later.

First, you'll want to know how many colors you've actually used in your image. To learn this

1. Choose **Layers, Merge, Merge Visible**. If this command is grayed out, you only have to do step 2.
2. Choose **Colors, Count Colors**. Paint Shop Pro reports to you exactly how many colors you've used. Remember that number, and click **OK**.
3. Click **Undo** to undo the merge.

Choose **File, Export, GIF Optimizer**. Up pops a dialog box that looks mightily like the one in Figure 24.3.

Figure 24.3

The GIF Optimizer command shrinks 16-million-color images down to 256 colors or less.

If you're using transparency as discussed earlier, on the **Transparency** tab choose **Areas that match this color**. Click the color box at the end of that option. A color picker appears. Select the color you were using to mark transparent areas (probably the last color on the grid) and click **OK**.

On the **Colors** tab, choose the **Standard/Web-safe** option and enter the number of colors in your image (which you're supposed to be remembering) into the **How many colors do you want** field. (This information will be used to compress the image a little bit more by not saving palette information for colors you didn't use.)

Top-Down Text

Avoid the **Interlaced** option if your image shows multiple lines of text; with the **Non-Interlaced** option on, the Web visitor will be able to read some of it while the rest is downloading.

On the **Format** tab, you get to choose how a Web browser displays a slow-downloading image. Choose **Non-Interlaced**, and the image will build from the top down. Choose **Interlaced**, and the image will appear fuzzy at first, and then grow sharper until it is at its full sharpness. This is cool looking, but makes slightly larger files.

When you have all the settings correct, click **OK**. A file browser appears, and you can enter a filename and select a folder to store the file. Click **Save**, and you'll have yourself a GIF!

Although GIF remains the primary graphics format, I also I explain how to save a copy of your graphic as a JPEG file in Chapter 28, "Photo Finish," because you'll mainly be using JPEGs to store photos.

Button-Making: More Fun Than Mutton-Baking

Many Web sites display a menu of graphical buttons that let you quickly navigate the site, like the ones shown in Figure 24.4. Sometimes these buttons are strung across the top or bottom of the page; more often, a column of buttons is on the left side of the page. Generally, each button has the same design; the only variation is the text on the button.

Figure 24.4

A row of buttons from my favorite site:
www.Gertler.com.

The easiest way to build buttons like that is to create them all as a single PSP file. Build the background of the button on the lowest layer. Add a vector layer, and then build the text for the first button on it. After you have the text looking right, copy that layer to a second vector layer, and use the text-editing tools to change the text of the second button. Repeat this with a new layer for each button's text. This way, you end up with a single PSP file, and if you want to change the background or font for your buttons, you can do it with one sweeping command.

To create the GIF files for the individual button, use the Layer palette to mark the background layer and the text layer for that button as visible. Mark the other text layers as invisible. Now your image will look like the button you want. Step through the process described earlier for saving a copy of this image as a GIF file. Repeat this for each button.

One Graphic, Many Buttons

You can create single images that lead to different Web pages depending upon where you click them. For example, you can set up a picture of your family so that if the user clicks your image, they go to a page about your hobbies. Click your spouse's image, and the user gets a page about your spouse's job. Click the picture of your dog, and up pops the financial results for your dog's business, International Doggytech Ltd. This effect is called an *image map*.

Rebuilt for the Web

The Image Slicer and Image Mapper are new in PSP version 7.

Paint Shop Pro can help you select what parts of the image link to what pages, and can generate the HTML code that you will need to add to your HTML page. To do this, choose **File, Export, Image Mapper**. The Image Mapper dialog box seen in Figure 24.5 appears.

Using this dialog box to create your image map is easy. Just follow these steps:

1. Find the area of your image that you want to make clickable. (The clickable areas are called *hot spots*.)

2. Select the drawing tool that matches the shape for your hot spot. There are separate tools for drawing circles, squares, and irregularly shaped hot spots (polygons).

3. Draw the hot spot. With the Rectangle tool, drag from one corner of the hot spot to the opposite corner. With the Circle tool, drag from the center to one of the edges. With the Polygon tool, click at each corner along the edge of the hot spot, then right-click once the last corner is in place. The hot spot that you draw will appear superimposed over the image.

4. In the **URL** field, type the Web address of the document that will open when the user clicks this hot spot.

5. In the **Alt text** field, type a name or description for this link. (Some browsers will display this text whenever the pointer is over the hot spot.)

6. Repeat steps 1 through 5 for each hot spot you want.

7. Use the **Format** drop-down menu to select if you want your image saved as a GIF or as a JPEG file.

8. Click **Optimize Image**. This will bring up the GIF Optimizer or JPEG Optimizer, as appropriate. Set the compression and transparency settings for this image, then click **OK**.

9. Click **Save As**. A standard file browser appears. Select a folder and enter a name for the HTML file, then click **Save**.

10. Another file browser appears. Select a folder and enter a name for the GIF or JPEG file, then click **Save**.

11. Click **Close** to close the Image Mapper.

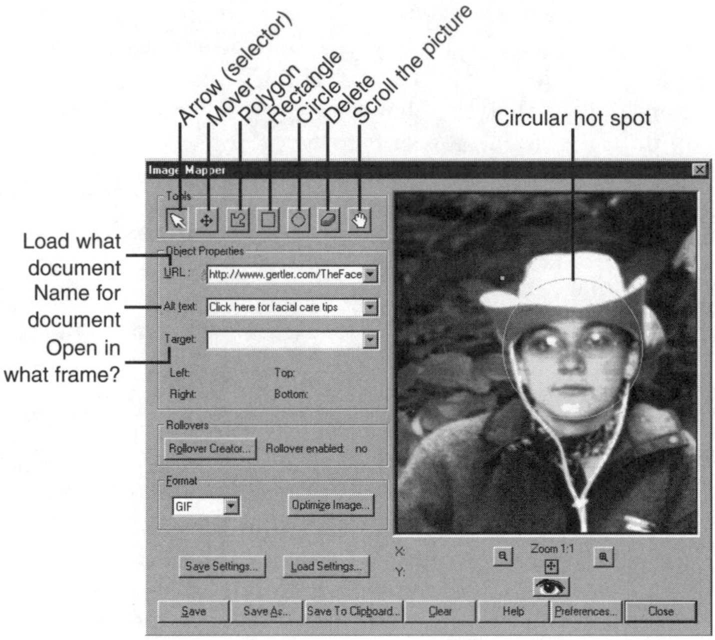

Figure 24.5

Image mapping: practicing cartography over photography.

If you make any mistakes along the way in drawing your hot spot, you can use the Arrow tool to reselect the area. Then you can edit the URL or use the sizing handles to adjust the size of the hot spot. You can even use the Eraser tool to remove hot spots altogether.

The HTML file that's created only has the image mapping information. Use your HTML editor to integrate this information with the Web page you're designing.

One Graphic, Many Graphics

You can break one larger image into several smaller images, and use the Table features of Web browsers to display them rebuilt into a single image. It's kind of like breaking a jigsaw puzzle down into individual pieces, and then having the Web browser rebuild them.

HugeTML

This book isn't big enough to teach you how to design Web pages. That's a big topic, and we've given it a book of its own: *The Complete Idiot's Guide to Creating a Web Page.*

Why would you want to do this? There are several reasons:

➤ You can reuse parts of your image. If you're showing a framed picture of your cat on your front Web page, you might want to reuse the frame on a later page with a framed picture of your grandmother, or you might want to reuse the cat without the frame on another portion.

➤ The pieces of the image can actually download quicker than the old complete image. In the case of a GIF file, this would be because each subsection has fewer colors than the whole, which makes for a smaller file. In the case of a JPEG file, you can set the important parts of your image to a very low compression rate to keep them clear, while setting the unimportant parts to a high compression rate to save space.

➤ You can build an image with more than 256 colors, break it down into sections that each have fewer than 256 different colors, and save them as GIFs with transparent areas.

PSP will not only help you slice your image into smaller images, it will even generate the HTML code needed to rebuild the image in the Web browser. To slice your image, choose **File, Export, Image Slicer**. As you can see in Figure 24.6, the Image Slicer dialog box looks a lot like the Image Mapper dialog box, only with a different set of tools.

When you start, your image is one big *cell*. To slice your image into smaller cells (each of which will be its own image):

➤ Slice a cell into several equal-sized cells by clicking **Grid** and then clicking the cell. A Grid Size dialog box appears, asking how many rows and columns you want the cell cut into. Fill in those values, and then click **OK**.

➤ Cut a cell into two side-by-side cells by clicking **Slicer**, pointing into the cell, and dragging just a bit downward.

➤ Cut a cell into a top cell and a bottom cell by clicking **Slicer**, pointing into that cell, and dragging just a bit to the right.

➤ Add a new slice clear across the image by clicking **Slicer** and then dragging from one edge to the opposite edge.

➤ Join two adjacent cells by clicking **Delete** and then clicking the border between the cells. (You can do this only if the joined cell would be a rectangle.)

➤ Create an empty cell with no image by clicking **Arrow** and then clicking the cell. Clear the **Include cell in table** check box. (The cell's image will still show in the image slicer, but the cell will be empty on the finished Web page.)

Figure 24.6

Stars and slices forever!

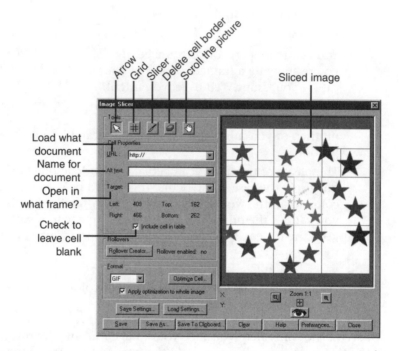

You can turn any cell into a link. Just click **Arrow**, click the cell, and then enter the address of the document to link to in the **URL** field.

Once you have the cells all sliced into shape, choose **GIF** or **JPEG** from the **Format** drop-down menu. Put a check in the **Apply optimization to whole image** check box, and then click **Optimize Cell**. The GIF or JPEG Optimizer dialog box appears, and you can set the compression rate, transparency, and so on.

With all your slices and optimization choices in place, click **Save As** and a file browser opens. Select a folder and type a name for the HTML file, then click **Save**. PSP will save each cell's image into a separate file in the folder you selected. The image file names will be based on the name of the image you were slicing up. For example, if you open the file cowboy.psp and slice that image, the file for the third cell in the second row might be stored as `cowboy_2´3.gif`.

Click **Close**, and the dialog box disappears to wherever it is that dialog boxes go on vacation.

Unique Formats

You can set a different compression rate or even a different file format for an individual cell. Clear the **Apply optimization to whole image** check box, click **Arrow**, and then click on the cell you want to change. Click **Optimize Cell**, and you can pick the settings for that cell.

Rollover Buttons (and Tell Tchaikovsky the News)

A *rollover button* is a button that changes when you point to it. This can be a keen effect; you can have your menu look fairly dim, and then have each button light up when you point to it. This way, Web surfers can be absolutely certain which button their pointer is on before they click.

While you're using the Image Slicer, you can give any cell a rollover effect. Click **Arrow**. Use the arrow to click the cell, and then click **Rollover Creator**. The Rollover Creator dialog box seen in Figure 24.7 appears.

Put a check in the **Mouse over** check box, and the folder icon to the far right of that option becomes highlighted. Click the folder icon, and a file browser opens. Use it to find the file that has the image that you want the button to change into. Click that file; then click **Open**.

Underwhelming Rollovers

Rollover buttons only work on browsers that support the JavaScript programming language. Make certain your buttons are clearly visible; don't rely on the rollover effect to make them clear.

Figure 24.7

The Rollover Creator has options for more than just rolling over.

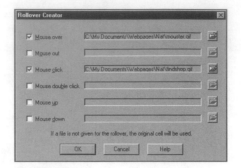

Rollover the Whole Image

The Rollover Creator button appears in the Image Slicer dialog box, but you don't have to slice the image before creating a rollover for it.

As you can see, there are other options you can set in this dialog box. Each option sets what image appears in the cell in reaction to certain mouse events:

➤ **Mouse out**   when the pointer moves off the image, on to something else.

➤ **Mouse click**   when the image is clicked.

➤ **Mouse double-click**   when the image is double-clicked.

➤ **Mouse up**   when the mouse button had been pressed down, but is released while the pointer is over the image.

➤ **Mouse down**   when the pointer is over the image and the mouse button is pressed down.

If you select one of these options, but don't select an image file to go with it, PSP assumes that you want that event to restore the image to its original state. People generally don't use all of those options. They use Mouse over to set the image that appears when the area is pointed to, and then they put a check in the Mouse out check box without selecting a file for it. That way, when the user slides the pointer away from the button, it returns to its original state.

After you've set your options, click **OK** to return to the Image Slicer dialog box. When you click **Save As** to save the sliced (or unsliced) image, PSP stores all the necessary rollover information in the HTML file. It also copies the rollover images into the same folder as the HTML file.

Fancy, Distracting Backgrounds

Back when the Web was young (which wasn't that long ago), one of the first special graphic enhancements added to Web browsers was the capability to show a *background image*—an image that would be repeated behind your text and your other images, filling your Web pages. Because everyone wanted to show off everything you could do with the Web, it seemed that every Web page had a repeating image of stars, or glowing lava, or the Web page designer's new niece.

Boy, was that a bad idea!

Those busy and loud images made the text very hard to read. Imagine trying to read this book if, instead of printing it on white paper, we'd printed the whole thing on fancy Christmas wrapping paper. It would strain your eyes, give you headaches, and make you not want to read the book.

These days, a much smaller portion of the pages use that sort of background, and those that do use it are generally using it more wisely. If you want to create such a background image, take a look at Chapter 11, "Fun with Fills," and read up on how to make your own repeating images for patterns. The same technique will let you design a repeating image for your Web pages. Here are a few tips:

➤ Save your repeating image as a GIF or as a JPEG with a low compression value. This will help keep a seam from appearing whenever the image repeats.

➤ Keep your entire image light if you're using dark text. Create a dark image for light text. This will help keep the text readable.

➤ When you design your Web page, you'll be able to set both the background image and the background color. Pick a background color that matches the main color of your background image; that way, it won't be such a shock to the reader's eyes when he's in the middle of reading your page and the background image finally gets downloaded.

➤ When in doubt, don't use a repeating image. It will never make text easier to read, and it can slow down your Web page.

The Least You Need to Know

➤ Save your PSP-created Web graphics as GIF files and your PSP-edited photo-graphic images as JPEG files.

➤ To save a GIF file, choose **File, Export, GIF Compressor**. To save a JPEG file, choose **File, Export, JPEG Compressor** (This is explained more fully in Chapter 28, "Photo Finish.")

➤ Graphics can really slow down your Web page, so use few of them, keep them small, and reuse the same graphic on multiple pages.

➤ You can create a group of similar-looking buttons as a single PSP file, putting the button background on the bottom layer and the text for each button on a separate layer. Use the **Layer Visibility** setting on the Layer Palette to make just the background and text for one button visible, and then save that button as a GIF file.

➤ Link different parts of your image to different Web pages by using **File, Export, Image Mapper**.

➤ Cut your image into multiple pieces with different compression settings by choosing **File, Export, Image Slicer**.

Chapter 25

Watermarking: Staining That Protects

In This Chapter

➤ What is a watermark?

➤ Embedding copyright and restriction information in your images.

➤ Reading information from images.

The World Wide Web is full of thieves. That should come as no surprise. The world is full of thieves, and on the Web, they can steal things quickly and easily. Oh, it's hard to steal a loaf of bread or an automobile over the Internet, but taking someone's intellectual property (their words, their drawings), that's easy.

If you want to raise a legal complaint about someone stealing your material, you may run into a problem. Just because you both have the same item doesn't prove they stole it from you; you may have stolen it from them! In some cases, the proof is easy. I just had to deal with a Web thief who made one of my articles part of their commercial site *including* the parts that said "by Nat Gertler." In other cases, it's harder. Even if you sign your Web images (which looks pretty silly unless you're doing something fancy), anyone with a good piece of image editing software can remove the signature quickly.

There is a way to embed your identity and a copyright date into your images so that it isn't blatantly visible, but you can prove its there when you want to. This technique is called *watermarking*.

Watermarking? Water You Talking About?

The term *watermark* comes from paper manufacturing. If you take a high-quality piece of paper and hold it up to the light, you'll probably see the manufacturer's name or symbol. A manufacturing trick has embedded that image in the paper so subtly that it cannot be seen in normal circumstances.

A *digital watermark* has much the same effect on your image. It makes very subtle color changes to your image, hiding the information in a way that a human being won't normally detect, but which a computer can read easily. This makes it very easy to prove that an image on someone else's Web site belongs to you; just run a watermark-reading program on the image, and your ID pops up.

Just Want Credit?

If you aren't worried about theft, but want your name in your Paint Shop Pro file, choose **Image**, **Image Information** (shortcut: Shift+I) and enter the info on the **Creator Information** tab.

Because of the subtlety of the watermarking effect, Paint Shop Pro's watermarking commands only work on images in 16-million-color or greyscale mode. The other modes just won't support subtlety. As such, for your Web images, JPEG files (which can store up to 16 million colors) are better designed to handle watermarking than GIF files (which are limited to 256 colors).

Watermarks are designed to be durable. This means that if someone takes your image and edits it, alters it, or changes its format, the watermark is still detectable. Even if someone prints your image, you can scan the printout back into the computer and show that your watermark is still there.

An ID 4U

The watermarking system supported by Paint Shop Pro is the Digimarc-brand watermarking system. When you create your watermark, what gets embedded is your own custom watermark ID, which Digimarc keeps track of. There's good news and bad news about this.

The *bad* news is that Digimarc makes much of their money by charging people for watermark IDs. They have to make a profit from something, and that's what they chose.

The *good* news is that Digimarc lets you get an ID and watermark the first 99 images you make for free. They only start charging you if you're going to watermark at least 100 images.

The *semi-good* news is that Digimarc offers another useful service, called *Marcspider*. This service is constantly scanning through the Web, finding all the pictures it can and checking their watermarks. If it finds a picture on another site with your watermark ID, Marcspider can let you know about it. This is only semi-good news, though, because Marcspider requires an annual subscription fee, even if you're creating less than 99 images.

To register for your ID, head on over to http://www.digimarc.com/register and follow the directions there. Beware, they will try to sell you some services! Those services can be a good deal if you need them, but you can always try watermarking first, and getting the services later. You have to be particularly careful, though, because they are trying to sign you up for a subscription. Be very careful reading over everything you're agreeing to.

After you've accepted Digimarc's terms and filled out the form, you'll be assigned an ID (six digits long) and a PIN (a two-digit number that your system will use to make sure you haven't mistyped your ID). When filling out the form, you also had to enter a password, which you will need if you ever need to update Digimarc's records about whom you are.

Tricks 'n' Tips

No Credit Card Needed

While Digimarc's form claims your credit card info is required, that's only true if you choose one of their more-than-99-images or Marcspider deals.

Creating Your Watermark

Adding a watermark should be done to a flattened, single-layer image, and it should be the last thing that you to that image. Any editing or effects that you do afterward may damage the watermark.

To watermark your current image, choose Image, Watermarking, Embed Watermark. The dialog box shown in Figure 25.1 appears.

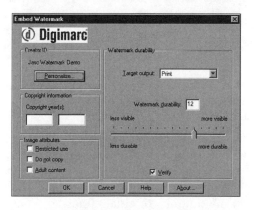

Figure 25.1

Before you make your mark, you must choose what mark to make.

If the words Jasc Watermark Demo appear above the Personalize button, you haven't entered your ID yet. Click Personalize, and a dialog box appears asking you for your Creator ID. Enter your PIN into the first field and your ID into the second field, and then click OK.

Next, it's time to enter the copyright years for your image. There are two fields for years. Usually, you'll only use the first one, putting the current year (and thus the year you created the image) in there. If your art is a reworking of an older piece, you may want to put two copyright years in it. For example, if you took a photo in 1999 and do some nifty graphics tricks in 2002, you could put both 1999 and 2002 into the fields.

Instant Copyright

Some folks think that you have to file federal forms to be able to claim copyright. This is not true! The moment you create something, that copyright is yours.

The program cannot handle dates before 1922, or dates after the current year. If you made your digital image before 1922, then you're enough of a genius to invent your own way around this dilemma!

There are check boxes that you can set to include the information that this image is restricted, not for copying, or that it includes adult content (such as the works of Aristotle, I reckon; those always confuse the kids). These check boxes won't actually prevent the image from being copied or prevent a minor from viewing the works of Aristotle. When someone checks the watermark, they'll be informed that you set these options. That's about it.

Frankenstein Versus the Invisible Man: Durability Versus Invisibility

You can set the durability level for your watermark, choosing how hard the mark will be to erase (accidentally or purposefully) through image manipulation. The immediate instinct is to make it as durable as possible, and set the durability to 16 on a scale from one to 16.

But there is a trade off. To make a watermark more durable, Paint Shop Pro will make it less subtle, which makes it more visible.

Don't worry very much about that. The Digimarc folks recommend a setting of 12 for images that will be printed, and a setting of 8 for images meant for the monitor (which uses bigger pixels, so the variations in them have to be more subtle to avoid detection). These levels should work fine.

Even if you set your durability to the maximum, the watermark doesn't really stand out. I tried starting with a solid white image so that the watermark dots would stand out immediately. Even so, the watermark wasn't clearly visible; it just made the white look a little dirty (as in didn't-use-bleach-on-my-socks dirty, not as in adult-material dirty). Even enlarging the image to nine times its original dimension merely left me wondering whether I had dust on the monitor. It was only with a lot of adjustments to the brightness and contrast of the image that I was able to get the clearer view of the watermark that you see in Figure 25.2.

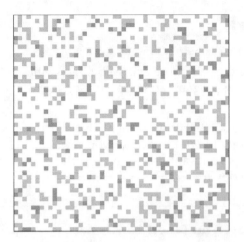

Figure 25.2

This is the way a water-mark looks to Superman.

After you've got your variables set, click OK, and the watermark will be added to your image. If you put a check in the Verify check box, Paint Shop Pro will immediately check to make sure that the mark is properly detectable.

Reading a Watermark

To read the watermark from any image, load the image into Paint Shop. If it's a multi-layered image, click the lowest entry on the Layer palette to make it the current layer. Choose **Images**, **Watermarking**, **Read Watermark**. A dialog box like the one you see in Figure 25.3 appears.

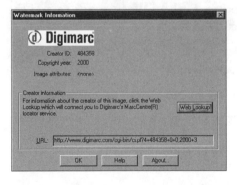

Figure 25.3

This is how those of you who aren't Superman have to read watermarks. Those of us, I mean. (Phew, almost gave away my secret!)

The watermark information doesn't have your name in it, but it does have your ID, which is linked to your name in the Digimarc database. Cooler still, it has a button marked Web Lookup; if you have an image that someone else created, click **Web Lookup**, and you'll be taken to the Web site of the image's creator (assuming that image creator told Digimarc his Web site address).

Changing a Watermark

You can't change a watermark.

After all, if you could change a watermark, those evil Web pirates who stole your image could just run a watermarking program and make it look like the image belongs to them.

After the watermark is there, you're stuck with it, so plan ahead. The safest route to go is to keep an unwatermarked copy of your image for your own use. That way, you can make all the additional changes you want. Just don't put the unwatermarked copy out where other people can copy it!

The Least You Need to Know

➤ A *digital watermark* is a code hidden subtly in the pixels of your image, which identifies the image as your creation.

➤ Paint Shop Pro can only add watermarks to 16-million-color and greyscale images.

➤ Web-bound color images that you want to watermark should be stored as JPEG files; GIF files don't have enough color depth to properly store watermarks.

➤ To apply for a digital watermark ID, head to www.digimarc.com/register and follow the instructions there.

➤ Choose **Image**, **Watermarking**, **Embed Watermark** to add the watermark to the lowest layer of your current image.

➤ You can read the watermark from any image by choosing **Image**, **Watermarking**, **Read Watermark**.

➤ A watermark, once added to an image, cannot be changed.

Chapter 26

Animation Shop 101: Picture Motions

In This Chapter

➤ Creating animations

➤ Putting images in an animation

➤ Transitioning from one image to the next

➤ Saving an animation for Web page use

A long time ago, before your grandmother was born, nothing moved. Movement hadn't been invented yet, you see. One day, cavewoman Goom and caveman Googam were standing around their cave, being perfectly still, because they had no other choice. They were standing around for a long time (although no one knew how long, because the clock's hands could not move). Eventually, Goom became so bored that she fell over in a stupor, bonking her head against the stone cave wall. Googam broke in laughter both from amazement (he had never seen anything move before) and from amusement (because pain is funny when it happens to other people). Googam was so infatuated with this concept of "motion" that he rushed out of the cave, hoping to head to the patent office and patent it. Unfortunately, he was immediately hit by a high-speed train that had also discovered motion, and Googam was never seen again.

The moral of this story: motion can make things less boring, but you can get carried away with it.

Animation Shop: The Free Movement Software

Paint Shop Pro comes with Animation Shop, a program that can make your images move, at no extra charge. It would be easy to assume that because it's a free piece of software (if you're buying PSP anyway), that it's not very useful or valuable. That assumption would be wrong.

Before you get too excited, thinking about the words *computer* and *animation* together—realize you won't be creating the next *Toy Story* using this software. You probably won't even be creating the next *South Park*. But if you want to create an ani-mated ad banner of your Web site or show a series of graphs, or have one photo from your family album fade into the next, this is the program for you.

For what it does, Animation Shop is a full, rich program. In fact, it's far too rich for me to cover it in depth. It deserves a book of its own. You should write the publisher right now and demand they have me write *The Complete Idiot's Guide to Animation Shop*. (No, wait, write and ask them to have me write *The Complete Idiot's Guide to Lying Around Drinking Daiquiris and Watching Dick Van Dyke Show Reruns*; I'm aching to do the research.) Instead, in this chapter and the next, I'll cover the basics of using Animation Shop to create good and useful Web graphics. This will be enough to give you a strong start on the great power of this tool.

Beyond the Book

These two chapters on Animation Shop should give you a good run-ning start on the basics. If you like what you see and want to learn more, use Animation Shop's help system. It goes into more detail on all the program's features.

What Is Animation?

We've all seen animation, and we think of it as moving non-photographic pictures. We're wrong. The pictures aren't really moving. An animation is a string of pictures shown in rapid succession. When the eye sees those pictures one right after the next, the brain gets fooled into thinking it's seeing some-thing move.

When you deal with Animation Shop, you'll be dealing with all of those individual pictures, which the program calls *frames*. You'll be able to see those frames individu-ally, add frames, and work on them one-by-one. Don't worry, not everything is so painstaking; there are plenty of commands that work on more than one frame at a time.

You Don't Need to Draw Every Frame

With Animation Shop, you can add frames to a new animation in four ways:

➤ Load an existing picture from a hard disk, including (but not limited to) pictures created with Paint Shop Pro.

➤ Draw a frame using Animation Shop drawing tools. They aren't as sophisticated as Paint Shop's Pro's drawing tools, but they are good for quick work.

➤ Create a series of frames by using an *effect* on a single frame. An example of an effect is a series of frames that make an image appear to spin.

➤ Create an effect that spans between two existing frames, making it look like one is moving away and the next one is appearing. An effect like this is called a *transition*.

Starting the Shop

To run Animation Shop, you can choose it from your Start menu; it should be in the same folder as Paint Shop Pro. You can also start the program directly from PSP, by choosing **File**, **Jasc Software Products**, **Launch Animation Shop**. When you do this, you'll see a display that looks like Figure 26.1, only you won't have a frames window or an animation window because you haven't started an animation yet.

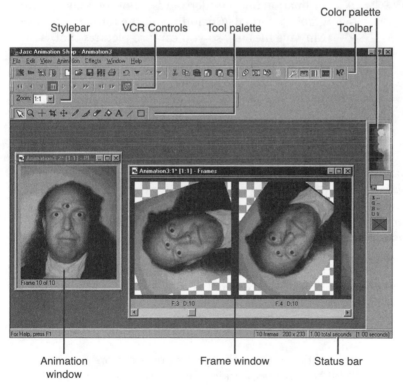

Figure 26.1

Animation Shop, home of lots of toolbars.

245

Play Around First

Before building your own animation, you should open one of the sample animations and see how it looks. Choose **File**, **Open** (shortcut: Ctrl+O) and select a file from the **Anims** subfolder of the Paint Shop Pro program folder. Choose **View**, **Animation**, and then press **Play** on the VCR Control toolbar.

Using the Layers

The use of separate layers for separate images can be handy for creating drawn animation. That way, in PSP you're drawing each frame on top of the last, the computer equivalent of drawing on tracing paper.

To Be Picture Perfect, Be Picture Prepared

Before you start a new animation, you're going to want to have images from which you'll be building your animation. Oh, sure, you could just use the program's built-in drawing tools, but why resort to using that low-level stuff when you have better programs?

The images that you use should be flat, either created as a single layer, flattened by using the **Layers, Merge, Merge All** command, or saved in some format besides PSP format. If you try loading a multi-layered image, Animation Shop treats the different layers as different images.

The images don't have to be Paint Shop Pro files; Animation Shop understands all of the major raster graphics formats (including all the formats that PSP can save files in), so you can use pictures that you've made with just about any program. All the pictures should be the same dimensions. Animation Shop can shrink or stretch pictures to fit the size of your animation, but you may not like the results.

Set Forth Upon This Continent a New Animation

To start creating a new animation, click **New Animation** (shortcut: **Ctrl+N**). A dialog box appears, hungry for simple information. Enter the width and height of your animation (in pixels; because animations are meant for the screen, there's no point to inch-measurements). Animation Shop can handle an animation as large as 32,767 pixels tall and 32,767 wide. They don't seem to be bothered by the fact that there isn't a display in the world that can handle that resolution. (That's about as many pixels as 2000 computer monitors set to standard resolution.)

For learning and experimentation, stick with small dimensions, no more than 200 pixels in each direction. This will keep things working faster, and you aren't so likely to run into memory and hard disk limitations when dealing with smaller animations.

There is one other decision to make: background color. This is the color that will fill the background if any of your images are smaller than the animation size or have a transparent background. It also shows up when you use certain animation effects. (For example, with the rotation you see in Figure 26.1, the background color fills the empty corner left by the rotating image.) Choose either **Transparent** (a good choice for many Web animations; it makes the file size larger, but lets the page background show through) or **Opaque**. If you pick **Opaque**, you can click on the color square and use the standard Paint Shop Pro color selector to choose your color.

Skip the Wizard

Animation Shop includes an Animation Wizard procedure that's supposed to make it easier to put together an animation. Really, it saves you very few steps, and will leave you with less of an understanding of what you're doing.

Click **OK**, and a new window opens with your animation in it. Actually, it's hard to call it an *animation* at this point; after all, it only has one frame, so it's really a still picture. Not only that, it's a *boring* still picture because it's just a rectangle filled with the background color you selected!

Adding Images (Two Images Plus Two Images Equals...)

Now it's time to take the images from your image files and put them into your animation. Choose **Animation**, **Insert Frames**, **From File**, and you'll be faced with the Insert Frames from Files dialog box shown in Figure 26.2.

Files already chosen

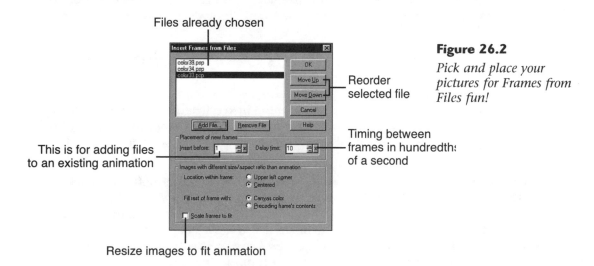

Reorder selected file

This is for adding files to an existing animation

Timing between frames in hundredths of a second

Resize images to fit animation

Figure 26.2

Pick and place your pictures for Frames from Files fun!

Click **Add File**, and a file browser appears. Use this to select a file to add to the list. (If you hold down **Ctrl** while clicking on the file names, you can select more than one image from the same folder at once.)

Use Your Movies

If you have short digital movies in MPEG format stored on your hard disk, you can open them as animations (choose **File**, **Open** and select **MPEG** from the Files of Type drop-down list) and add titles and effects.

The files are listed in the order they will appear in your animation. To rearrange the files, click the file you want to move, and then click **Move Up** or **Move Down**.

You'll also need to set the time between frames on your animation in the **Delay Time** field. This time is measured in hundredths of a second. Set the number small (say, 2), and your animation will fly by (unless you add a lot of frames, which will make it a large file). Set the number high (say, 50), and your animation will start to look jerky. If you're going to be adding transitions and effects, this number isn't so important; you'll be able to set the timing of those effects individually.

Click OK, and the selected images are added to your Frames window. You can expand the window by dragging a side edge, letting you see more than one frame at a time. You can also use the scroll bar at the bottom of the window to look through your images. If you see a ghostly copy of the previous frame over each frame, choose **View**, **Onionskin**, **Enabled** (shortcut: Shift+O) and that copy will go away.

If you're creating each image from your animation by hand in PSP, you can skip to the end of the chapter and read about viewing and saving your animation. But if what you have is a series of still images, and you want to liven them up, read on. (Not that there's anything wrong with still images; you can use Animation Shop to have a simple slide show, as long as you use a fairly long delay time between images.)

Transition: That's "No, It Is'n Art" Spelled Backward

To create a transition from any one image to the next, click the **Arrow** button and use the arrow pointer to right-click on the image you want to transform from. Choose **Insert Image Transition**, and the Insert Image Transition dialog box shown in Figure 26.3 appears.

Make certain that the option **Animation Frame** is selected for both the **Start With** and **End With** fields. Next, select a transition style from the **Effect** drop-down list. There's a number of interesting effects with interesting names, and the best way to find out what they do is try them all. If you have a check in the **Show Preview** check box, the transition will be displayed in the Preview area. (It may take the program a few seconds to prepare the transition for preview.)

Going from this image...   ...to that image

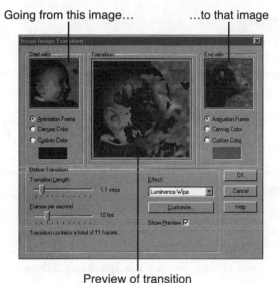

Preview of transition

Figure 26.3

Changing babies is normally a pain in the neck, but with a transition you can easily change a baby—into a mountain goat!

The Science of Art

Transition Talk

Filmmakers divide transitions into five types:

➤ A *cut* is where one image just disappears and another simply appears in its place.

➤ A *fade* is where two images appear superimposed briefly, generally with the old image fading out and a new image fading in.

➤ A *wipe* is where piece by piece, the old image disappears and the new image is in its place.

➤ A *reveal* is where the old image appears to be pulled aside, to show the new image already in place. (This includes *splits*, where different parts of the old image move in different directions.)

➤ A *cover* is the opposite of a reveal; the new image slides into place over the old image.

Each transition in Animation Shop falls into one of those five categories.

Manual Transition Tuning

There are several ways you can fine-tune your transition. You can make it go slower or faster by sliding the **Transition Length** slider; it can take as long as 10 seconds. You can also adjust its smoothness by changing the **Frames per second** slider in the Insert Image Transition dialog box.

Click **Customize**, and you'll be presented with a small dialog box full of options for the specific transition style you have selected. (Some of the effects don't have any such options, so the customize box is greyed out.)

Transition Completion

Once you've got all the settings as you like them, click **OK**. A series of new frames are inserted into your animation. These frames contain the transition.

If you've got a series of still images and your transitioning from each to the next in series, you'll have to keep using the **Effects, Insert Image Transition** command. This won't be as much of a pain in the neck as it sounds, because Animation Shop always remembers the last settings you used with the command. Because of this, you can repeat the same style of transition without having to repeatedly set the settings.

Effectively Inserting Effects

 To apply an interesting animated effect to a single frame image, use the Arrow pointer to right click on that frame in the Frame window. From the pop-up menu, choose **Insert Effect**.

The Insert Image Effect dialog box looks a lot like the Insert Image Transition dialog box, without an End With option selection. It works the same way, too. Choose an effect style from the **Effect** drop menu, and the effect is previewed in the preview window. Try out the various effects to see what they do. I'm a fan of *pixelate* (which reduces the apparent resolution by a series of steps, until your image is just a handful of colored squares, as shown in Figure 26.4) and *spiral* (which makes it look like your image is being flushed down a toilet).

Figure 26.4

Baby Ben gets pixilated.

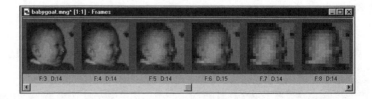

There is one additional option that you didn't have with transitions: choose **Run Effect in Reverse Direction**, and the effect will run backward. Pixelate will start with your image as a handful of huge pixels, and sharpen it until you have the full image. Spiral makes it look like your image is being, ummm, flushed out of the toilet. (When you set this option, the Preview is not reversed; you have to imagine it running backward in your head.)

A Little Text About Text Effects

You may want to insert words over your pictures. For example, you may want to put the word Baby over a picture of a baby so that no one gets confused and thinks it's a goat. Of course, you could have just added some text in Paint Shop Pro—but then the text would be standing still, and that's boring. If you have a still picture, you might as well have moving text to liven it up!

With the arrow pointer, right-click the frame you want to have text moving across. Choose **Insert Text Effect** from the pop-up menu. As you can see in Figure 26.5, the Insert Text Effect dialog box looks a lot like the Insert Transition dialog box, but with some significant differences.

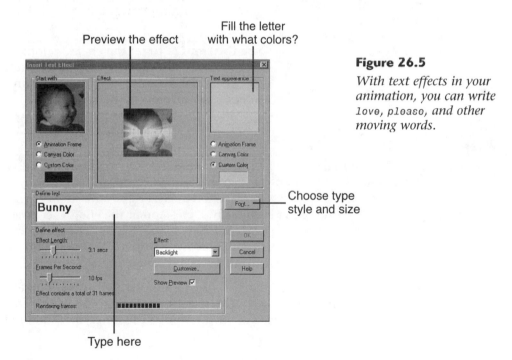

Preview the effect

Fill the letter with what colors?

Choose type style and size

Type here

Figure 26.5

With text effects in your animation, you can write love, please, *and other moving words.*

For the Start with option, select **Animation Frame**. Type the words you want to animate into the **Define Text** field. That's the basics.

Next, click the **Font** menu, and you'll get an Add Text dialog box that lets you select the typestyle and the size, as well as whether the text should be bold, italic, underlined, and so on. You can even choose the **Antialias** option to make your animated text merge with your picture as smoothly as possible (although antialiasing isn't as important with a moving item, because the human eye tends to blur moving objects a bit anyway). As you set the options, the Add Text dialog box displays a preview of what your words look like in that style and size. (Unfortunately, it doesn't display the text over the picture, making it hard to pick a size that will look right on the frame.) Click **OK** when you have the right style and size.

Tricks 'n' Tips

Still the Best?

While animated text can look cool, some effects make it hard to read. If you're more concerned with read-ability than nifty animation, put the text on the original image in Paint Shop Pro.

Click **Custom Color**, and then click the color square to choose what color the text should be. Or, if you want to be fancy, choose **Animation Frame** in the Text Appearance area, and the letters will act as a window onto the frame that follows the one you're adding text to.

Choose an effect from the **Effect** drop list. My favorite is **Backlight**, which creates the appearance that a harsh light is passing behind the edges of your letters, shining forward. It's a real Hollywood-style effect.

Click **Customize** to set the effect options. For most effects, this includes setting where on the image the text will appear, usually defaulting to setting it dead center on the image.

Don't Stop for Effects

You've seen TV. You know that when the words Guest Starring Lawrence Olivier show up at the beginning of an episode of Wacky Melvin's Humdrum Adventures, the action doesn't come to a stop. No, Wacky Melvin goes right on walking, juggling, and yodeling as if those words aren't even really there! And at the end, when Wacky Melvin and Sir Larry are playing pattycake, they don't suddenly freeze when the image starts to fade out. They go right on playing. If you have an animation going, why should it have to stop to have an effect or to display text?

It shouldn't have to, and it *doesn't* have to. If you want to apply text or an effect over a range of existing frames, first you have to select the range of frames you want to effect. Use the arrow pointer to click the first frame in the range, and then hold down **Shift** and click the last frame.

A Range of Effect

To apply an effect over the selected range of frames, right-click on one of the frames and choose **Apply Image Effect** from the pop-up menu. As you can see in Figure 26.6, the Apply Image Effect dialog box looks a lot like the Insert Image Effect dialog box, but it lacks the controls to set how many frames the effect stretches over. (You already told it how many frames by selecting the range of frames.)

Figure 26.6
Not all babies know how to wave properly.

Choose the effect from the effect drop-list, watch the preview, and click **Customize** if you want to fine-tune it. When you're done, click **OK**, and the effect will be applied.

Text on the Range

To apply a text effect over a range of frames, select the range, and then right-click on the range and choose **Apply Text Effect**. When the Apply Text Effect dialog appears, set your options and you're on your way!

Toon-Time: Watching Your Animation

You can see your animation at work at any time simply by dragging the slider at the bottom of the Frames window, moving the frames past the current area of the display. This won't use the proper frame timing (the speed of the display depends strictly on the speed you drag at), but it's a handy way of quickly checking the animation and finding a specific frame you're looking for.

To view the animation at the proper speed, choose **View**, **Animation**. The Animation window opens up. When this window is selected, you can control the animation using the VCR Control toolbar shown in Figure 26.7.

The animation continues to play while you're working. Make a change to a frame, and that change automatically shows up in the playing animation. You can even zoom in and out on the playing animation by using the + (plus) and – (minus) keys on the number pad at the side of your keyboard.

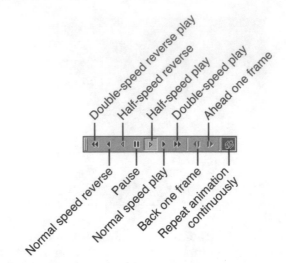

Figure 26.7

*Half-speed reverse play?
My VCR doesn't have
controls like that!*

Making the Save

To save your animation to a file, make sure that the Frames window, not the Animation window, is currently selected. Choose **File**, **Save As**. A standard file browser appears, letting you choose the folder and filename for your image. You also get to use the **File of Type** drop-down list to select the animation file format used to save it. If you're creating animations for the Web, there are only three of these formats that you really have to know about:

➤ *Animation Shop Animation (*.mng)* format is the program's native format. This is no good for putting the animation on your Web page because people's Web browsers aren't set up to be able to understand it. However, because it saves every frame of the video precisely, it's good to keep a copy of your work in this format, in case you want to work on it later.

➤ *CompuServe's Graphic Interchange (*.gif)* format is one that almost every graphic Web browser can understand. (There are some older browsers that won't play the animation, but even they will still show the first frame of the animation—a good reason for putting the important shot first.) Anytime you see little bits of decorative animation on a Web page, you can bet it's a GIF file. The down side is that GIF files have a severe color limitation; if your animation has color photos or fancy light effects, the GIF version is likely to be visibly degraded.

➤ *Video for Windows (*.avi)* format can handle more complex colors than the GIF format. It's not as widely supported as the GIF format, and it really isn't designed to have graphics integrated into a Web page of other material. Rather, you have a link to your AVI file on your Web page. When some people click on the link, the animation will be shown in the Web browser. For other people, a separate player program will start up and display the animation. And for yet other people, the animation won't play at all. It all depends on their setup.

If you choose to save your file in GIF or AVI format, a Wizard will start to help you select the compression level for your file. The more you can compress your file, the faster it will download to people's computers. (People don't like waiting around a long time for animations to download. As a rule of thumb, it takes someone using a dial-up modem about 1 second to download each 2 kilobytes of animation. If you make an animation that's one megabyte long, it will take about 8 minutes to download, which is far too long for an animation that plays in a few seconds.)

Think Small

The smaller your animation, the smaller your files. An animation that's 50 pixels wide and high makes a file that's 75% smaller than one that's 100 pixels wide and high.

The downside to compression is that it degrades your picture quality. The more you compress, the worse your animation looks. (This is why it's important to save an undegraded copy of your animation in Animation Shop's native file format.) If you have plenty of space on your Web site and the only people who visit your site have high-speed connections, feel free to use a very low compression rate. Otherwise, you'll have to choose your own tradeoff between size and quality.

GIF: Gosh, Interesting File

When you choose to save a GIF file, the compression system will step you through making the following decisions:

1. A slider lets you choose four compression levels, between **Better Image Quality** (large files) and **Smaller File** (less quality). Choose the level that suits your needs, and then click **Next**.

2. The compression now takes place. A series of progress meters keeps you up to date on the progress of the compression (the bigger your file, the longer it will take; with a large animation, it may take quite a while). When the compression is done, click **Next**.

3. The uncompressed and compressed versions of your animation are displayed side by side. If you're not happy with the result, click **Back** twice to return to step 1. Otherwise, click **Next**.

4. Animation Shop shows you the resulting file size, along with rather optimistic estimates of how long it will take different types of modems to receive this file. If the file is too big and the times are too long, you can click **Back** three times to return to step 1, where you can choose a smaller file setting. Otherwise, click **Finish**, and you're done!

One interesting thing about GIF files: Most browsers don't wait for the whole animation to download before they start playing the file. Rather, they will show each frame of the animation as it's received. As such, the animation may look like it plays through once very slowly, and then continues repeating at the standard speed.

AVI: 'at's Very Interesting

If you chose to save your file as a **Video for Windows** file, the compression routine will walk you through the following steps:

1. Choose **Create new or overwrite existing AVI file**, and then click **Next**.

2. On a drop-down list, choose between **24** and **8** bits of color per pixel. If your animation has color photos, choose 24, to get good reproduction (that's 16-million-color mode). If it's made up of simple drawings, 8 should be fine (that's 256 color mode). Click **Next**.

3. If you chose 24 bits of color, skip to the next step. Otherwise, you'll have to choose how it picks which 256 colors. If you can count on your viewers having fairly new computers, choose the **Optimized Octree** and **Error Diffusion** options. Otherwise, choose **Browser Palette** and **Nearest Color**. Click **Next**.

4. Now it's time to choose the compression algorithm. For Web use, choose **Cinepak Codec** (it will work on more computers than any other choice). Use the **Compression Quality** field to set the tradeoff between image quality and file size (a lower number means lower image quality but smaller files.) This will have to be your call. Click **Next** when done.

5. Your next decision is how many frames per second you want to include. This should match the frames-per-second of your animation; for example, if you chose a delay of 20 hundredths of a second between your frames, your animation has five frames per second (because one second divided by 20 hundredths equals five), and you should set this setting to **5**. Click **Next**.

6. The program now sets to converting and compressing your animation. This can take a while. If your animation is a long one, this is a good time to step out and get yourself a donut (and get one for me, while you're at it). When the **Finish** button is clickable, you're good to go. Click the button.

The Least You Need to Know

➤ To create a new animation, choose **File, New Animation**.

➤ Load saved images as frames in your animation by choosing **Animation, Insert Frames, From File**.

➤ Select frames using the Arrow pointer. Click on a single frame to select it. Select a range of frames by clicking the first frame and then Shift+clicking the last one.

➤ Right-click a selected frame and choose **Insert Image Transition** (to add frames that go from this image to the next), **Insert Image Effect** (to add frames that warp or change this image), or **Insert Text Effect** (to add frames that superimpose moving text over this image).

➤ Select a range of frames and right click to choose **Apply Image Effect** (show an effect over the range of frames) or **Apply Text Effect** (add moving text over this range of frames).

➤ When you choose **File, Save As** to save your file, you'll then be able to select a file format. Use **CompuServe Interchange (*.gif)** if you're creating little animations to put on the Web page, or **Video for Windows (*.avi)** if you're creating Web video that can be linked to.

Chapter 27

Animation Shop 201: Wizards and Tricks

In This Chapter

➤ Edit your animation

➤ Send frames to Paint Shop Pro

➤ Effective frame building in Paint Shop Pro

➤ Make text banners quickly

The previous chapter gave you the basics of using Animation Shop. This chapter will give you more tricks that will let you polish your work and create neat things easily. Even this chapter has to leave many things untouched; delve into those Animation Shop menus and see what you can discover.

Get Out Your Scissors: Editing Your Animation

It's easy enough to add frames to your animation. After a while, you might find that you've added too much and made some mistakes along the way. "This is supposed to be an animated version of the company's sales charts! Why did I slip that picture of Uncle Mortie into there?"

To get rid of those frames with Uncle Mortie, select them, right click on them, and choose **Delete**. Bang, Mortie is gone.

But what if you want to keep Uncle Mortie? What if you love him so much that you want to move him to the front of the animation? Select his frames, right-click on one of them, and choose **Cut** (shortcut: **Ctrl+X**) to move those frames to the Clipboard. Then, right-click the first frame of the animation and choose **Paste**, **Before Current Frame** (shortcut: **Ctrl+L**). To place Uncle Mortie after the current frame, choose **Paste**, **After Current Frame** (shortcut: **Shift+Ctrl+L**).

It's a Drag

You can move individual frames by dragging them. If you drag frame 1 to the margin between frames 2 and 3, you end up with the frames in the order 2, 1, 3. If you drag frame 1 on top of frame 3, frame 3 disappears and you end up with just 2, 1. You can even drag a frame from one open animation to another!

What's the Delay?

You can see a frame's current delay setting under the frame in the frame window, where it shows something like F:15 D:10. That means this is the fifteenth frame in the animation, with a delay setting of 10 hundredths of a second.

Does Uncle Mortie deserve his own animation? You can cut out his frames as described previously, or just copy his frames to the Clipboard without removing them by choosing **Copy** (shortcut: **Ctrl+C**) rather than cut. Right-click again and choose **Paste**, **As New Animation** (shortcut: **Ctrl+V**). Bang! It's an original Mortietoon! You can also use cut or copy to move the frame into another program, pasting it there.

Want to speed Uncle Mortie up or slow him down? No, you don't have to give him caffeine or gin and tonics. Instead, select his frames, right-click, and select **Frame Properties** (shortcut: **Alt+Enter**). There, you can adjust the frame delay by setting a new value in hundredths of a second.

The second tab of the Frame Properties dialog box is the **Comments** tab. On a nice large field there, you can attach a comment to the frame, for later reference. You can use it to remind yourself how you made this frame, or to keep track of things you still want to do to this panel, or just to store limericks in.

Choose **Animation**, **Animation Properties** (shortcut: **Shift+Alt+Enter**), and you get a dialog box that allows you to change the background color. Click the **Looping** tab, and you can choose whether the animation *loops* (repeats) endlessly, or a fixed number of times, or only runs through once.

Want to shrink Uncle Mortie down to mini-Mortie? Choose **Animation**, **Resize Animation** (shortcut: **Shift+S**), and you'll find the dialog box shown in Figure 27.1.

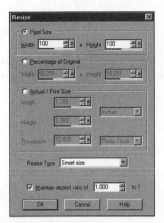

Figure 27.1

Resize your animation for fun and profit.

If you leave the check in the **Maintain aspect ratio** check box, you can simply change the **Width** field, and the **Height** field will change to match (or vice versa). This way, your animation won't look squished or stretched. It will merely look smaller or larger.

Returning to the Paint Shop for a Touch–up

You're looking at your picture of Uncle Mortie, and you realize he's missing something. To be specific, he's missing the clown makeup that he always used to wear to birthday parties. (And to graduations. And to synagogue, for reasons that you never could fathom.) Animation Shop does have painting tools that you could use to paint that on, but they're wimpy tools compared to the painting tools that Paint Shop Pro has. It's time to send Uncle Mortie to the PSP for a touch-up!

To make Uncle Mortie up just right, do this:

1. Select the frame or frames that you want to touch up.

2. Right-click the image and choose **Export Frames to Paint Shop Pro** (shortcut: Shift+X).

3. Paint Shop Pro opens up and displays the selected frame as an image. If you had multiple frames selected, they will be layers of that image; use the Layer palette to select which one is visible.

4. Make your touch-ups, and then close the image window by clicking on the **Close** (**X**) button. The changes are automatically transferred back to Animation Shop.

Seventh Heaven

Frame Forwarding Frenzy

The ability to send multiple frames from Animation Shop to PSP and have them arrive as a layered image is new with Animation Shop 3 (the version that comes with Paint Shop Pro 7).

261

Making Motion

Animation Shop is well designed to twist, warp, and transform. However, it's not really designed to do the sort of animation we usually think of as animation: characters in motion against backgrounds. We have to rely on our abilities with Paint Shop Pro to design the individual frames of such things, and use Animation Shop to combine those frames into finished images.

Simple Motion

A simple motion is one where the object that's moving really isn't changing at all. For example, let's say you want to create an animation of a blimp flying from right to left across a cloudy sky:

1. Start a new image, and draw the cloudy sky as a background.

2. Create a new layer, and draw the blimp on that layer (my attempt at this is shown in Figure 27.2). Save the file in Paint Shop Pro format as `blimp.psp`.

Figure 27.2

Good grief, it's a blimp!

3. Drag the blimp layer so that just the nose of the blimp is poking in from the right-hand side. Choose **File**, **Save Copy As** and save it in the Zsoft Paintbrush format as `blimp01.pcx`. (Why a PCX file? Because saving that way automatically saves as a single flat layer, and that's what we need.)

4. Drag the blimp layer one blimp-length left. Choose **File**, **Save As**, and save this as `blimp02.pcx`.

5. Repeat step 4 (drag and then save as the next higher file number) until the blimp has disappeared off the left side.

6. In Animation Shop, start a new animation, and use the **Animation, Insert Frames, From File** to select the PCX files and build an animation out of them, like the one shown in Figure 27.3.

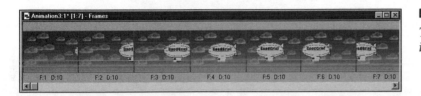

Figure 27.3
The miracle of blimp-imation.

You're not limited to how many layers you have. You could have a blimp moving in one direction while a plane flies in the other direction by putting them each on a separate layer and moving them both between file-saves.

Complex Motion

A complex motion is one where the thing that's moving is also changing its appearance as it does so. Consider an animation of a cat walking across the screen from right to left. If I drew a still picture of a cat and then used a simple motion to move it, the cat's legs wouldn't be moving. It would look like the cat was sliding across a sheet of ice (and not very realistically; cats on slippery ice tend to panic and go sprawling every which-way).

What we need to do is to draw a series of pictures of a cat in motion, against a steady background. We start as we did for the simple motion: draw a background, and then on a separate layer, draw the picture of the cat at the far right, starting to walk. For the first shot, we'll have the cat's left front paw and right rear paw stepping forward.

Next, we create a new layer with the cat a little more to the left, and it's now placing its weight on the left front and right rear paws. It may sound tough to make the cat look the same (consistency in drawing is one of the real tricks of being an animator or a cartoonist), but there are a couple of cheats you can use:

➤ You don't have to start from scratch. To create the new layer, right-click the first cat layer on the Layer palette, and choose

The Science of Art

Trickier Than It Sounds

Notice how I talk about drawing a cat walking, but I don't have illustrations of such drawings. Drawing people and animals in motion is a tricky art in itself. If you want a good tutorial on doing such animation, my professional animator friends recommend Preston Blair's book *Animation: Learn How to Draw Animated Cartoons*.

Duplicate from the pop-up menu. This gives you a new layer with a copy of the cat. (What kind of cat? A copycat, of course!) Erase the legs, and redraw them in the new position, and then slide the layer a bit to make it look like the cat has moved.)

➤ You can look at the original cat while you're drawing the second cat. The best way to do this is to adjust the Opacity Level slider of the first cat layer down to about 50 percent. As you can see in Figure 27.4, a ghost image of the previous positions helps you in both drawing and positioning your figure.

Figure 27.4

Put each frame's foreground on different layers and lower the opacity of the lower layers to use them as easy reference from drawing and positioning.

You repeat this effort a couple more times. For the third layer, the cat has his right front and left rear paw stepping forward. For the fourth frame, the cat is starting to put its weight. And after doing this, you've found your cat has made it about a third of the way across the screen, and you start to freak out. "I can't keep redrawing the cats legs! There must be more to life than that."

Don't worry; you're done with those legs. Now you have what animators (in all their beer-fed wisdom) call a *cycle*—a series of shots that make up a repeating motion. With just those four frames, you've got a basic cat walk down. Now would be a good time to save your file in Paint Shop Pro format (as cats.psp, perhaps).

To get the finished animation out of this file

1. Make all the layers fully opaque, and use the grouping commands to turn the four cat layers into a single group. (See Chapter 20, "Egging on Layers," for more on how to do this.)

2. Use the visibility toggles on the layer palette to make every layer invisible except the background and the first cat layer. Use the **File**, **Save Copy As** command to save this in Zsoft Paintbrush format as cat01.pcx.

3. Make the first cat layer invisible and the second layer visible, and then save a copy as cat02.pcx. Repeat this for the third and fourth layers (cat03.pcx and cat04.pcx).

4. Drag the layer group so that the cat on the first layer is where the cat should next be stepping (a little to the left of where the fourth-layer cat was).

5. Repeat steps 2 and 3 for cat05.pcx through cat08.pcx. If this doesn't bring the cat all the way to the left edge, repeat step 4, and keep dragging your cat cycle further over and saving the four files until the cat has finally walked out of the picture.

6. In Animation Shop, start a new animation, and use the **Animation**, **Insert Frames**, **From File** to select the PCX files and build an animation out of them.

Bang-Up Banners

Banners are used on the World Wide Web for all sorts of purposes, but the most common use is for advertising. When folks throw around the term *banner* in relationship to the Web, they usually mean those wide ads that spring up at the top of many Web pages. However, those ads are becoming less popular and less effective. More advertisers are using smaller banners, often with a little animation, that can sit beside the main content on a Web page.

You can build an animated text banner easily enough using the standard animation tools. If you want to throw one together more quickly, just reach for the *Banner Wizard*, and let it step you through the process.

Choose **File**, **Banner Wizard** (shortcut: **Shift+B**). The wizard opens and forces you to make your first decision: Should your banner have a **Transparent background**, an **Opaque background** (in which case you click on the color square to get a color selector, letting you choose which color background), or **Use a background image** (in which case you click **Browse** to select an image file).

After you've made that decision, click **Next**. The wizard then asks you what size banner you want. You can choose between six different standard banner sizes, from the tradition *full banner* (468 pixels by 60 pixels, like the one seen in Figure 27.5) all the way down to the currently popular *micro button* (88 by 31). You can also choose to set your own dimension or, if you chose **Use background image** in the previous step, to use the dimensions of that image. Click **Next**.

This display asks you how long you want the animation to last (in tenths of a second), how many frames you want per second (anything more than 10 is a waste), and how many times you want the animation to loop (repeat). Set these values, and click **Next** to move on to the next form.

Figure 27.5

A Banner Wizard-created banner, using the Backlight effect.

Get your Peanuts books at AAUGH.com

On this form, enter the text that should appear on your banner. There's also a **Set Font** button; click it and you'll get a font dialog box where you can choose the typestyle and size of the lettering. After you have the look of your words set up, click **Next**.

Tricks 'n' Tips

Contrast Counts

Generally, light text on a dark background gets the most attention.

The next form lets you choose between **Opaque text** (a solid color; click on the color box to get a color selector) or **Image text** (text filled with a picture; click **Browse** to select the image). Then click (wait, you've probably already guessed it…) **Next**.

This brings you to the final form of the wizard. Use the **Transition** drop-down list to select what style of text animation you want. (These are the same styles offered by the Insert Text Effect command.) Choose one, and the effect is previewed in the preview window. After you have the effect you like, click **Finish**, and the animation will be generated!

The Least You Need to Know

➤ You can use the **Cut** (shortcut: **Ctrl+X**) and **Copy** (Ctrl+V) commands on the pop-up menu to move selected files onto the Clipboard. Use the **Paste, Before Current Frame (Ctrl+L)** and **Paste, After Current Frame (Shift+Ctrl+L)** commands to put them in a new place in the animation.

➤ Right-click and choose **Frame Properties** to change the timing of a frame.

➤ To resize your animation, choose **Animation, Resize Animation** (shortcut: **Shift+S**).

➤ Send selected frames to Paint Shop Pro for editing by right-clicking on the selection and choosing **Export Frames to Paint Shop Pro** (shortcut: **Shift+X**).

➤ Exported animation ranges arrive in PSP as a multi-layered image, one layer per frame. When you've edited the frames, close the image window and your updates will be applied to the animation in Animation Shop.

➤ To quickly throw together an animated text banner, choose **File, Banner Wizard** (shortcut: **Shift+B**).

Part VI
Advanced Concerns

After all of Paint Shop Pro's abilities you've already read about, it turns out there are even more?!? Yikes! How do they expect you to use all of them?

They don't. Paint Shop Pro is like a pillow: to one person, the pillow is something to sleep on; to another, it's stuffing for a Santa costume; to a third, it's a weapon for a pillow fight; and to a particularly unwise person, it can be lunch!

Photo Finish

You got all excited. You were going to take the family photo album and scan the pictures in, creating a cutting-edge 21st century digital photo album. But when you scanned them in, you discovered that you ended up with a digital collection of scratched, faded, discolored images.

How did that happen? The answer becomes obvious when you look back at the old photo album and discover that it was filled with scratched, faded, discolored photos. But you don't have to settle for that. This is the digital age! You can tune up those photos and turn them into sharper, better images. Oh, Great Aunt Matilda still won't look like Miss Nebraska and Crazy Uncle George will still have hair growing in odd spots, but that's what they're supposed to look like. Using PSP, it's easy to make Matilda and George's eccentric looks come through clearly.

Phixing Phaulty Photos

If you could take the image you see through a camera viewfinder and put it up on your computer, you'd have a nice, clear photo. Alas, we still don't have that direct eyeball-to-PC link yet. We have to use other tools to get images into the PC, and often those tools aren't perfect. They create problems of their own, including problems that you can fix with Paint Shop Pro.

Scanning in Scratches

Little scratch lines on your scanned photos come from two different sources. Sometimes, the original photo (or the negative it was developed from) is scratched. This is particularly true on older photos, which have been lying around with plenty of chances to be scratched. Other times, the scratches come from your scanner itself. The scanning bed might be dirty (clean it!) or there may be dirt or hair on one of the internal optical components.

 If you just have a few scratches on your image, click **Scratch Remover**. This tool covers up scratches by blurring them with parts of the surrounding image. You can see the Tool Option palette for the Scratch Remover in Figure 28.1.

Figure 28.1

Using the Scratch Remover to remove a scratch is as easy as using a scratch to remove an itch.

Starting from Scratch

The Scratch Remover tool is brand new in version 7.

There are two choices to make here. The Scratch Remover works by blurring an area around the scratch so that the scratch is covered up. The **Width** field selects how wide a path gets blurred; this is measured in pixels. The two **Selection Boxes** buttons set the shape of the path. Click the box with the tapered-ended image if you have stray scratches on the original photo. Click the box with the rectangle if you have long straight scratches that run the full length of the your image (these come from scanner dirt).

Point to one end of a scratch, and then drag to the other end. As you drag, an outline appears showing the area that PSP is going to blur, as you can see in Figure 28.2. When you release the mouse button, the blur occurs.

Figure 28.2

The Scratch Remover selecting an area.

If your image has a lot of scratches, you don't have to handle them one-by-one. Instead, choose **Effects, Enhance Photo, Automatic Small Scratch Removal**. This effect goes through your image and blurs anything that might be a scratch. Unfortunately, that includes a lot of the detail of your image (particularly if you're working on an image destined for the screen, rather than one that's at the higher resolutions used for print).

The Automatic Small Scratch Removal dialog box has just two settings. The **Sensitivity to Scratches** field takes a number from 0 to 100; the higher the value, the more your image is blurred. Even when set to zero, the blur is noticeable. The other choice you have to make is **Type of Scratches**. Choose **Light** if you have the white marks that come from scratched photos, or **Dark** if you have the black marks that come from scanner problems or scratched negatives.

No More Moiré

If you've ever tried to scan in a printed photo from a magazine, you might've been surprised with the results. When you see the picture on your computer screen, you might think you're looking at it through a screen door, because there can be a subtle but visible grid lines on your image. This is called a *moiré pattern*.

To eliminate a moiré pattern, choose **Effects, Enhance Photo, Moiré Pattern Removal**. The Moiré Pattern Removal dialog box offers two settings, **Fine details** (which blurs the picture to achieve its effects) and **Remove bands** (which washes out your colors). Each value can be set from 0 (no effect) to 15 (way too much effect). Because this is an Effect dialog box, you can see a preview of how your settings will change the image. Experiment with the settings until you find something that gets rid of the pattern without destroying the better portions of your picture.

Avoid the Problem

Your scanner software may have a built-in moiré pattern remover. Generally, using this when you scan is more effective and precise than trying to fix the image later.

Artifacts of the New Age: Fixing Digital Photos

You'd figure that digital photos are already perfect. However, digital cameras often degrade a photo in order to be able to cram more photos into memory. They use a compression method called *JPEG* (short for *Joint Photographic Experts Group*, the folks who developed the compression method). The same compression format is used for most photos that are published on the Web or distributed by email. The JPEG system adds square areas that aren't quite the right color. The more the image is compressed, the larger and more visibly wrong these squares (called *artifacts*) become.

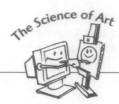

The Science of Art

A Pattern of Patterns

Moiré pattern is the term given to patterns that are made by putting one pattern over another. The reason you get them when scanning in a magazine photo is that the magazine photo is printed as a grid of dots, and your scanner is trying to read it as a grid of dots. The problem is that the scanner's grid doesn't quite line up with the picture's grid. For some scanned points, the scanner is reading the exact spot where the ink hit the paper, which will create a strong color in the scanned image. For other areas of the scan, the scanner is reading the point between two dots of ink, getting a more washed-out color. These areas of strong colors and washed-out colors form a pattern, which is the moiré pattern you see.

Purposely created moiré patterns can be very artistic. They're often used for hyp-notic light effects. Another place you're likely to see moiré patterns is on TV when someone wears a shirt or tie with thin horizontal stripes. The pattern of the shirt combines with the horizontal lines that make up your TV image, creating a strange strobe effect.

If the color variations are noticeable, try choosing **Effects**, **Enhance Photo**, **JPEG Artifact Removal**. The JPEG Artifact Removal dialog box has two settings; the **Strength** setting lets you choose from four levels of artifact removal effect, each of which blurs the image a little more. (Even the strongest effect doesn't blur it very much.) The **Restore Crispness** setting (0 to 100) sharpens your image to make up for the blurring. All in all, this is a very well-made tool, quite effective at eliminating the signs of compressions without really hurting the rest of your image significantly.

Seventh Heaven

A Photogenic Release

The JPEG Artifact Removal command, Moiré Pattern Removal command, and all the other Enhance Photo effects are new in Paint Shop Pro 7.

Creating Captivating Captures

The digital video revolution is well under way, giv-ing us lots of revolting digital video. Ever more peo-ple are hooking their video cameras up to their PC, or piping their TV images through the computer. Sometimes they're storing video on their PC, and sometimes they're taking single images from the video stream and capturing it onto their PC.

A video image is an interesting format. It's made up of a series of horizontal lines, called *scan lines*. A single video display is made up of two images, called *frames*. One frame goes on every odd-numbered scan line, while the other frame (broadcast one sixtieth of a second later) goes on the even-numbered scan lines. This technique of mixing two partial images is called *interlacing*.

While these frames are hitting your TV screen 60 times per second, you don't notice the interlacing effect. However, when you capture a single image from a video display, you're actually getting two interlaced frames, and they may not quite match up because of the fraction of a second that passed between the recording of the two frames. (This is particularly likely if the video shows something moving, or the camera is in motion.)

To clear this up on a video image you're editing, choose **Effects**, **Enhance Photo**, **Deinterlace**. This command keeps alternating rows of pixels from the image; each pixel on the other rows is replaced with an average between the pixel above it and the pixel below. The one option you have on the Deinterlace dialog box is whether you keep the odd-numbered rows or the even ones. There is no standard right answer; try both settings and see which looks better in the preview display.

For more information on digital video, ask your bookseller for *How to Use Digital Video* by Dave Johnson.

Overlooking the Obvious

Be sure to look at any video captures with the zoom setting of 1:1. PSP will often open such pictures at a 1:2 setting; at that level of zoom, you're only seeing every other line, so you won't be able to see any interlace problems.

Gonna Wash That Red Right Outta My Eyes

Sometimes when you photograph people and animals, their eyes turn glowing bright red. This can be very handy if, say, you're trying to write an article about how your entire family is demonically possessed. On the other hand, you want to fool people into believing that your family *isn't* demonically possessed, you may want to eliminate the red.

Choose **Effects**, **Enhance Photo**, **Red-eye Removal** to correct the red-eye problems with your image. As you can see in Figure 28.3, the Red-Eye Removal dialog box has much larger

Those Eyes Ain't Red from Crying

Red-eye is caused by the bright light of the camera's flash being reflected off of the retina at the back of the eye. You can avoid it by not having your subjects look directly at the camera, or by using one of those detachable flashes and holding it away from the camera.

preview displays than most Effect dialog boxes. This is because these are used for more than just previews; you'll actually have to work in the left preview display.

Figure 28.3

Red-eye removal with the Auto Human Eye technique: a few clicks, and the red is gone.

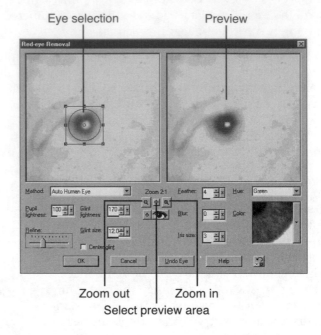

Eye selection   Preview

Zoom out   Zoom in

Select preview area

Quick Eye Correction for Humans

To quickly correct red-eye in humans

1. On the **Method** drop-down list, choose **Auto Human Eye**.

2. Using the **Zoom In**, **Zoom Out**, and **Select Area** buttons, position the eye you want to correct in the preview window, as large as possible.

3. Point to the center of the *pupil* (the dark area of the eye, which is what's showing up red) in the left preview display, and then drag to the outside edge of the *iris* (the colored area of the eye). Around the iris appears a circle in a square with sizing handles, which you can use to adjust the eye size.

4. On the **Hue** drop-down list, choose the person's eye color.

5. On the **Color** drop-down list, you'll see from 6 to 17 variations of that eye color. Choose the one that best matches the person's eyes.

6. Adjust the **Refine** slider. Set the value too high, and the person's iris color will be painted completely around the pupil, even if that covers over their eyelid. Set it too low, and the red won't be covered. Fiddle with it until the iris is covered with the iris color without spilling out over the eyelids.

7. Repeat steps 2 through 6 for all the eyes that the pictured person has.

Quick Eye Correction for Beasts

No, this isn't a section on teaching buffalo to use Paint Shop Pro. Animals' eyes are different than humans', and the fine folks at Jasc Software made sure the tool will work with these ocular oddities.

Working with animal eyes is just like working with human eyes, except:

➤ From the **Method** drop-down list, you choose **Auto Animal Eye**.

➤ When selecting the eye, just select the pupil. (The sizing handles will let you adjust for a non-circular pupil, and the selection will include a rotation handle so that you can select a tilted oval.)

➤ Don't bother with the **Hue** drop-down list. From the **Color** drop-down list, you'll select from one of three examples of animal eye shape.

Tricks 'n' Tips

They've Got to Be Red

Unlike most effects, Red-eye Removal will not work on a greyscale picture. It only works in 16-million-color mode. Of course, you can't have red eyes in a grey picture, so this isn't a problem!

Precise Pupil Picking

If you don't want to tint the iris color, or are dealing with an odd pupil shape, you can carefully select just the pupil. If you choose **Freehand Pupil Outline** from the **Method** drop-down list, you just draw a line around the pupil. If you choose **Point-to-Point Pupil Outline**, you click on points around the pupil's edge, going around the pupil and double-clicking when you get back to the starting point.

With either method, you then have to pick the type of eye from the **Color** drop-down list; you can choose one of three animal eyes, or a human eye.

Tuning the Eye

There are a number of adjustments you can make to the eye:

➤ Adjust the **Pupil lightness** setting to change how dark the pupil is.

➤ The *glint* is the white reflective spot on the pupil. Use the **Glint lightness** field to adjust how white it is, and the **Glint size** field to change how big it is. Click the **Center glint** option to set the glint right in the middle of the pupil; otherwise PSP tries to keep the glint in the same spot that it appears to be in the original photo.

➤ Increase the **Feather** setting to blur the outside edge of the pupil with the iris, and the outside edge of the iris with the eye around it. Setting a **Blur** setting blurs the entire eye area.

➤ Adjust the **Iris Size** setting to change how much of the eye area is iris, and how much is pupil.

As you change each of the settings, the effect can be seen in the right preview window.

Color Clarification and Tone Tuning

Colors often look wrong on photographs. Sometimes it's due to poor lighting when the photograph was snapped, or old film. Maybe you took too long to get the film developed, or the photo has faded with age, or your scanner isn't precisely tuned and thus turns all of your skin tones a bright green. Oh, sure, having green photos of yourself and your kin may be handy when it's time to send out your homemade St. Patty's Day greeting cards, but you may want to be able to fix the colors for other uses.

There are a number of commands on the **Effects**, **Enhance Photo** menu designed to adjust the colors and tones of your image:

➤ **Automatic Color Balance**—Adjusts the warmth of the image between a warm orange tone and a cool blue.

➤ **Automatic Contrast Enhancement**—Increases or decreases the contrast of the image, while aiming to keep your image basically bright or basically dark.

➤ **Automatic Saturation Enhancement**—Makes your colors richer or less rich.

➤ **Clarify**—Increases the sharpness of your image.

➤ **Fade Correction**—Livens up images that are dulled from age and poor storage conditions.

➤ **Manual Color Correction**—Adjusts the color tones of the selected area to match a color you select. This is great for making trees greener, making tans richer, and making blackened redfish more red and less black.

Some of these effects are similar to standard color adjustments on the Color menu. However, the Enhance Photo effects have options that are fine-tuned for working with photos. For example, the Automatic Saturation Enhancement includes an option that will protect skin tones, making sure your people don't turn glow-in-the-dark.

Edgy Choices

Photographing still objects in the studio tends to be the art of arrangement, getting everything set up just right and framed perfectly in the camera viewfinder. Quality photographing in the real world, particularly photographing things in motion, is more about getting the camera pointed in roughly the right direction, and then when you get the picture, trimming off the parts that you don't want.

I've already talked about the mechanics of cropping the edges off a picture, in Chapter 5, "Selecting and Cropping: Tools for a Picky Farmer." "How do I crop?" is an easy question. "What do I crop?" is a much tougher one.

An easy trap to fall into is to automatically put the biggest or primary object in your image right in the center. That can look fine, but often it makes the image static and loses what the image is truly about. For example, if you're taking a picture of a field with a tree in it, the instinct may be to crop it so that the tree is right in the center. If you do that, the image becomes about the tree. If the tree is about a third of the way from the edge, instead of dead-center, the image becomes as much about the open space as it is about the tree. (Figure 28.4 shows a good example of this at work.)

Figure 28.4

Keeping the church just off-center in this shot makes sure that the viewer sees the entire gorgeous environment.

Achieving Balance

Some people are concerned that their images be *balanced*, but that doesn't mean that the images have to be symmetrical. Photographers talk about something called *negative space*, which is a fancy way of saying an area where there's basically nothing. There may be a blank wall, a sky, a flat-colored backdrop—just empty background. Negative space has a name because it's important; it can actually have as much of an impact as a physical object. In the off-center tree picture, the presence of the tree is actually balanced by the presence of a strong negative space.

However, there are times when you really want your image to be unbalanced. An unbalanced photo can create a sense of motion. For example, if you're shooting a picture of a race car zooming from left to right, you may want to crop it so that the car is at the far right. The eye of the person looking at the photo will scan across the image quickly toward the right, which creates a motion effect. Creating an

Tricks 'n' Tips

Studying Balance

The next time you go out to the movies, watch carefully where the people are placed in conversational scenes. They're usually placed off-center, which helps make sure that their environment is as important to the picture as they are. A lot of this effect is lost when watching movies on video tape, because they've cropped the movie to fit the TV screen, generally cropping off the background and negative space.

unbalanced image can also make the image's subject seem eerie or unusual, or can encourage looking at a common item in an uncommon way.

A Real Frame Job

If you're creating pictures for your Web site and you want it to look like a museum or a gallery, choose **Image**, **Picture Frame**. This command puts a frame around your picture, as you can see in Figure 28.5

A wizard takes you through several steps of adding a frame. In the first step, you select the type of frame from dozens listed on a drop-down list, with a preview of each frame displayed. After you select a frame, click **Next**.

If you picked a non-rectangular frame, you will be asked what color to fill the outside edges of the image with. Choose a color, and then click **Next**.

Figure 28.5

A coral beach in a marble frame—ah, texture!

Finally, choose whether you want **Frame inside of the image** (which means that the frame covers over the edges of your image) or **Frame outside of the image** (your image size is made larger, to accompany the existing image plus the frame). Click **Finish**, and the frame is added. The frame is created on a new layer all its own, above all the other layers of your image. Your original image is still there on the lower layers, easily editable.

Saving Your Photos

You can save your photo the same way that you save any other Paint Shop Pro image, and you probably should. Keeping a copy of your photo in the PSP format means that you have a precise version of your photo that you can save at any time. That's a good method for keeping your own copy, but it's not very good for sharing with people. The file sizes are fairly large, making them slow for downloading or displaying on the Web. Instead, you'll want to save them in the JPEG file format. Any computer with a graphics Web browser can view JPEGs, and the JPEG file format is a very powerful compressor.

The best way to save a file as a JPEG is to choose **File**, **Export**, **JPEG Optimizer**. Up pops the JPEG Saver dialog box shown in Figure 28.6.

> *Tricks 'n' Tips*
>
> ### Flat Border for a Flat Image
>
> You can give your image a solid border in the current Background Solid Color. Choose **Image**, **Add Border**, and you'll be able to choose the size of the border in pixels. This only works with flat (single-layer) images.

Uncompressed image   Compressed image

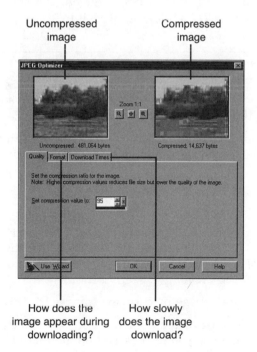

How does the image appear during downloading?   How slowly does the image download?

Figure 28.6

The more you compress the image, the fuzzier it gets.

On the **Quality** tab, set a value from 1 to 99 in the **Set compression value to** field. A low number means a larger file, but a high-quality image. A high number means a much smaller file, but a lower quality image. When you set this value, the compressed image preview window shows you how your picture looks compressed at that rate. This preview window can be zoomed in on and moved about in the same way as the preview windows on Effects dialog boxes.

You'll rarely want an image compression rate higher than 80, because at that point the artifacts caused by the compression scheme look quite blatant (although you can get some cool abstract effects by setting the value to 95 or higher). When you set a value, click on the **Download Times** tab. There you will find estimates of how long this image will take to download over different modem speeds at the current resolution. (These estimates are a little on the optimistic side, but they're close enough.)

Click the **Format** tab, and you'll choose how your image appears while it's downloading over a slow Internet connection. Choose **Standard**, and the top of your image appears first; then more and more of your image appears until the whole thing is revealed. Choose **Progressive**, and a fuzzy version of your image appears first. Then the image grows sharper and sharper until the whole thing is in place. (This option usually makes slightly larger files that download more slowly, but is often worth it, because people will more quickly get a sense of what your whole picture looks like.)

After you've selected your quality and format, click **OK**. A file browser appears, and you can enter a name for this file and select a folder to place it in.

The Least You Need to Know

➤ If you just have scratches on your image, click **Scratch Remover**, and then drag from the one end of the scratch to the other.

➤ If you scan in a printed photo, use **Effects, Enhance Photo, Moiré Pattern Removal** to eliminate any phantom pattern that appears.

➤ Clean up downloaded images or compressed digital camera images by choosing **Effects, Enhance Photo, JPEG Artifact Removal**.

➤ To eliminate glowing red eyes from your picture, choose **Effects, Enhance Photo, Red-eye Removal**. With the **Method** field set to **Auto Human Eye**, point to the center of the pupil, drag to the outside of the iris, and then select a **Hue** and **Color** for the eye, and adjust the **Refinement** so that the color doesn't cover the eyelid.

➤ Add a picture frame around your image by choosing **Image, Picture Frame**.

➤ Choosing **File, Export, JPEG Optimizer** will let you see the effects of various JPEG compression rates, helping you select a compression rate that will keep your file small while maintaining image sharpness.

Chapter 29

Leggo My Logo

> **In This Chapter**
>
> ➤ Design a strong logo
>
> ➤ Make the logo fit your business
>
> ➤ Avoid logo problems

Every business should have a *logo*, a symbol or text design that you can put on your letterhead, display on your Web page, or brand onto your cattle. A good logo can go a long way in building name recognition for your business. If your business is already known and loved, your logo instantly confers that respect on your product.

Paint Shop Pro is a fine product for designing logos. Still, just owning the program does not make you a good logo designer.

Give Your Logo a Goal

Not all logos are alike—which is a good thing. If everyone's logo were alike, they would be pretty pointless! Different businesses have different goals for their logo. Before you start designing, you should ask yourself what your goals are.

Some people want their logos to indicate what their company does. A plumber's logo might show pipes, or a tobacconist's logo might show pipes of a different sort. Other folks want logos that carry an attitude; a party store's logo should look festive, while a funeral parlor's logo should look respectful.

A lot of companies have logos that really aren't meant to confer much of an image. Consider the Golden Arches, the famed logo of the McDonald's fast food chain. It doesn't show you a restaurant or a hamburger, and it really doesn't suggest speediness or family-friendliness or any of a number of attributes that might describe the restaurants.

It doesn't have to.

What a logo like that offers is recognition. It's a simple, basic logo that you've probably been seeing since you were a kid. Seeing that logo should automatically make you think of the restaurant and the burgers.

Words Versus Pictures

Some logos are basically words, the name (or an abbreviation of the name) for the business and product. Other logos, such at the Golden Arches, the CBS television eye, or the AT&T death star, are primarily images, strong symbols. That doesn't mean that you can't have any text (some versions of the CBS eye have the letters CBS in the middle), but the picture does most of the work. You can mix pictures and text, but you should know which part is key and which part is decorative.

If you have a long name that you want to include in your logo, the text will end up being the key part. The larger you make the symbol, the less room you have for text.

Finicky About Fonts

The font you choose and how you place it can suggest a lot. Some fonts look casual, more like handwriting. These would be good for creating a sense of friendliness or even artiness, which is great for some things, but would be wrong for an investment company or a security device. Those things would need a more serious-looking font, something that looks sharp and precise.

These days, Windows comes with a fair number of fonts and a lot of programs you buy will come with additional fonts. If you don't like any of the fonts you have, you can buy CD-ROMs with hundreds of fonts to expand your collection.

A lot of the fonts that are out there are too ornate for almost any logo uses. An ornate font is hard to read, and all the details of the font will get lost if you have to print it fairly small. Also, if you're going to be bending or warping your logo's text at all, extra details tend to confuse matters more. Skip those old English typestyles.

Typographers sort fonts by whether they have *serifs*, those little lines and ticks at the end of the main lines of the letter. For example, the text you're reading right now has serifs. The X is not just a pair of lines crossing; at the top and bottom of each line you see a small tick. The text on the front cover of this book doesn't have serifs, so the fonts used there would be considered *sans serif* (without serifs).

Most fonts used in logos have no or few serifs. Serifs are helpful to the eye when you're reading a large quantity of text, but tend to interfere with quickly reading and recognizing small amounts of text.

The spacing between letters makes a difference. Letters that are widely spaced suggest calmness, control, and class. If the letters are tight or overlapping, it suggests eagerness and activity (an impression that can be increased by using *italics*).

Logo Shop Pro

When designing logos in Paint Shop Pro, you should stick to the vector tools. Logos are generally made up of strong and precise lines and shapes, which are really vector strengths. Logos can also require a lot of fine-tuning of the sort that vector objects handle well.

Resizable Advantage

Vector objects are smoothly resizable, which is very handy for logos. After all, you might be using the same logo on business cards and billboards, and need to adjust the logo for each.

The bad news is that when you resize a vector object, there's one part of it that doesn't resize: the stroke width. If you take a 100-pixel wide circle with a 5-pixel stroke and then use the resize handles to shrink the circle to 20 pixels across, you'll still have a 5-pixel wide stroke. This stroke will look very thick, and keep the logo from looking the same at the smaller size, as you can see in Figure 29.1.

Vector Is Better

If you have a vector version of your logo and you need a raster version, you can just flatten a copy of your logo image. However, if you drew your logo as a raster object, you'd have to totally redraw it to turn it into a vector.

Figure 29.1

Shrink the logo, and the line thickness seems to take over.

There are two bits of good news related to this. One is that you can change the stroke width on your resized objects; just adjust the stroke width in the Vector Properties dialog box for each object. The other good news is that you probably shouldn't be using strokes anyway. Logos work better made of strong, simple, solid pieces, and stroke outlines work against that.

Improving Your Font One Node at a Time

If you can't find the exact type style you need, don't panic. There's no rule that says that you have to use an exact specific type style. Instead, build your font text using the typestyle that's closest to what you need. Then choose **Objects**, **Convert Text to Curves**, **As Character Shapes**. Now you'll be able to edit the nodes on your letters, as you can see in Figure 29.2. Simplify them by removing nodes. Exaggerate them by stretching nodes out of place.

Figure 29.2

It takes a mess of nodes to make a logo.

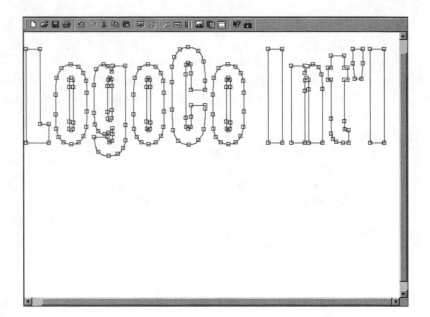

A Practical Example

A fair while back, I worked for a certain high-tech company that no longer exists. This company had a smart and capable designer on staff. She designed a logo that looked like the one shown in Figure 29.3. (As they used to say on Dragnet, "only the name has been changed to protect the innocent"; I've replaced the name of that high-tech company with the name of my own publishing company.)

This is actually a very nice logo. It looks good very small or very large. It's not fancy, but it's clean and to the point, which matched the corporate image. The upward direction of the letters suggests moving ahead, moving forward, and soaring.

Figure 29.3
A good, basic, uplifting logo.

A Hidden Meaning

The designer ran into one practical problem, however. When she would send the logo out to some other company for them to put it on letterhead or labels or mugs or whatever, the other company wouldn't put the logo at the correct angle. The designer decided that the logo needed a straight horizontal line built into the top of the design, so she did it in a fairly abrupt manner, which you can see in Figure 29.4.

Figure 29.4
The Not About Comics logo.

There are two problems with this logo. The first is obvious: it's not that attractive. The added bar looks mechanical, unneeded, and interferes with the simplicity of the design.

The second problem has to do with the nature of the company. Being a high-tech place, it was filled with engineers, and often did business with other engineers. In engineering and logic diagrams and equations, a bar over something has a very specific meaning: it means *not*, or in other words that whatever is under the bar is false. As such, to a techy with a sense of humor, the logo you see would mean Not About Comics.

Hidden meanings like that are something to look out for. Show your logo to a few knowledgeable friends before committing to it. (I once did some work for a company whose animated logo showed a man standing on a rotating earth. The only problem was that the earth was rotating *backward*—which is actually an accurate word to use in describing this company, but I'm sure it's not what they meant to evoke.)

An Unintended Picture

The designer's next stab was the design shown in Figure 29.5. This is actually a very nice design in a lot of ways. It incorporates that top line without the line seeming forced, it's bold and stands out well. It was a good idea having the letters go all the way to the edge, suggesting that the company is not constrained and is going "outside the box," to use a current expression.

Figure 29.5

A sharp-looking logo.

Still, there was something that bugged me about this logo, something that I couldn't quite name. The designer understood my concern and had a vague, uneasy feeling about it too. Because neither of us could define our discomfort, she thought we were likely both being paranoid.

She got the logo all ready to show to the corporate vice president. As she was taking it to his office, I suddenly realize what the problem was. I rushed from my desk on the other side of the building and caught her just in time.

"It's a guillotine blade," I whispered.

She took a look at the flat-topped, slant-bottomed design, and muttered a mild epithet. Once she recognized the shape, she couldn't get it out of her mind. We did not want our company image connected to a blade that chops people's heads off. It's easy to get caught up in the design and miss its effect (see Figure 29.6). Again, showing the design to other folks should help you avoid this.

Figure 29.6

The final logo.

She went back to her desk and went to work, and quite quickly reworked the design into what you see in Figure 29.6. This design works. It looked good on the company letterhead, on the front door of the offices, and taking up the side of the shipping boxes. If the company's product had been as cutting-edge, functional, and compelling as this logo, the company might still be in business today.

Other Things to Worry and Fret About

Logo design is an art, not a science. That doesn't mean it's a do-as-you-please effort, however. Here are some other things that you need to keep in mind, both when working your own logo and looking at the logos of others. (It's a good idea to spend a while looking at other logos before preparing your own.)

Limit Your Colors

Logos tend to use strong, solid colors for very practical reasons. The more colors you use, the more difficult it is to produce items bearing the color, and the more expensive it will be, to boot.

A logo is not a place for subtleties, gradients, and patterns; strong simple color use catches the eye better, particularly when the logo will be printed small. People who want a gradient effect in a logo use a series of ever-thickening lines of solid color instead.

Shrinkability

Your logo will sometimes be printed very small. Think of how it will look in the corner of a business card, or at the bottom of an ad. You can use the **Zoom** tool to zoom out, seeing a small version of your logo.

Using simple, solid colors will help with this, as will avoiding details and outlines. Simple shapes reduce more effectively than complex ones.

Be Anti-Antialiasing

Remember that antialiasing works by mixing the colors of pixels at the edge, effectively creating additional colors. Turn off all antialiasing settings on the objects that make up your logo. The only time you want to antialias your logo is when creating a low-resolution version of it for your Web site.

Faxibility

If your business is at all successful, your logo will be passed around and copied on various documents, and it won't always be in color. When your logo is photocopied or faxed, you still want it to be recognizable and readable.

For a quick test of what your logo will look like when photocopied or faxed, first try choosing **Colors**, **Greyscale**. That will give you a sense of what your image will look like on a very good photocopy, one that turns colors into shades of grey. That's a best-case scenario.

Next, click **Undo** to restore your image to color. Choose **Layers**, **New Adjustment Layer**, **Threshold**, and set the threshold value to about 128. As Figure 29.7 shows, this should give you an idea of what your image will look like on a cheap photo-copier or fax, one that doesn't pick up any shades of grey. (Of course, it won't show the lowering of resolution and the fuzziness that such reproduction can cause.) Again, click **Undo** to restore your image.

Figure 29.7

The threshold test shows that the logo at the top may leave you with a par-tial logo after faxing.

Confusability

Get to know other folk's logos, particularly the logos of your competitors. Make cer-tain that your logo doesn't look like theirs. That's one of the things that makes simple logos so tricky; so many of the simple ideas have been taken. A while back, the NBC television network spent about a million 1970's bucks creating and applying a new logo, only to find out that they had managed to re-create the Nebraska Public Television logo (which had been designed for $35.00).

Your logo should identify you clearly, not confuse the customer.

The Least You Need to Know

➤ Design your logo using only vector tools.

➤ Use fonts with few or no serifs.

➤ Keep your design simple, and use as few colors as possible.

➤ Avoid using stroke outlines and antialiasing.

➤ Show your logo to others to make sure that they don't see any unexpected images or connotations.

➤ Try to make your design unique, so it's not confused with competitors' logos.

Your Own Custom Paint Shop

In This Chapter

➤ Change your file locations and preferences

➤ Add and remove buttons

➤ Save your open window arrangement

➤ Add additional effects and tools

If you work at a desk, you probably have it set up just the way you want it. The cup of pencils is right at arm's reach, the keyboard is just at the height that you want it, and that all-important jar of emergency-only peanut butter cups is in the second drawer on the right, awaiting your twice-daily emergency.

Now imagine that every day when you went home from work, someone came in and took your desk and put a brand new desk in its place. Your items would all be placed up against the far edge of the desk. You'd either spend a lot of time every morning getting things back as you like them, or you'd learn to work with everything in the awkward place that those desk-switchers left it.

Neither option is a good one. If you're not reorganizing PSP to better match the way that you work, you're in a very similar situation.

Some References to Your Preferences

The main control for setting up PSP as you like it is the Paint Shop Pro Preferences dialog box shown in Figure 30.1. You can open this by choosing **File**, **Preferences**, **General Program Preferences**.

Figure 30.1

Paint Shop Pro Preferences offers plenty of preferences to pick from.

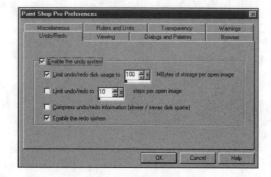

There are about 60 different options and settings you can set here. You can take some time flipping through the various tabs and seeing all the different things you can change. Here are some highlights:

➤ Paint Shop Pro puts up warnings in a lot of situations where you're doing something big, and allows you the chance to back out of what you're doing. Some people rely on these warnings, but others find it very annoying to have the computer continually question their commands. If you're in the latter group, click the **Warnings** tab. You'll be able to pick and choose which warnings you want.

➤ When you start up PSP, the program launches a screen telling you that you're starting PSP. If this seems wasteful to you, clear the **Show splash screen when application starts** check box, which you'll find on the **Miscellaneous** tab.

➤ When you install the program, it assumes you'll be working on images intended for computer monitors. As such, it sets up all the ruler and grid measurements in pixels, and sets a default image resolution of 72 pixels per inch. If you are usually designing things for print, go to the **Rulers and Units** tab. There you can switch to working in inches or centimeters, and change the default resolution as well.

➤ If you use the graphical file browser, the program has been creating a new file in each directory you browse. This file has a thumbnail of every image in the directory. PSP uses this file the next time you browse to that directory, so it doesn't have to make new thumbnails for all the images. Doing this saves time, but it does add some disk clutter. If you don't want that disk clutter, choose the **Browser** tab and clear the **Save Browser files to disk** check box.

➤ When you zoom in or out on an image, the window resizes to match the new image size. If you keep your windows carefully arranged and don't like that resizing, clear the first two check boxes on the **Viewing** tab.

➤ Tired of the gray-and-white checkerboard pattern that PSP uses to show you where your image is transparent? Try the **Transparency** tab, where you'll be able to change the colors and the sizes of the squares.

When you're done setting the preferences you like, click **OK**. Your preferences will now take effect not only for the images you are currently working on, but for every image that you work on until you change the preferences again.

Where Are the Files Filed Away?

Paint Shop Pro relies on a lot of files to work. Every texture, gradient, brush, pattern, frame, and shape has its own file. You can change where it looks for those files by choosing **File**, **Preferences**, **File Locations**. As you can see in Figure 30.2, the File Locations dialog box has a tab for each type of support file. Most of the tabs look like the one pictured in the figure.

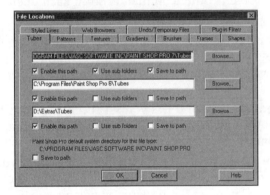

Figure 30.2

You can set three different directories for each type of file.

As you can see, there are places for three different directories for tubes; the same is true for each of the other elements. Why would you want three different directories? You might want to have one directory for the tubes that come with PSP, another for tubes that you download from other folks, and a third for tubes that you create yourself. You can pick and choose which tubes you want to use for each project by using the **Enable this path** check box for each folder.

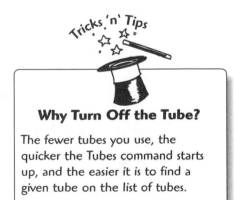

Why Turn Off the Tube?

The fewer tubes you use, the quicker the Tubes command starts up, and the easier it is to find a given tube on the list of tubes.

Tricks 'n' Tips

Where Are Your Web Browsers?

If you use the Preview In Web Browser command, check the **Web Browsers** tab of the File Locations dialog box. You can use this to set up as many as three different Web browsers to use for previewing.

To change a folder (or to add a new path in place of one of the empty entries) click the **Browse** button at the end of that folder's field. A folder browser will appear, which you use to select the folder you want.

There are two other options for each folder. Put a check in **Use sub folders** if you want PSP to check in this folder for any other folders that have tubes (or gradients, or whatever tab you're working on). The **Save to path** check box is used to select which folder your new tubes (gradients, whatever) get saved into. (Some tabs, such as the **Textures** tab, don't have this last option. That's because PSP doesn't have a way to create and save your own textures.)

Other Preferences

The **File**, **Preferences** menu has several other commands on it. Each opens a dialog box with its own uses:

➤ The **CMYK Conversion Preferences** and **Color Management** commands are both used mainly to help you prepare your work for a commercial printer. You'll learn more about them in Chapter 31, "Digital Laundry Day: Separating Colors."

➤ The **File Format Preferences** command lets you set specific options for dealing with PostScript, PCD, RAW, and WMF files. If you don't know what those are, you don't need this command!

➤ Use the **File Format Associations** command to tell Windows that you want PSP to be your main program for certain types of files. That way, if you're using Windows Explorer or the My Computer file browser, you can double-click on any file of these sorts and automatically open that image in PSP.

➤ The **Monitor Gamma** command doesn't keep an eye on your grandmother, as its name implies. Instead, it brings up the Monitor Gamma Adjustment dialog box shown in Figure 30.3. Use this command to make sure your monitor is showing the right color brightness by sliding the sliders until the color of the inner rectangle matches the color of the outer rectangle.

➤ The **Autosave Settings** command helps you choose whether to save a backup of your image as you work, and how often the image gets saved.

Match this color...

...to this color...

...by sliding this slider

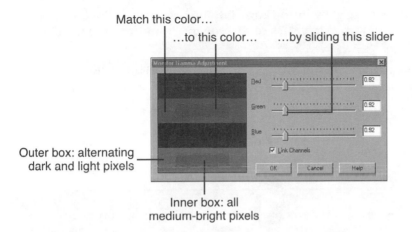

Figure 30.3

Adjusting your monitor gamma ensures an even distribution of pixel brightness.

Outer box: alternating dark and light pixels

Inner box: all medium-bright pixels

Toolin' Around with the Toolbars

The Toolbar, Tool palette, and Color palette are a key part of your PSP workspace, and an important part of your customization. The easiest thing you can do is change their location. As you can see in Figure 30.4, the toolbar and tool palette can be moved to either side or the top or bottom edge, or even left floating in the middle of the workspace. Drag them into position by dragging on the top edge of a vertically oriented button set, or the left edge of a horizontal set. They will automatically reorient themselves to match whichever edge you put them against.

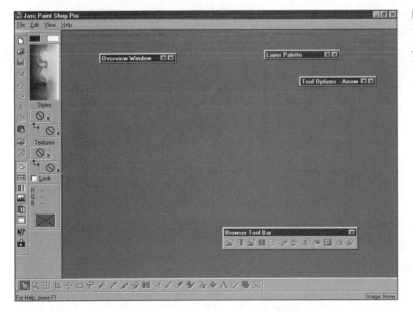

Figure 30.4

They're your toolbars, so stick them where you want 'em!

The Color palette can be dragged by its top edge, but it won't stick to the top or bottom edge of the work area. It can only stick to the sides or be adrift in the middle of the workspace.

You can also close any of these items that you don't need. Just right-click on any toolbar, and a menu appears from which you can pick and choose which item to close or open.

Bring 'Em Back Alive

Remember, if you close all the toolbars and palettes, you can return the Toolbar to the screen by pressing **T**.

Extra Toolbars

Paint Shop Pro has three more toolbars available. By default, they're turned off, but if you can turn them on via the menu that appears when you right-click a blank area on any toolbar or palette. As you can see in Figure 30.5, these toolbars are:

➤ **Effects Toolbar**—has buttons for various commands from the Effects menu.

➤ **Photo Toolbar**—has buttons for Effects commands that are particularly useful with photos, plus a button for the command that loads images from a digital camera.

➤ **Web Toolbar**—has buttons for the Web tools (Image Slicer and Image Mapper), plus buttons for saving you image in standard Web formats, for previewing in your Web browser, and for interacting with Animation Shop.

A Trio of Toolbars

The Effects, Photo, and Web Toolbars are all new in PSP version 7.

You shouldn't leave all of these toolbars open, because they take up a fair amount of your screen, leaving less space for your image. Instead, just open the one toolbar that you need for the project your working on, and then only if you use that toolbar's commands often. Otherwise, you may as well just stick with using the menu commands.

Web toolbar

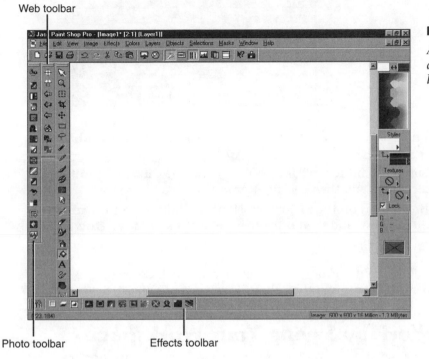

Figure 30.5

A few more toolbars, and there'd be no space left for your image.

Photo toolbar   Effects toolbar

Button-Picking for Fun and Profit

Buttons on the toolbar are the quickest way to get at your commands. As such, your button space should be devoted to the commands that you actually use frequently, and you shouldn't bother having buttons for commands you never used.

To change the buttons on the toolbar, first right-click on the toolbar. From the menu that appears, choose **Toolbars**. On the Toolbars dialog box that appears, click the name of the toolbar you want to add buttons to, and then click **Customize.** The Customize Toolbar dialog shown in Figure 30.6 will appear.

Seventh Heaven

Buttons for Everyone

Although previous versions of PSP let you add certain commands to your toolbar, version 7 is the first one where every single command is available.

297

Figure 30.6

PSP has more buttons than an entire marching band's outfits.

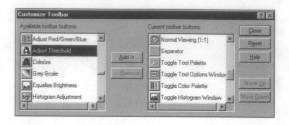

➤ Add a button to the toolbar by finding the command on the **Available toolbar buttons** list, click it, and then click **Add**.

➤ Remove a button from the toolbar by finding it on the **Current toolbar buttons** list, clicking it, and then clicking **Remove**.

➤ Rearrange the buttons on the toolbar by selecting a button on the **Current toolbar buttons** list, and then using the **Move Up** and **Move Down** buttons to change its position.

When you have all the right buttons in the right places, click **Close** on the Customize Toolbar dialog box, and then click **Close** on the Toolbars dialog box.

Save Some Work by Saving Your Workspace

You're working on a big project. You have several images open, in varying sizes and zooms. Your palettes aren't where you usually want them to be, you've got them someplace special just for this project. Every command you need to use is on a button on a toolbar. It is comfort, it is perfection. Then you have to work on another project that you want things in different places for, but you know you'll have to come back to the first project again.

Tricks 'n' Tips

Sharing Your Shop?

If you're sharing your PC with another PSP user, use the workspace commands to save the layout you like with no image documents open. That way, the other user can rearrange things all they want for their own convenience, and you're just a few clicks from returning to your favorite setup.

Don't worry, you can save and reuse that wonderful screen layout. Choose **File**, **Workspace**, **Save** (shortcut: **Shift+Alt+S**) and PSP prompts you for a name for this layout. Enter a name, and it's saved! If you have any unsaved files open, PSP now prompts you to save them.

To return to that layout, choose **File**, **Workspace**. At the bottom of the submenu, you'll find a list of recently used layout settings. Choose the one you want from the list. If the one you want is not there, choose **Load** (shortcut: **Shift+Alt+L**). A file browser opens, which you can use to select the layout file that you're looking for.

Adding Features and Filters

Paint Shop Pro has a huge list of commands and a huge list of effects. It may have everything you ever need. That doesn't mean, however, that it has everything you could ever think of.

It certainly doesn't have every feature that other people can think of. Other folks prove this by inventing their own effects and tools, which you can then add on to your copy of Paint Shop Pro. These add-ons are called *plug-ins*.

Plug-Ins Are Meant for Another Shop

Most of the plug-ins that are out there weren't originally designed for Paint Shop Pro. Instead, they were designed for another program called *Photoshop*, which is somewhat more popular and a lot more expensive than PSP. The folks at Jasc Software were smart, and started designing PSP so that it would work with most Photoshop plug-ins.

As it turns out, you don't need some of the plug-ins out there. They offer features that Photoshop doesn't have (or didn't use to have) but which are built into PSP.

Obtaining Plug-Ins

You can go to a good computer store and purchase commercial plug-ins. Generally a commercial plug-in set offers a large number of effects or some very special tools. Often, a good commercial plug-in set will cost you more than PSP cost you.

Plug-ins can also be downloaded. Many of the available downloadable plug-ins are free demonstration versions of commercial packages (generally offering a few example effects), while others are designed by fans and being given away for free.

Don't Make the Mac Mistake

Because Photoshop is available for Macintosh computers, many plug-ins are offered in Mac editions. These won't work on your PC.

Here are some good sites for finding plug-ins:

➤ www.state-of-entropy.com provides mostly free plug-ins, although some of them are really Filter Factory filters, for which you'll need to go to…

➤ pico.i-us.com, where you'll find the program *Plug-in Commander* (PiCo), which can convert Filter Factory filters into plug-ins. PiCo is available in a free version and a more-powerful commercial version. This site also offers free plug-ins and commercial tools.

➤ www.thepluginsite.com has a lot of good links with ratings for various plug-ins.

➤ www.alienskin.com is the home site for a commercial plug-in manufacturer, with downloadable demos.

➤ www.flamingpear.com is the home site for BladePro, a popular commercial plug-in for creating 3D textured and reflective effects.

Installing Plug-Ins

Before you install your first plug-in, choose **File**, **Preferences**, **File Locations**, and choose the **Plug-in Filters** tab. There you'll see the name of the folder path where your plug-ins are to be stored (generally, a subfolder named Plug-ins in your main PSP folder). Copy the path of this folder down.

Exit PSP before installing any plug-in. If you've downloaded a plug-in and the file extension starts with .8b, you just have to move that file into your Plug-ins folder. If you bought a commercial package or demo, you will have a file with an .exe extension; this is an installation program. Run the installation program by double-clicking the filename.

Some installation programs try to suggest a folder where the plug-in should be installed. This folder will almost always be *wrong* because the installation program assumes you have Photoshop rather than PSP. When it suggests this folder, click the **Browse** button and use the folder browser to locate your Plug-ins folder; then continue following the steps instructed by the installation program.

Plugging Away

When you restart PSP, you'll be ready to use the plug-in you just installed. Open an image that you want to work with, and then choose **Effects**, **Plug-In Filters**. All of your plug-ins will be there. Many will have their own submenus of individual effects.

No Command?

If your Effects menu doesn't have a Plug-in Filters command, that means that PSP didn't detect your plug-in. Make certain that you placed it in the correct directory. If that's okay, choose **File**, **Preferences**, **File Locations**, click the **Plug-in Filters** tab, and make sure there's a check in the **Include sub-folders when searching for filters** check box.

As you can see in Figure 30.7, the plug-in's dialog box may look very different from the usual Paint Shop Pro plug-in dialog box. Still, the controls should be easy to figure out. (Some plug-ins don't have a dialog box at all; what could be easier than that?) Most commercial filters will have a **Help** button that you can click for more information.

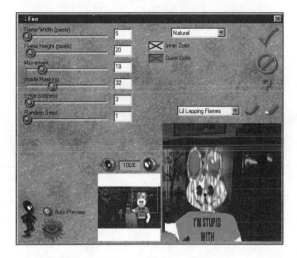

Figure 30.7

The Eye Candy filter set includes Fire, an effect that lets you set your selection ablaze.

If you want to reuse the plug-in effect you used most recently, choose **Effects**. The command you want will be listed right between **User Defined** and **Plug-in Filters**, saving you the trouble of diving through the submenus.

The Least You Need to Know

➤ Choose **File, Preferences, General Program Preferences** to adapt the program to your way of working.

➤ Show PSP where to find textures, gradients, plug-ins, and other relevant files by choosing **File, Preferences, File Locations**.

➤ Drag your toolbar, tool palette, and color palette where you want by dragging the top edge or the left edge.

➤ To add new buttons to the toolbar, right-click the toolbar and choose **Toolbars**. On the dialog box that appears, click on the name of the toolbar and then click **Customize**.

➤ Save the layout of your screen, including all open images, by choosing **File, Workspace, Save**. Then you can bring back that layout by choosing **File, Workspace, Load**.

➤ Plug-ins let you add new effects and tools to Paint Shop Pro.

Chapter 31

Digital Laundry Day: Separating Colors

In This Chapter

➤ Get a better prediction of how your printout will look

➤ Prepare your image for commercial printing

Most people just print out their drawings on their inkjet printer, and they're happy so long as the sun isn't green and the cows aren't purple. That keeps life easy, and the results are good enough for most uses. If you're preparing for commercial printing, however, you may need to pay a bit more attention to getting the right colors coming out of that high-quality professional printing press. For that, you'll need to consider *proofing* and *separation*.

Proofing Proves Useful

Your printer prints in color and your screen shows images in color, but they're not really the *same* color. Oh, reds are still red, but the scarlet on your screen may print out as a burgundy. Monitors and printers make up colors in different ways, so its not surprising that they don't quite match. Even different printers use different methods, so the color is apt not to match on the same drawing printed on two different printers.

Windows has a built-in *color management* scheme that lets you try to emulate the colors on one device with another. It's not perfect, but it is an improvement. Paint Shop Pro helps you take advantage of this scheme. After you set up color management, you can use your system to *proof* (art-folk talk for previewing) how the image will look in the final printing.

Setting up color management is a bit of a pain in the neck, but if you need it, it's worth the effort. What makes it a pain in the neck is that you need to have a *color profile* (a file that contains information on how a device's colors look) for your printer, one for you monitor, and one for the machine your commercial printer will be using.

Be a Pro Profile File Installer

Let's check out which profiles are already on your computer, and tell your computer which device the profiles should be used with. To do this

1. Using Windows Explorer or the My Computer file browser on your Windows desktop, surf on over to \Windows\System\Color. If your system doesn't have a Color directory, you're probably using an older version of Windows that does not include color management.

2. All the files listed in here are color profiles with the .icm file extension. Right-click the first file on the list, and choose **Associate** from the pop-up menu.

3. Click the **Profile Information** tab on the Profile Properties dialog box that appears. As you can see in Figure 31.1, this shows you what printer or monitor the profile was meant for. If it's a printer, it will tell you what print mode and paper this particular profile is for. If this is not a device or mode that you use, skip to step 5.

Figure 31.1

This profile is for a Canon BJC-5100 printer, in regular printing mode, printing on some of that expensive glossy film.

4. On the **Associate Device** tab, check to see whether the device this profile goes with is listed. If it's not, click **Add** and choose your device from the list that appears, and then click **Add**.

5. Click **OK** to close the Profile Properties dialog box.

6. Repeat steps 2 through 5 for all the profiles listed in \Windows\System\Color. If you don't find an appropriate profile for your monitor, choose the profile

named sRGB Color Space Profile and associate that with your monitor. (If you don't find the appropriate profile for your printer, go to the manufacturer's Web site and see if new drivers are available.)

Profiling the Printing Place's Printer

This part is probably the biggest pain in the neck: you want to get a copy of the .icm file for the device that your commercial printer uses. There are a couple of ways of going about this.

You can try asking the commercial printer for a copy of its .icm file. They may or may not have it, may or may not know what you're talking about, and may or may not be willing to help you. If you do get the file from them, copy it into your \Windows\System\Color folder. Use the steps described earlier to associate this profile with *your* printer. It doesn't matter that the profile wasn't meant for your printer; you need to associate the profile with something, and your printer will do.

If your commercial printer can't help you with that, find out the manufacturer and model of printer device they are using. The manufacturer may have a Web site where you can download the driver for its printer. You might have to install that driver on your PC in order to get the .icm file. Or the manufacturer may have the .icm file itself available for downloading.

Can't Get the Profile?

Use the profile for your printer that sounds closest to the paper and printing style that the commercial printer will be using. It's not a great compromise, but it's better than nothing.

Putting Proofing Profiles in Paint Shop Pro

Now it's time to set up Paint Shop Pro to work with color management. With Paint Shop Pro open, choose **Files**, **Preferences**, **Color Management**. The dialog box shown in Figure 31.2 appears.

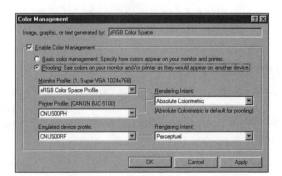

Figure 31.2

I like to do color management. I like coloring my boss pink, and the company president purple!

1. Click the **Enable Color Management** check box to put a check in it.
2. Click the **Proofing** option.
3. On the **Monitor Profile** drop-list, select the profile for your monitor.
4. On the **Printer Profile** drop-list, select the correct profile for your printer, print mode, and paper.
5. On the **Emulated Device Profile**, select the profile for the device the commercial printer is using.

The last choice to think about is the lower of the two drop-lists marked **Rendering Intent**. (The upper one should have automatically been set to **Absolute Colorimetric**, which is what you want.) From this lower list, choose

➤ **Perceptual** if you're proofing photographs or realistic, many-colored drawings.

➤ **Relative Colorimetric** for proofing a simple drawing with a few colors.

➤ **Saturation** for proofing things like graphs, where the exact color is not as important as the relative richness of the color.

Click **OK** when done, and you can now use your monitor and your printer for more accurately proofing what your finished item will look like. *Don't expect miracles!* Your $50 printer isn't going to start producing output like a $50,000 digital press. You'll just get a somewhat more realistic color sense out of it.

Color Separating: Four Colors for Color Printing

A lot of commercial printing is done using what is called *four-color process*. You may recall that all colors displayed on the monitor are actually made up of RGB dots—that's *Red, Green, Blue*. Printers generally use what art geeks call *CMYK Colors*. The letters in CMYK each stand for one of the four colors used. C stands for *cyan*, sort of a light blue. M stands for *Magenta*, an edgy form of red. Y stands for *Yellow*, which is, well, yellow.

And the K? *K* stands for *blacK*. I kid you not.

Each page passes through four presses, one for putting each color on the page. To set that up, the printing company needs one image for each of the four colors, showing where that color goes on the page. The process of creating these four images is called *color separation*.

Pulling the Colors Apart

Nowadays, you will usually let the printing company take care of separations. They know how to handle it best for their presses. There may be cases, however, when you're doing most of the *prepress* (the steps between designing the item and actually having it printed) for your publication.

A Whole Separate World

Computers have changed the world of color separation tremendously. For example, consider comic books. It used to be that one person, called a *colorist*, would color in a copy of the page and indicate which shade of green the Incredible Hulk would be in an individual panel. The colorist had very few greens to choose from, each described as a certain percentage of cyan, magenta, yellow, and black ink. Then a group of little old ladies working for a color separation company would look at the color indications and see that the Hulk's green was made up of cyan and yellow. These ladies would put down, by hand, a Hulk-shaped blob on a page that shows where the cyan goes, and another Hulk-shaped blob on the yellow page. Each blob would be shaded to indicate how much of that color was to be used. This method produced very rough-edged colors and a very limited palette. You could only have solid colors; no fading sunsets or glowing scepters.

Modern comic book colorists work on computers, where they can use as many colors as they want and do as many coloring tricks as they want. The computer can separate the colors automatically, much more cheaply, quickly, and precisely than a room full of little old ladies.

Printing color separations in Paint Shop Pro is as easy as separating candy from a baby. First, choose **File**, **Page Setup**. In the Page Setup dialog box, choose the **CMYK Separations** option. Click **OK**. Next, choose **File**, **Print**. Choose the **Print Registration Marks** option. (This prints crosshairs that the printer will use to make sure the four images get properly aligned.) Click **OK**, and the separations print out.

Gimme an M, Gimme a C, Gimme a K, Gimme a Y

You can preview how much of each color is going to be used on each part of your image. Choose **Colors, Split Channel**, **Split to CMYK**, and four new flat greyscale images open up, as shown in Figure 31.3.

Each of the four colors gets its own greyscale image, which shows you how much of that image's color is in each pixel. Black means that there will be none of that color ink used to print that pixel, while white means there's as much of that ink as possible used to print that pixel, and grey means somewhere in between. This is actually

307

counter-intuitive; on the black separation, for example, everywhere you see black in the image means there will no ink, and everywhere you see white means there will be black ink! Everything looks like a photographic negative.

Figure 31.3

Baby Ben gets separated. Notice how his blue jumper shows up as pure white (full ink) on the cyan plate.

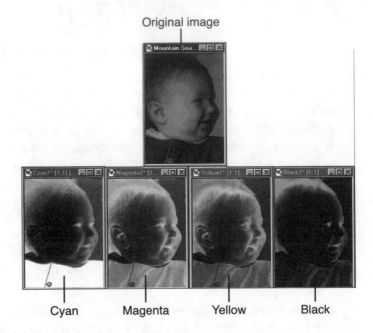

If you want to, you can alter these separations. You can draw something on the cyan image, for example, so that it will only show up in solid cyan, which can create a very strong image. After you're done messing with the images, you can recombine them into a single image by choosing **Colors**, **Combine Channel**, **Combine from CMYK**, and then clicking **OK** on the dialog box that appears. A new, flat image will be created.

Separation to Perfection

If you are a pre-press wizard, you can fine-tune PSP's separation system to separate around the strengths and weaknesses of a certain press. You really have to know the press and separation terminology well to do this. To get to the dialog box where you can create these settings, choose **File, Preferences, CMYK Conversion Preferences**. Click **New** to create a profile for a new printer, and then type a name for that printer and click **OK**. Now click **Modify**, and you'll find yourself with a dialog box meant for high-end fine tuning.

The Least You Need to Know

➤ *Proofing* is using your system to view what your image will look like when printed out from some other device. Paint Shop and Windows rely on special color management files that indicate how different printers and monitors handle colors.

➤ To set up the color management files for your system, go to the folder \Windows\System\Color, right-click on each file name, and choose **Associate**. The **Profile Information** tab will show you what device the profile is for; use the **Associate Device** tab to associate this profile with that device.

➤ Set up proofing by choosing **File, Preferences, Color Management**. Choose the options **Enable Color Management** and **Proofing**, and then choose the correct profiles for you monitor, your printer, and the printer that the final product will be created on.

➤ Four-color printing presses use *color separations*, a series of four images that will be printed in cyan, yellow, magenta, and black, adding up to a single full-color image.

➤ To set-up to print color separations, choose **File, Page Setup** and click the **CMYK Separations** option.

➤ When using **File, Print** to print your separations, be sure to choose the **Registration Marks** option so that the printer will be able to align the four images.

Installing Paint Shop Pro

Before installing Paint Shop Pro, close any other programs you have running. This keeps other programs from interfering with the installation, and will also keep you from losing data if something goes wrong with the installation and it crashes your machine.

If you have downloaded Paint Shop Pro (the evaluation version is available at www.jasc.com), locate the file you downloaded using Windows Explorer or the My Computer explorer located on your Windows desktop. When you find the icon for the file, double-click it to begin the installation process.

If you've purchased Paint Shop Pro on CD-ROM, insert the CD-ROM into your CD-ROM drive. The installation program will begin immediately.

Once you have the installation program running

1. An opening animation plays. Once it's done, click **Install**.

2. A dialog box appears welcoming you to the installer. Click **Next**.

3. Click **I accept the terms of the licensing agreement**. Click **Next**.

4. Click **Complete**. Click **Next**.

5. The installer tells you it's ready to install the program. Click **Install**. (The installation process may take several minutes.)

6. A set of options appears. Click **Finish**. A file listing the latest information on the product appears. Read through this file then close your editor window.

7. If a dialog box tells you that the system has to be rebooted before Paint Shop Pro can be run, click **Yes**, and the reboot will take place. Then you're ready to run Paint Shop Pro. If that dialog box doesn't appear, you don't need to reboot; Paint Shop Pro is now ready to go!

Tricks 'n' Tips

Start Me Up?

If inserting the CD-ROM doesn't automatically start the installation program, double-click on My Computer on your desktop. In the window that opens, double-click the icon for your CD-ROM drive.

Buttons and Menus and Mice, Oh My! Working Wonders with Windows

In This Chapter

➤ Control the computer using the mouse

➤ Start and handle programs using Windows 95, Windows 98, or Windows NT

➤ Use buttons and menus to give commands

➤ Complain about your computer using the right words

This appendix is about *Windows*, the program that handles how you control all the other programs. A number of different versions of Windows are around, but you're probably using Windows 95, Windows 98, or Windows NT. These all work pretty much the same.

Maybe this is the first time you've used your computer, or maybe it's not. If you have used a computer before, you probably know most of the stuff in this appendix, but read it over anyway to become comfortable with the terminology used in this book. (For example, did you know that we are no longer calling the W key "the W key?" Instead, we're calling it the *Harold Stassen Memorial Digital Wuh-Sound Input Device*.)

A Mouse in the Hand

Attached to your computer is probably a white lump with two or three buttons on it. You use this device to control the computer. The Geeks in Charge of Naming Computer Things (GICONCT) decided that because you would be spending so much time with your hand on it, they should name it after something you would never put your hand on. It's called a *mouse*. You use the mouse by putting your hand on it and sliding it across a flat surface (usually a *mouse pad* made for just such usage).

Try sliding your mouse around. When you slide it, you should see something move on your computer screen. When you slide the mouse side to side, it also moves side to side. When you slide the mouse forward, it moves up the screen, and when you move the mouse back, it moves down the screen. This thing is called a *pointer*, and it's under your command. It will follow you to the edge of the Earth—or at least the edge of the screen.

Missing a Mouse?

If your computer doesn't have a mouse, it probably has a *trackball* (push your hand across the top of the ball, and the pointer is pushed in the same direction) or a *pad* (drag your finger across this flat rectangle, and the pointer is dragged similarly).

The Point of the Pointer

The pointer is used to point to different things on the screen. When you want to give the computer a command about a certain part of what's being displayed, you use the pointer to tell the computer which part.

The pointer takes on different shapes at different times. Usually, it's an arrow, which makes a very clear pointer. When you're pointing to an area of text, the pointer might turn into something that looks like a thin, tall capital *I*. This is called an *I-bar*, and it's handy because you can put the thin vertical bar of the I between two letters, letting you point to a specific place in the text.

Sometimes the pointer turns into a picture of an hourglass. This means that the computer is busy doing something, and you have to wait until it's done. If you get sick and tired of seeing the hourglass, it's either time to get a faster computer or time to go do something else, like whittling. (If you can whittle yourself a new computer, you can do both at once!)

Clicking's a Snap!

It's not enough to point to something to give a command. After all, the pointer is always pointing to something. You have to have a way of letting the computer know that it's time to act on what you're pointing at, and that's what the mouse buttons are for.

The mouse has at least two buttons. The left one is the one that you'll use most of the time. When we talk about *clicking* something, we mean that you *point* to it with the pointer and then press the left mouse button. Don't hold it down, just push down and then let up on it quickly. To *double-click* something, you point at it and, instead of clicking once, you click twice.

Right-clicking is just like *clicking*, only you use the right mouse button rather than the left one. You won't do this nearly as often.

If your mouse has three buttons, you probably won't be using the middle one, at least not in the beginning. That third button is there mostly for advanced users, who can set it up to do special things with certain programs.

Tricks 'n' Tips

Lefties Are All Right!

If you have a mouse that's set up for left-handed use, you will use the right button for normal clicking and the left button when we tell you to right-click.

Clicking a Button

On your screen is a rectangle with a little colorful Windows symbol in it and the word **Start**. It's probably in the lower-left corner of the screen. (If you don't see it, try pointing to the very bottom of the screen; a gray bar should appear with **Start** at the left end.) This is a *button*, a rectangular area on screen that, when you click it, issues a command to the computer. At this point, the **Start** button is probably the only button on your screen, but soon you'll have more buttons on your screen than there are on a dry cleaner's floor!

Notice how the button looks like it's pushed out from the gray bar that it's on. Try clicking the button, and you'll see two things. One is that the button looks pushed in. This means the button is currently *active*, that it is having an effect. The other is that a list of items appear above the button (see the following figure). This list, called the *Start menu*, shows a number of commands that you can give to the computer. Pushing the Start button told the computer to show you the commands. Click the button again, and the list disappears and the button appears pushed out again.

Try *right-clicking* the big open background area of the screen display (this is called the *desktop*). A short list of commands that you can choose pops up. This is called a *shortcut menu*. By right-clicking many things in Windows, you get a menu of commands that apply to what you clicked. Right-click the desktop, and you get a shortcut menu of commands that can change the desktop. Right-click a strawberry, and you get a strawberry shortcut menu, which isn't half as good as a strawberry shortcake menu!

315

Figure B.1

Pressing the Start button made the Start menu pop up.

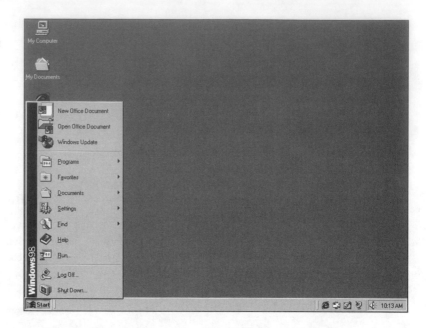

Dragging Ain't No Drag!

Sometimes, you have to move something from one part of the screen to another. This is called *dragging*, and it's quite easy. To take a swing at it, let's try dragging one of the *icons* around your desktop. (The icons are the little pictures with words underneath. Each one stands for a different program, file, or device on your computer.)

Find the icon with the picture of a computer on it (it probably says **My Computer** underneath it). Point to that icon. While pointing to it, push down the left mouse button and hold it down. With the button pressed down, slide the mouse around. A transparent copy of the image follows your pointer. It's the ghost of your computer!

Slide the pointer over to an area of the desktop where the ghost icon isn't overlapping any other icon. Let go of the mouse button, and one of two things happens:

➤ The icon disappears from where you dragged it and reappears where you moved it, or...

➤ The icons rearrange themselves in neat columns, with the icon appearing in a new spot.

If the second thing happened, it doesn't mean your dragging didn't work. Your copy of Windows is set up to keep the desktop tidy, and the moment it saw that something was out of the group, it neatened everything up. If your real desktop worked as well as your computer desktop, you'd always be able to find a pencil when you needed one!

In either case, you can put things back to the way they were by dragging the icon you moved back to where you took it from. If the rearranging icons covered up the place where the icon was before, drag it just a bit higher on the screen than the icon that took its place, again making certain the ghost icon doesn't overlap any other icon.

When You Need a Menu

You've already seen how the Start menu and the shortcut menu can appear when you need them, hiding away like squirrelly, umm, squirrels the rest of the time. Menus provide access to tons of commands without taking up a lot of screen space when you don't need them.

Start Up the Start Menu, You Upstart!

Click the **Start** button again. Take a look at the Start menu. Each line has a picture and a word or phrase explaining what that command does. Some of the lines also have an arrowhead at the right edge, pointing toward the right. The arrowhead indicates that ancient native peoples used these menus, probably while running Windows 1273.

Actually, the arrowhead means that that command brings up another menu. Slide your pointer up the menu. Notice how, as the pointer passes over each command, it changes color. This color change is called *highlighting*. Just like the way that blue water in your toilet shows you that Tidy Bowl is there for you, the colored bar shows you that that command is there for you. Click the line marked **Programs**.

Programs had an arrowhead on it, so that means that another menu will appear next to it. It may be just one column, but it may be several. Find the line marked **Windows Explorer** (it should be near the end of the last column), and click it. This starts a program that lets you sort through the files on your disks.

Why Don't You Drop Down and See Me Sometime?

A big rectangle appears onscreen, filled with all sorts of stuff in it. This is the Windows Explorer *window*, the area of the screen where the Windows Explorer program displays controls and information (see the following figure).

At the top of a window are two bars. The first, called the *title bar*, has a name for the window. On the Windows Explorer window, it says Exploring followed by the name of your hard disk.

Tricks 'n' Tips

Managing Menu Mishaps

If you accidentally bring down the wrong menu, don't worry. Just click the menu name again, and that menu disappears!

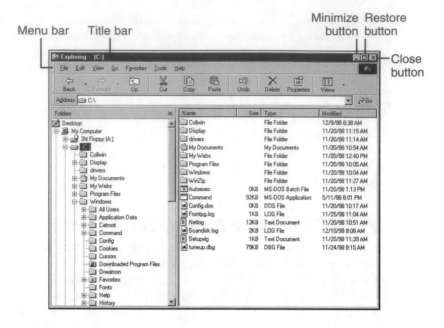

Figure B.2

Your Windows Explorer window may look different depending on your Windows version and settings.

The second bar is called the *menu bar* (as opposed to, say, a *bar menu*, which would have a list of drinks and prices for those 10-year-old boiled eggs they keep in a jar). It has a series of words on it. Each word is the name of a menu. Try clicking the word **View**. A menu of commands appears below it—these are commands that have to do with the way that the program is displaying the list of what's on your disk. Try clicking the command **Refresh**. This tells the program to recheck what's on the hard disk and to display the information again; you should be able to see when the display is being redone.

Some programs try to keep their menus simple using a system called *personalized menus*. This means the program guesses which commands you're likely to use and shows only those commands when you click the menu. At the bottom of the menu will be a down-arrow. Click the down-arrow, and the rest of the commands become visible.

Keyboard Kwikies!

Sometimes you don't want to keep moving your hand back to the mouse and then back to the keyboard, you just want to keep typing. Reaching your foot for the mouse is too much exercise after a while! Luckily, there are ways to give menu commands without clicking the menu.

If you click the **Edit** menu, you will see some commands with things like **Ctrl+V** or **Ctrl+A** on the end of them. This tells you the shortcut for that command. For example, the **Ctrl+V** on the end of the Paste command means that you can do a Paste command at any time by holding down the key marked **Ctrl** and pressing the key marked **V**. Other keys you might see referred to include the **Shift** key and the **Alt** key. If a menu item is followed by **Shift+Alt+X**, for example, that means that you can issue that command by holding down the Shift key and the Alt key, simultaneously, and tapping the X key. Of course, if you're new at typing, you might need both hands and your nose to do this.

On the menu bar, one letter of each word is underlined (for example, the V in View is underlined.) This means that you can bring the menu up by holding down the **Alt** key and pressing the underlined letter's key (such as **Alt+V**). On the menu that appears, one letter in each command is underlined; just press the key for that letter (such as the R in Refresh) to issue that command. So, in full, to get the refresh command, press **Alt+V**, and then let go of the Alt key and press the **R** key. It may sound like a lot of work—but if you think that's a lot of work, you should talk to your grandpa, who will tell you that real work is carrying 16 tons of rocks a mile up hill every day, just to earn your lunch (a rock sandwich). (Of course, your grandfather actually sold shirts for a living, but that's no reason why you should have it easy!)

Grey Means No Way

Most of the menu commands are in easy-to-read lettering, probably black. If you see one that's almost the same color as the background (probably grey), it means that you can't use this command now. (These are commands that only work under certain conditions.)

Windows Don't Have to Be a Pane!

If you're using several programs simultaneously, you can end up with a screen full of windows, overlapping and even completely hiding each other. This can make your desktop as messy as that "stuff" drawer in your kitchen, where you *know* there's an almost-working 9-volt battery, if only you could find it! Luckily, there are tools that let you move around windows, change their size, and even hide them for a while (very handy if you're playing Space Bunny Attack and hear your boss coming).

Wipe Away Your Window

At the right end of a window's title bar are three buttons. The first, which has a straight line in it, is the *Minimize* button. Click this, and the window disappears! Don't worry, it's not gone for good, so you can still help the Space Bunnies save the galaxy. If you look at the *taskbar* (the bar with the Start button on it), you'll see a button with the title of each window you are currently using. Click the button that has the title of the window you just minimized, and the window reappears, good as new, with each Space Bunny still intact.

Seize the Size!

The middle button will have one of two pictures of it. If it has two overlapping rectangles, this window is currently in *Full-Screen mode*, so that it automatically takes up all the screen space available. When a window is in Full-Screen mode, you can't move it or change its size. It is seemingly invincible, but for one fatal flaw, its Achilles' Heel (or, for those of us with more modern heroes, its Kryptonite). If you click this button (called the *restore* button), it goes from Full-Screen mode to *Resizable* mode, and then you can do what you want with it! You've torn down all of its defenses!

If the middle button has just a single box on it, the window is already in Resizable mode. Clicking this button (called the *maximize* button) will put the window into Full-Screen mode. This is good if you want to see as much as possible in the window. (More Space Bunnies!)

Become a Mover and a Shaker... and a Resizer!

For you to move a window, it has to be in Resizable mode. Point to the window's title bar and then drag it. Depending on how your computer is set up, you may be dragging the whole window or just an outline of it. Drag it up, drag it down, drag it, drag it all around! When you let go of the mouse button, the window will now be where you dragged it to!

If you want to change the size of a window, point at the lower-right corner of the window. The pointer will turn into a slanted arrow with arrowheads in both directions (like a "two-way" street sign would look, if there were any need for such things)! Try to drag the corner, and you'll find that you're moving the corner of an outline of the window. Move it so that the outline is the size that you want the window to be, and then release the mouse button. The window will now appear in the rectangle. With a little practice, you'll get so quick at dragging that you'll be ready for the drag races!

Wiping Out the Window

The button on the far right of the title bar, the one with an **X** in it, is the *Close* button. After you finish using a window, click this and the window disappears. This also tells the computer that you're done using the program that opened the window; so if you're running a program where you create a file (like a word processor), be sure you've saved the file before clicking this.

Let's Rap About Dialogue!

Sometimes, a program wants to ask you for information. To do that, it uses a *dialog box*, a type of window. Most dialog boxes don't have a menu bar and can't be resized, but they can be moved around. More importantly, you give the computer the information it wants with one. Or, if you don't want to buckle into the computer's demands, you can just ignore the dialog box. Of course, then the computer won't do what you want it to, but sometimes it's important to show who is boss!

A dialog box is a basically a form. Just like paper forms can have blanks to fill in, boxes to check off, items to circle, and so on, computer forms have a lot of different ways of getting information. After all, filling out a form on a computer should be just as much fun as filling out a paper one!

To see some of these in action, click the **Start** button, and select the **Find** command. When the second menu (sometimes called a *submenu*) appears, pick the **Files or Folders...** command. (The ... at the end of a command name lets you know that if you select that command, you'll get a dialog box (see the following figure). You can't complain that you weren't warned!)

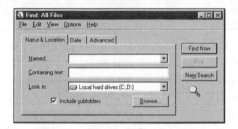

Figure B.3

A dialog box.

Tab: It Isn't Just for Dieters Any More!

On the Find File dialog box, you can see a file folder shape with a form on it. At the top of it, in the tab where the name of the folder would go, are the words **Name & Location**. Next to it are two other tabs, just like if you got a set of good file folders with the staggered tabs. Click one of those other tabs, and another form appears. Clicking the three tabs, you can easily choose which form you want to work on!

A Text Field Is the Type for Type

Check the **Advanced** tab and the **Name & Location** tab. On one of them (depending on which version of Windows you're running), you'll find a white area marked **Containing Text**. This is a *text field*, one that you can type into. To put some words into that field, click in the field, and then type. You can use the cursor keys and the Backspace key to correct any typos you make. Or, you can leave your mistakes in, and just confuse the computer!

Drop Down and Give Me Twenty!

On the **Advanced** tab is a field labeled **Of type**, which has a button at the end with a down arrow. This is a *drop-down list*, good for choosing one item from a list of items. Click the button (the *drop-down button*, which is a better name for it than *Mildred*), and a list of items will appear under it. Click any item, and the list goes away, and that item appears in the field.

What the Scroll Is That?

At the right side of the *drop-down list*, you will see a vertical bar with a box inside it. This is a *scrollbar*, which sounds like a wizard's tavern. Actually, it's Windows's way of telling you that it has more to show you than it can fit in the area it has to work in. The bar area represents the whole list. If the box is at the top of the bar, it means you're seeing the start of the list; if it's at the bottom of the bar, you're looking at the bottom of the list.

To see more of the list, just drag the box down the bar. The lower you drag it, the farther down the list you will see. (If you see a sideways scrollbar at the bottom of a display, it means that what the computer is trying to show you is wider than the space it has. A sideways scrollbar works just like a regular one, if you're lying down!)

Check Out the Check Box!

Click the **Name & Location** tab. At the bottom of the form you'll see a little box marked **Include subfolders**. This is a *check box*. It either has a check mark in it, which means *yes*, or it's empty, which means *no*. To change a check box from checked to unchecked (or vice versa, or even the other way 'round), just click it!

Option Button, Option Button, Who's Got the Option Button?

Click the tab marked either **Date Modified** or just **Date**. At the left of the form, you'll see two columns of circles. These circles are called *option buttons*. These "buttons" are used to select one thing from a small list of choices. You use them to select one from a list of choices, and when you select one by clicking it, a dot appears in the circle. You can only have one button selected in each column at a time; when you click one, the dot disappears from the previous selection.

Try clicking the lowest option button. When you click it, the field next to that option turns white; but if you then select the button above that one, that field turns gray. That's because that field is only used if you use that option. When it turns gray, the computer is telling you that you don't have to fill it in. Think of the fields like fields of snow—a white field is good to be in, but stay away from the gray ones!

The Least You Need to Know

➤ Sliding the mouse across your desk moves a pointer on the screen.

➤ *Clicking* means to point the pointer at something and press once on the left mouse button.

➤ *Double-clicking* means to point at something and press the left button twice, quickly. *Right-clicking* means to point at something and press the right button once.

➤ A *menu* enables you to select from a list of commands by clicking the menu name to bring up the list and then clicking the command you want.

➤ A *dialog box* is a form that the computer displays, asking you for information.

Speak Like a Geek: The Complete Archives

Graphic artists and computer engineers like to make up new words to describe the various pieces of the computer and the things you use these pieces for. Even worse, they like to take already existing words like *mouse* and *window* and give them new meanings.

Here's a cheat sheet for you. With it, you should be able to understand what they're talking about, and even spit it right back out at them!

adjustment layer   A type of image layer that transforms the appearance of the layers beneath it.

Airbrush   A painting tool that adds color lightly and builds up color if you continue to drag across the same spot.

alpha channel   A storage space in your image file that can hold masks and selection shapes.

antialiasing   A computer imaging technique where diagonal lines and curves are made to look less jagged by combining the color of the edge of the line with the color on top of which it is being drawn.

artifact   A square area of distorted color on an image, caused by the image being stored in a lossy compressed format.

background   The raster layer at the bottom of your layer stack.

background color   This term is used for two different things. It refers to the color of a new blank image when you first create it, and it also refers to the color used when right-clicking with the brush tools or the fill tool.

background image   An image that is repeated to fill up the background of a Web page.

banner   A Web graphic in one of several standard sizes, usually used for advertising.

blend mode   The way in which the color on the current layer is combined with colors on the lower layers to create the visible color.

BMP   Short for *bitmap*, BMP is a standard non-compressed format for image files.

cel   In animation, a drawing on a clear surface. One or more cels are put on an animation background to create an image.

channel   PSP tracks your image internally by separating into sections of information, such as the red channel, green channel, and blue channel, each of which holds information about where that color is mixed into the image.

check box   A small white square that you use to select an option. Click on the square to put a check mark in it (which means you want the option); click again to take the check mark out.

click   Clicking on something is when you point the pointer at it, and then press and release the left mouse button once. (If you're using a left-handed mouse, you'll use the right button.)

Clipboard   A storage area in your PC's memory that holds the most recent item you copied or cut.

close button   The button with an X at the right end of a window's title bar. Clicking on the image's Close button closes the image while leaving the program open. Clicking on the Close button on the program's title bar closes the document and the program.

CMYK   The system of four different color plates used in four-color printing; short for *cyan*, *magenta*, *yellow*, *black*.

color management   PSP and Windows feature designed to help you predict how an image will look on one printer or monitor using another printer or monitor.

color profile   A file that describes how a given device displays color, used in color management.

color separation   The breaking down of an image into the component colors used on different printing plates in four-color printing.

copying   Storing a copy of whatever is currently selected into an area of memory called the *Clipboard*.

Crop   The tool used to cut off the edges of an image.

crop marks   Marks beyond the edge of a printed image, indicating where the edge of the image actually is.

curved segment node   A node on a vector object that marks the end of one curved segment and the start of another.

cycle   To repeat an animation.

dragging   Moving the mouse with the left button pressed down. To drag an object, point to it, press, and move. (Left-handed mice use the right button.)

dialog box   A window that appears when the computer wants information from you. It can have a mixture of tabs, buttons, fields, check boxes, and radio buttons in it.

dithering   A process of faking a color that's not on an image's palette by alternating dots of related colors that are on the palette.

document   Any single picture, letter, report, spreadsheet, presentation, or other item that you've created and stored on the computer.

double-clicking   Pointing to something with the mouse pointer and pressing and releasing the left mouse button twice, rapidly. (If you're using a left-handed mouse, use the right button.)

downloading   Copying a file from another computer to yours, using a modem connection or a network.

drop shadow   A shadowy image generally placed slightly below and to the right of an image, to create the illusion that the image is floating above the page.

Effect   A category of commands that transform the current selected area of a raster layer.

evaluation version   A free-sample version of Paint Shop Pro, which will only work for a fixed amount of time unless you pay to have the program registered.

feathering   Fading out an area's color beyond the edge of the area.

field   A white rectangle where you can type information that the computer wants.

filled   Describes a shape that is not just a hollow outline.

float   To hover a selection above the current layer so you can move the selection without destroying the image beneath it.

Flood Fill   The tool used to fill areas with a color or design.

folder   The information on the hard disk is organized into *folders*. Each folder has a name, and inside each folder there can be files or more folders.

font   A type face in a given size.

font size   How big your letters appear.

foreground color   Also called Stroke Color, this is the color used when using a paint tool or the Fill tool.

frames   Used both in referring to the individual pictures that make up an animation and the picture frame designs that can be added around your image.

GIF   The *Graphical Interchange Format*, a type of compressed image file with the extension `.gif` that can store images of up to 256 colors, and can include transparency and animation.

gradient   A fade from one color to the next, or across several colors.

graphics   The term that Web and print designers use for images.

greyscale   An image made up solely of 256 shades of grey.

grid   A network of lines that PSP can superimpose over your image to make it easier to line up things.

handle   One of a set of squares placed around the rectangle that displays a selected area or vector object, which you can drag to resize, rotate, or deform.

highlighted   Displayed in a different color in order to be made visible.

histogram   A graph showing the distribution of colors within your image.

hovering   Holding the stylus close to the surface of a pressure-sensitive tablet without actually touching the tablet.

HTML   Short for *HyperText Markup Language*, this is the format used to store displays on the World Wide Web so that your Web browser can understand it.

hyperlinks   Areas of a document (such as a Web page) that one clicks to be shown another document.

image map   A system of designating various areas of an image as hyperlinks to different documents.

interlaced   Describes an image that is presented as non-consecutive lines of pixels first, followed by the remaining rows of pixels being filled.

jaggies   Unsmooth edges to diagonal lines and curves, caused by the square nature of pixels.

JPEG   Short for the *Joint Photographic Experts Group*, this is a format for image files that supports 16.7 million colors and lossy compression. The filenames have the extension .jpg or .jpeg.

layer   An image is made up of one or more superimposed layers, which combine to form the image. A single layer can have only a raster image, a vector image, or adjustment information.

loop   An animation segment that can repeat smoothly.

lossless compression   Any method of reducing the amount of file space that an image takes up, which doesn't alter the image it holds.

lossy compression   Any method of reducing the amount of file space that an image takes up, which alters the image it holds.

Marcspider   A service that searches the Web to see where images with your watermark appear.

marquee   An animated outline that appears around the edge of a selected area.

mask   A channel that contains information showing which parts of the current layer should effect the image.

Moiré pattern   A pattern formed by one pattern being combined with another, such as you see when scanning in a printed image.

negative space   The areas of an image that are basically empty.

nodes   The series of points that are used to define the outline of a vector object.

opacity   How non-transparent a layer or pixel is.

opaque   Describes something that you cannot see through at all.

Paint Shop Pro   An image creation and editing program manufactured by Jasc Software.

palette   Palette is used to mean two very different things in Paint Shop Pro. It can mean the set of colors that you have to draw with in an image, or it can mean a movable area of your screen display (such as the Tool Options palette).

pasting   Taking whatever's in the area of memory called the *Clipboard* and putting it into your document.

pattern   A repeating design with which you can fill areas of your image.

PCX   An image file format with lossless compression.

perspective   The appearance that one end of an object is further from the viewer and thus appears smaller.

Photoshop   A popular Paint Shop Pro-like program manufactured by Adobe.

picture tube   Also called simple *tube*, a file that contains a series of related graphics that can be quickly applied to an image.

pixel   Short for *picture element*, the individual rectangles of solid color that are the smallest units used to make up a computer-generated image.

pixelate   An effect where the image appears to be made up of a few very large pixels.

plug-in   Any add-on program that gives PSP additional features or effects.

PNG   A compressed image file format that many Web browsers support but which is not used very often yet.

pointer   A small picture on the screen that moves when you move the mouse. The picture is usually an arrow, but sometimes it can be a small bar or a finger.

pressure-sensitive tablet   A computer input device that consists of a flat surface and a pen-like stylus; dragging the stylus across the surface drags the pointer across the screen in the same direction. The tablet can also detect how hard the stylus is pressed.

proofing   Previewing how an image will look on a given printer or monitor.

prepress   The steps needed after designing the content of a work and before that work is printed commercially, such as proofing and color separations.

PSP   Abbreviation for Paint Shop Pro.

raster   Describes image sections and tools that treat the image as a grid of pixels (as opposed to *vector*.)

registration marks   Marks outside of the main image on printouts of color separations, used to make sure that the colors are properly lined up in the final printing.

resolution   Either a measurement of the entire image height and width in pixels, or a measurement of the number of pixels per inch of the image.

retouch mode   Any one of 19 image-altering functions that can be performed by the Retouch tool.

right-click   Right-clicking on something is when you point the pointer at it, then press and release the right mouse button. (If you're using a left-handed mouse, you'll use the left button.)

right-dragging   Holding down the right mouse button while moving the mouse. (If you're using a left-handed mouse, you'll use the left button.)

rollover button   A Web graphic that changes appearance when you point to it, such as a button that becomes highlighted.

sans serif   Describes a type face in which the letters don't have little tic marks or small lines at the ends of each major line.

saving   Copying the document you're working with (including all new changes) onto a disk.

scan lines   The individual horizontal lines that make up a video display.

scanner   A computer peripheral that can create an image of a printed page or photograph.

screentip   A small box that appears beside your pointer, giving you information about the item to which you're pointing. Also known as *tooltips*.

scroll bar   A scroll bar is used to let you select which part of a document you want to see, when that document is too big to show in the space provided. There's a box on a bar. The box shows the relative position of what you're seeing in the document. Drag the box to see another part, or use the up and down buttons at either end of the scroll bar to move up or down in the document. (Sideways scroll bars have left and right buttons.)

selecting   Indicating to the program what areas of your image you want your following commands to work with.

serif   A little line or tic mark at the end of the main stroke of a letter.

Start button   A button on the left edge of the taskbar that you click on when you want to start a program.

straight segment node   A point in a vector object that indicates the start and/or end of a straight line.

stroke   The outline that goes around a shape.

stylus   The pen-like object used with a tablet.

tab   Named dialog box buttons that let you select which set of settings you want to work with; click on a tab, and the settings having to do with the name on the tab appear.

tablet   A computer input device that consists of a flat surface and a pen-like stylus; dragging the stylus across the surface drags the pointer across the screen in the same direction.

TIFF   A file format for losslessly compressed images.

tooltip   A small box that appears beside your pointer, giving you information about the item to which you're pointing. Also known as *screentips*.

transparency lock   A feature that prevents changing the opacity levels in a layer.

tube   Short for *picture tube*.

undo   A feature that takes back your last command.

Usenet   A standard discussion system on the Internet.

vector objects   Image portions that are worked with and stored as a series of nodes and the lines and curves that connect them.

watermarking   A method of embedding a computer-readable mark into your image, which can be used to identify who created and owns that image.

Web browser   A program that lets your computer show you the displays on the World Wide Web, as well as any other displays stored in HTML format.

window   A moveable, resizable rectangular area of a computer.

wizard   A program feature that steps you through the decisions used in a complex task.

World Wide Web   A system that lets you see information displays stored on various computers that are connected to the Internet. To see these displays, you need a connection to the Internet, and you need a Web browser.

Index

U - V